BEYOND *ENDURANCE*

D1369174

BEYOND *ENDURANCE*

An Epic of Whitehall and the South Atlantic

by

NICHOLAS BARKER

with a foreword by
SIR REX HUNT CMG

LEO COOPER

First published in Great Britain in 1997
Reprinted in this format 2002 by
LEO COOPER
an imprint of
Pen & Sword Books Ltd
47 Church Street
Barnsley
South Yorkshire
S70 2AS

© Nicholas Barker, 1997, 2002
ISBN 0 85052 879 8

A catalogue record for this book is
available from the British Library

Typeset by Phoenix Typesetting, Ilkley, West Yorkshire.

Printed in England by CPI UK

TO THE *RED PLUM*
AND ALL THOSE WHO
SERVED IN HER AND SUPPORTED HER

CONTENTS

ACKNOWLEDGEMENTS AND AUTHOR'S NOTE

Much of this story was recorded on cassette. Had it not been for the wordsmith skills of Clive Kristen I am not sure how much shape and coherence would have emerged. Clive has been my Navigating Officer in charting the course of this book. His ingenuity and writing experience have helped to keep me, for the most part, clear of the rocks. It has been a fascinating voyage for both of us. I am also indebted to Maureen Ann Kristen for her technical and word-processing skills without which it would not have been possible to maintain momentum and revise a manuscript within a reasonable time framework.

The book was originally intended to be more autobiography than history, but I was persuaded by my publishers to tell the story of *Endurance* first and leave the rest of my life story for a possible later volume. In this book I endeavour to explain how we stumbled into an unnecessary war against a friendly nation. I had a duty to perform which always came before any personal feelings I had about incompetence in Whitehall and elsewhere. I accept that my interpretation of events in London and Buenos Aires may conflict with the received version of history or the views of some senior officials, civil and military, of the day. I hope that this core part of my narrative will be read as the informed account of a Naval Officer who was at the sharp end of events. It should be added that I have always taken a keen interest in geo-politics and have been regularly baffled by far-reaching political and diplomatic manoeuvres and recommendations that all too often have disastrous consequences. As likely as not this has been manifest through over-intelligent indecision.

To make sense of my commentary on internationally significant events, which may still have far-reaching consequences, the reader should know something of the whole man, warts and all. I am not a natural rebel, far from it. There have, however, been a number of occasions during my Naval life when I believed that principle required me to stand my ground. Fourteen years after the Falklands Conflict there is no rancour or bitterness, merely the intent to put the record straight. My account is to my mind both fair and truthful. Readers will judge this for themselves.

For this opportunity to put the record straight I am deeply grateful to my publisher, Leo Cooper. I know Leo views this volume as the final part of his 'Falklands jigsaw'. That being the case, his patience in waiting for its completion is immeasurable. I must also express my gratitude to Tom Hartman for his editorial skill and advice, and to Ewen Southby-Tailyour for his help with the illustrations.

I am equally grateful to members of the South West Atlantic Group, and particularly to Lords Buxton, Callaghan and Hill-Norton. I must also express my deepest thanks to the Hon Alexandra Bergel (Ship's sponsor to the *Endurance*), Sir Vivian Fuchs, Commander Ranken and the late Admiral Irving. There are many others, too numerous to mention by name, who fought the campaign to save HMS *Endurance* and to secure her replacement. They are, to my mind, the unsung heroes of this story.

I must also note my thanks to the Macadam family, who have been invaluable in their support and their enlightened views of government policy both in the UK and Argentina. They helped considerably in providing me with a unique and broad-based perspective.

But a sailor's view of the world is, almost by definition, different. After almost 40 years in the service I have nothing but admiration for the men of the Royal Navy and Royal Marines. The Naval Officer is now better educated and better qualified to represent his country in the remotest corners of the world. He works cheerfully within a framework of ever-increasing constraints and cutbacks, takes the constant acceleration of technology in his stride and rarely complains when his view of the world is ignored by an officialdom cocooned in isolation and ignorance.

I sincerely thank Sir Rex Hunt for providing the foreword to this book and by making my task much easier by completing his own account *My Falkland Days* some time ago. Many thanks also to Roger Perkins for his advice and permission to loot sections of his excellent book *Operation Paraquat*, and to Andrew Lockett, Neil Munroe and David Wells, co-authors of *Season of Conflict*.

I have cherished memories of the late Lord Shackleton, who was a constant source of both advice and inspiration, and the late Lady Buxton whose writing provided a most refreshing view of life on board *Endurance*. Both these wonderful people did much to shape the content of these pages.

Lord Buxton has been another esteemed source of advice and encouragement for which I am enormously grateful. I also wish to record my thanks to my agent, Peter Knight, his assistant Ann King-Hall and my own former secretary Hilda Knowles. Each of them has taken an interest in this project that goes far beyond the call of duty.

Finally I thank my wife, Jennifer, for her support and common sense, my children for many ideas and contributions, and my former wife, Elizabeth, for her compassion to the families of the ship's company.

NB
October, 1996

FOREWORD

BY SIR REX HUNT CMG
FORMER GOVERNOR OF THE FALKLAND ISLANDS

Forewords are usually written after reading the book, but I wrote the following in 1982 when Nick Barker was in mid-career in the Royal Navy with a fine record behind him and glittering prospects ahead. Nevertheless, it is I think a fitting introduction to the autobiography of a truly courageous and outstanding man.

* * *

I am writing this in the guest cabin of HMS *Endurance*. The Argentines have surrendered and we are steaming along the East Falklands coastline from Stanley where twenty-one British ships now lie peacefully at anchor, to Fitzroy, where *Sir Galahad* was mortally hit and *Sir Tristram* severely damaged by Argentine bombs a few weeks ago.

I last sat here in December, 1981, on a memorable trip to South Georgia, recalling with my wife happy memories of previous voyages on board *Endurance*. There were carefree incidents like snowballing on the upper deck as we nudged our way through the spectacular Le Maire Channel; the Chief Bosun's Mate dressed up as one of Shackleton's men off Elephant Island; skiing on Deception Island; stuck in the ice off James Ross Island; drinking beer with the Senior Ratings. But that was another world. So much has taken place since then.

On 12 December, 1981, the night after our arrival at St Andrew's Bay, I trapped my finger in the cabin door and lost a nail. In less time than it took to grow a new one the Argentines occupied the Falkland Islands and South Georgia, the British assembled a task force and transported it 8000 miles across the ocean, recaptured South Georgia, landed at San Carlos, marched across East Falkland, recaptured Stanley and sent over 10,000 Argentines packing.

This fine ship – which was about to be cast aside by the Ministry of Defence – put paid to an Argentine submarine, knocked down two helicopters, damaged a corvette and took the surrender of the garrisons at South Georgia and Southern Thule. Not bad for an 'unarmed' merchantman on her last trip!

I was, of course, delighted that HMS *Endurance* earned a reprieve. I can, however, understand that some people might think that her Captain went to inordinate lengths to guarantee her continued commission. Something less than engineering a full scale Argentine invasion might have served to prove his point! But one has to admit that, like everything else about *Endurance*, it was done with great style. And, unlike her illustrious predecessor, she survived to tell the tale. The Captain of the *Santa Fe* apparently had the opportunity to determine otherwise and perhaps for sentimental reasons decided not to deliver the *coup de grâce*.

The man whose name is synonymous with the first *Endurance*, Sir Ernest Shackleton, died on board the *Quest* in Grytviken Harbour on 5 January, 1922. His 'Number One', Commander Frank Wild, described how they took him to the hospital and placed him in a room they had shared seven years before. The next day they carried 'The Boss' to the little church situated at the foot of snow-covered mountains. There they said goodbye 'to a great explorer, a great leader and a good comrade'.

'The Boss' whose name will now be forever associated with the second *Endurance* is Nick Barker. Although there is no longer the opportunity to win the first of Wild's accolades I imagine his Number One, Mike Green, would confirm the other two. Come to think of it, I'm not sure that Nick does not qualify for all three, for I remember exploring uncharted seas off James Ross Island and being filled with admiration at the coolness on the bridge as the seabed suddenly shoaled from 40 to 9 metres. The only people having kittens were myself and the television team – landlubbers all and lacking in *sang froid* and the Nelson

Touch. All I could think of was Bill Stephens, the Marine Engineering Officer, who explained that he had to stop the engine before putting it into reverse. So, with *Endurance* the days of exploration are not over.

I shall never forget the anxiety we felt for *Endurance* during those days at the end of March, 1982. We knew the Argentine fleet was at sea; we did not know where. We did however know that *Endurance* was heading west towards us from South Georgia. We dearly longed to see her return, of course, but with hindsight I am heartily glad she did not make it. Another day and she would have been there. I do not think she would have stopped the invasion but she would have tried and would almost certainly have been sunk with considerable loss of life.

As it was, she returned to South Georgia and thus began what must have been one of the strangest hide and seek games in military history. We all have reason to be grateful to Nick Barker, not only for successfully conducting the campaign to save his ship from the Whitehall axe, but also from the Argentine Navy. Thanks to him *Endurance* endures.

Wild said of Shackleton: 'Of his hardihood and extraordinary powers of endurance, his buoyant powers of optimism when things seemed hopeless, and his unflinching courage in the face of danger I have no need to speak.'

If Wild had been alive today I am sure he would say the same about 'The Boss' of the second *Endurance*. I salute Captain Barker and all who sailed with him.

South Shetland Islands

King George Island

Nelson I.

Greenwich I.

Bransfield Strait

Deception I.

Hope Bay

James Ross I.

Seymour I.

BELLINGSHAUSEN

SEA

ANTARCTIC PENINSULA

Cape Disappointment

WEDDELL

SEA

Adelaide Island

Rothera

Larson Ice Shelf

Marguerite Bay

The Antarctic Peninsula

Miles

0   50   100

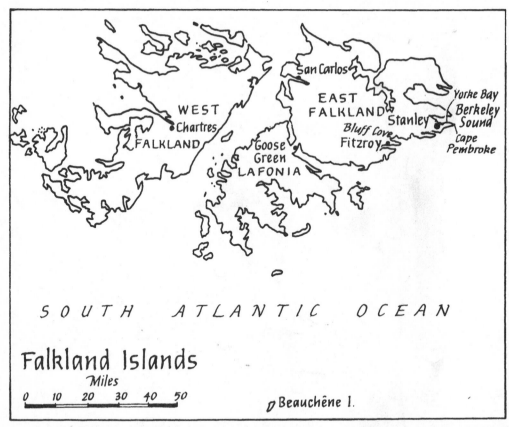

WEST
FALKLAND
Chartres

San Carlos

EAST
FALKLAND
Stanley

Yorke Bay
Berkeley
Sound

Goose
Green
LAFONIA

Bluff Cove
Fitzroy

Cape
Pembroke

SOUTH   ATLANTIC   OCEAN

Falkland Islands

Miles

0   10   20   30   40   50

Beauchêne I.

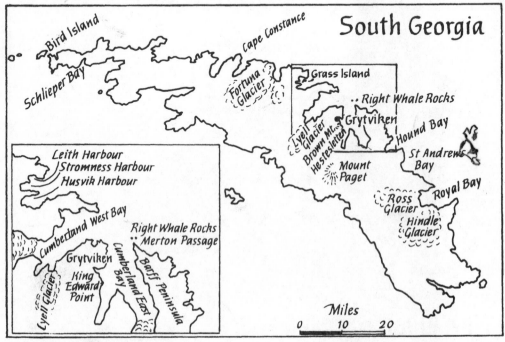

Bird Island

Cape Constance

South Georgia

Schlieper Bay

Fortuna
Glacier

Grass Island

Right Whale Rocks

Lyell
Glacier
Brown Mt.
Hestesletten

Grytviken

Hound Bay

St Andrews
Bay

Mount
Paget

Ross
Glacier

Royal Bay

Hindle
Glacier

Leith Harbour
Stromness Harbour
Husvik Harbour

Cumberland West Bay

Right Whale Rocks
Merton Passage

Grytviken

Lyell
Glacier

King
Edward
Point

Cumberland
Bay

Cumberland East

Barff Peninsula

Miles

0   10   20

INTRODUCTION

1 April, 1982

It was a chill early morning. The sea was rough and the ship was heading westwards in a force ten gale. We were all accustomed to the violent pitching and rolling motion, but this time it felt much worse. The foul weather, the danger presented by the enemy and the political situation in which we found ourselves combined to create a nausea of frustration. The situation was as dark as the day. We had to work out a practical plan as soon as possible.

Commanding a ship can be a lonely business. When things are going well there is nothing more satisfying. I had been fortunate enough to command a number of ships, but never before had I felt so alone or betrayed.

'This is the worst day of my life,' I wrote in my diary. Why had the MOD not listened to my warnings? Why hadn't the government repeated the strategy of 1977 and sent a small deterrent force to the South Atlantic? It had worked then. Why not now?

The Argentine amphibious force had landed on the Falklands beaches near Port Stanley. It was highly likely that another landing would take place on South Georgia, 400 miles away. HMS *Endurance* was half way between the two areas, heading towards the Falklands. Our ship stood alone as the only British presence in the South Atlantic. this was the culmination of years of political bungling, diplomatic misunderstanding and disastrous intelligence assessment.

I gathered together my tactical team. There was Francis Ponsonby, a former submarine Captain, who by fortunate coincidence was on board with a team making a film about the Royal Navy in the Antarctic. I was also able to turn to Bill Hurst, my senior and much trusted Navigating Officer, and to Tony Ellerbeck, our courageous Flight Commander. Unhappily we were without Mike Green, my second-in-command. Mike had been struck down with peritonitis a month earlier in South America. Despite Mike's absence I felt we had a strong, sensible and mature command team. From their reaction I knew I reflected the mood of the moment.

'There must be something we can do to zap these bastards,' I said.

Looking round the communications office I read the determination on their faces. Such was the urgency of the moment it was easy to ignore the chatter of radio sets and teleprinters, and the kaleidoscope of lights and displays. The signals had been pouring in. When Port Stanley went off air we thought of our ship's Naval survey team we had recently left there. The last communication had them shredding documents in Government House, accompanied by the distant rattle of machine-gun fire. We knew there were sixty or so marines dug in defensively. The 'last resort' was the small detachment around Government House. Faced by the first invasion wave of 2000 Argentines, they kept the flag flying for hours longer than expected.

The British Antarctic Survey radio confirmed the fall of Stanley. Ham radio operators from the UK told of the great victory claimed by the Argentines. Our covert helicopter over South Georgia had confirmed the worst. Our options were limited. We had left our Royal Marines on the ground in South Georgia. We were threatened by an Argentine group of two frigates, two destroyers, a submarine and a support tanker. The Argentine Group Commander, Cesar Trombetta, had invited us to surrender South Georgia. We told him to 'get stuffed'. Further communications were ignored, but it would have been difficult to place a bet on our survival as things stood. Further breaks in radio silence could seal our fate. Despite all this, the mood of my command team echoed my own. We had to do something positive.

The obvious target was the tanker. Was it worth trying to ram it with the ice-breaking bow before turning east and down sea for South Georgia to support our Royal Marine Detachment? Here was something positive. I felt better. A plan was beginning to form. If nothing else we could leave the Argentine groups of ships without fuel. Without their 'filling station' these gas guzzlers could find themselves in a perilous situation drifting towards South Georgia. Then we could attack with our short-range helicopter-launched guided missiles. The alternative was a probably suicidal attempt to enter the harbour at Port Stanley in the vain hope of deterring an already committed amphibious operation.

There is irony in remembering that this was to be the final commission of the *Endurance*. John Nott, the Secretary of State for Defence, had included the ship in a package of swingeing defence cuts which included the sale of the aircraft carrier HMS *Invincible*. He had charted a course for maritime diplomacy that was depressingly similar to the one set by government for national industries and services. He was deaf, not only to the advice of the First Sea Lord, Sir Henry Leach, but also to Lord Shackleton, perhaps the most acknowledged expert on the South Atlantic. More surprisingly, perhaps, he had refused to heed the warning delivered by a group of more than 300 peers and MPs (led by Lords Shackleton, Buxton, Callaghan and Hill-Norton) who believed that the withdrawal of HMS *Endurance* would precipitate military action by Argentina. The firm impression was that the Government didn't give a damn about the South Atlantic until political necessity forced their hand. Now they had to do something. And afterwards, when it was all over, there was a greater irony. This little war became Margaret Thatcher's finest hour.

When it came to talking to the media I was as firmly muzzled as a pit bull terrier with his MOD minder leading him round the show ring. There would be no hint of controversy, and no leaks to the press. The message was loud and depressingly clear: 'You may have been right, Captain Barker, but on no account are

3

you to say so.' There was a General Election looming in mid-1983. No one, particularly Government and military service officials, were to undermine Mrs Thatcher's reputation as a war leader.

The subsequent enquiry was like the débris of a paint factory explosion. There was little of substance left, and that which did survive was whitewashed. This was not the fault of enquiry chairman Lord Franks, an academic of integrity. But the intention was always to clear the government. This much I had suspected then. Later I had it confirmed personally by a member of the Board of the Enquiry.

Sadly these were the politics of the 1980s. Dog eat dog: an 'enterprise culture' becoming a contract culture with its noose growing ever tighter around the neck of community spirit. Arrogance and rudeness replaced courtesy and integrity. The message was loud and clear – 'Look after Number One'. This brought out the least attractive aspects of the British character. Greed and self-interest came first: the weakest could go to the wall. One immediate and obvious symptom of the new establishment was the way that political mistakes were covered up at almost any cost. The British model of 'firm but fair' was replaced by a dictatorial arrogance. An early casualty of this approach was defence policy.

John Nott was a hatchet man appointed to sort out any 'old buffers' still prepared to stand their ground. He had the advantage of being able to rely on powerful political allies and the Civil Service. None of them had much respect for the intellect of senior serving officers. The mission was to stop inter-service rivalry and massively to cut the cost of procurement. This policy led directly to the bloody nose we received when the Argentines invaded the Falklands.

Did we learn from our mistakes? I don't think so. Every year the axe falls more heavily and Whitehall continues to bungle. The Prime Minister is poorly advised, and government departments are put through the mangle as never before. The theory is that if you reorganize and restructure regularly enough things will eventually get better. This is a smokescreen. Changes that do not address fundamental management and commitments first – purposeful channels of communication and a thorough understanding of what is expected of each department and individual within it – are doomed. Sometimes it feels as if we are all invited to take part in a massive game of Musical Chairs: every time the music stops, some poor bastard is out on his ear. Perhaps this begins to explain why our confidence and self-respect as a nation is often low, and why our standing in the world continues to decline at a pace that few would have thought possible a generation ago.

I probably feel these things strongly because I have a real sense of pride in my country and pride in my service. I'm not a political animal in any formal sense. I have never been associated with a political party. But from my upbringing and later experiences I've formed an unshakeable belief that given the opportunity (and the right kind of leadership) we do things very well. There are still roots of excellence everywhere and we have young men and women of ability and commitment. But it's not enough. We need leaders of vision and integrity. We should encourage initiative. We should not be frightened to shout down those who constantly say, 'Better not'. Above all, we should have courage and we should care. All these qualities can be found in our history and traditions. And what happened in the Falklands in 1982 was proof that these foundations of British character still exist.

I was promoted to Captain RN in December, 1979, and appointed to command HMS *Endurance* in May, 1980. I had just completed two years with the Ministry of Defence and had already enjoyed a number of sea-going commands. *Endurance* was considered to be a special appointment. Certainly it was unlike any other command. It was considered necessary to be briefed by the appropriate departments of the Foreign and Commonwealth Office. There were also briefings from the British Antarctic Survey and Scott Polar Research Institute at Cambridge. Finally there were the 'normal' military courses which are an integral part of any Naval sea command.

Ironically, just a few months before the *Endurance* appointment, I joined the Maritime Tactical School for a special study period where we considered defence aspects of a Task Force at sea. One of our main recommendations was 'Air Early Warning' for the fleet. The demise of the carriers *Ark Royal* and *Eagle* meant that we had lost the fixed-wing Gannet aircraft, our tactical eye in the sky. The Harriers and helicopters that were to play such an important part in the Falklands Conflict were not fitted with Air Early Warning equipment. This meant that the British taskforce had to rely solely on shipborne radar which could only detect an incoming raid up to 200 miles. In tactical terms this could be described as a Local Warning System. Sadly, it proved largely ineffective as the enemy aircraft often approached close to the surface of the sea below radar cover. The recommendations of the Maritime Tactical School were digested by the appropriate departments in both the MOD and by the Commander in Chief's staff at Northwood. No action was taken. We also expressed reservations about the reliability of the Air Defence Missile, the Sea Dart System, though there was genuine enthusiasm about the short-range Sea Wolf because of its speed and accuracy.

It's easy to be wise after the event, but when the British Task Force was put to the test these observations proved to be prophetic. Again, with the benefit of hindsight, it is fair to claim that the Task Force performed admirably despite these major deficiencies in our armoury.

At least some lessons have been learned. Some Sea King helicopters were later fitted with Air Early Warning Radar and the Sea Dart System has been upgraded. It's also true to say that satellite surveillance and the shipborne intelligence systems have improved almost beyond recognition. But why did it take a war and the associated loss of life to convince our moguls that the Navy should be provided with the fundamental tools of the trade?

I had been invited to join a most exclusive club. My officers and ship's company were not much different from those of the Shackleton era, or any of those courageous ships' companies in the 1939–45 War. What we saw once again was Britain at her best in a backs-to-the-wall situation.

It's an odd thing. Here is a story about party political arrogance, ill-judged frugality in government departments and the incompetence of mandarins in the corridors of power. But it is also a tale of extraordinary loyalty to Queen and Country and a highly professional fighting service. And, for my money, the officers and men of the *Endurance* matched up to the highest traditions of the Royal Navy.

Chapter 1

SOUTH ATLANTIC BRIEFING

Until the Conflict I think it is true to say that very few British people knew where the islands were, or indeed that they were British. Those who had heard of the Falklands most frequently placed the island group somewhere off the west coast of Scotland.

I had already seen for myself that Argentina was a nation of great culture and a proud historical tradition, and, even under the Junta, was probably one of Britain's closest allies outside the Commonwealth. The Conflict of 1982 focused attention on a neglected and little understood, part of the world. Until that time British politicians had taken what they would certainly have claimed to be a firm stand on behalf of the Falkland islanders. Significantly, however, they had avoided any decision over sovereignty. In part this was to avoid damaging relations with Argentina, or worse still causing provocation, but it was never clear what the Argentines would do if provoked.

The Falkland question is one aspect of a much larger problem – the political and economic future of the South Atlantic region. The economic potential of the area, has always been promising and since the Conflict it has lived up to the most optimistic forecasts.

My preparations before joining HMS *Endurance* in 1980 had filled me with enthusiasm. I was longing to get south and work in that extraordinary environment. But no preparation, however thorough, can adequately prepare for the magic of the Antarctic. It can be never less than a privilege to catch a scent of the pioneering exploits of men like Amundsen, Scott, Shackleton, Fuchs, and Hempleman-Adams. There were the modern luminaries too, many of whom I have had the privilege to come to know. Stephen Venables, Monica Kristianson and Ranulph Fiennes continued a tradition of Antarctic heroism. And, there is a marvellous heroic link through the late Lord Shackleton, and his father, Sir Ernest.

Sharing a similar wealth of experience, and a deep understanding of wild life of the region is Lord Buxton, the former head of Anglia Television and the Independent Television Authority. I was also greatly influenced by Dr Richard Laws, the Director of the British Antarctic Survey, Dr John Heap, who led the Polar Department at the FCO, and Robin Fearn who was responsible for South America and the Falklands at the Foreign and Commonwealth Office.

Charles Swithinbank and the late Nigel Bonner at the British Atlantic Survey were instrumental in helping me to understand the scientific ambitions of British exploration. They also passed on their unquenchable thirst for further knowledge. This has stood me in good stead ever since.

The wild places of the world all have their special magic. During two sea-going commissions in the Middle East I had come to learn something of the Bedouins and nomads of those vast desert tracts. That was during the 60s, and it seemed to me that they were much the better for having assimilated little of 'modern civilisation.'

But the Antarctic is the wildest and most beautiful desert on earth. There are no nomadic tribes and no disease. In the Antarctic there are very different environmental hazards – from wind, sea, ice and intense cold.

But there is life there aplenty – untamed and, for the most part, unexploited. Here too a permanent 'deep freeze' creates unexpected problems. Garbage, for instance, survives for years and so must be burnt. Climatic changes are more sudden than anywhere else within my experience, and when the weather seriously misbehaves sea conditions in the South Atlantic are probably more severe than anywhere else on earth.

The four and a half million square miles of the Antarctic are uniquely isolated. Much of the rock surface beneath the ice is below sea level, so the sheer volume of frozen water is almost unimaginable. One calculation suggests that if the ice cap should melt the mean sea level around our planet would rise by 100 metres. For me that figure is perhaps the best possible illustration of the threat of global warming.

'Endurance' is a symbolic name. The first *Endurance* – of Sir Ernest Shackleton's expedition of 1914–16 – was marooned and crushed in the Weddell Sea. But Shackleton's complete company survived after he and five others battled 800 miles from Elephant Island to South Georgia to find assistance. Shackleton had been a member of Scott's 1901 expedition, but this was his finest hour. In the darkest days of 1982 we were very short of food and pursued by the Argentine Navy in weather that was perfectly bloody. I called for that 'extra little bit of British grit.' The Ernest Shackleton story was all the inspiration we needed.

I also came to understand the wider role of the Navy in the Antarctic. Indeed the name of the ship itself provided some pointers. The first *Endurance* had been bought by Shackleton for the purpose of exploration. Soon enough the name became synonymous with bravery and leadership, and, quite literally, endurance. I began to understand what a privilege it was to follow this tradition.

Dr John Heap's Foreign Office briefing was meticulous. The US-brokered 1961 Antarctic Treaty was one of the few that actually worked. 'British Antarctica' had no more recognition than the territorial claims of Chile and Argentina. The continent was in effect a No Man's Land where national sovereignty did not apply. In theory this meant there should be no political dimension other than the co-operation of the various national organizations in the interest of science. In theory too the exchange of information could be more complete, or at least more open, than in any other situation in the world. And to a very large extent that level of co-operation did exist. When unfettered by political directives, scientists are the first to recognize that vested interests are well served through co-operation.

Atmospheric science was also a well-established discipline in our Antarctic bases. It was the British Antarctic Survey who 'discovered' the hole in the ozone layer in the early 1980s. As the climatic and meteorological impact began to be calculated there was a bandwagon of publicity. One impact of this, following the Conflict, was that quite a large grant was given to the Antarctic Survey. Until that time research funding had been sparse. That momentum has been sustained. Increasing concern about global warming, skin cancer, and other problems associated with ozone holes, means that there is now a multinational dimension and commitment to Antarctic atmospheric research.

Antarctica has a considerable impact on climatic conditions throughout the world. It is often argued that an understanding of the world's weather could properly begin with the cold continent. There is earth science evidence (the Gondwana Theory) which suggests that the geological provinces of the southern continents could be matched across the intervening oceans, providing evidence of the former conjunction of these land masses. One example of this is the way the Andes extend geologically into the Antarctic peninsula. The inevitable geophysical conclusion of this is that Antarctica must hold vast mineral wealth. Statistically this is likely to be equivalent to the total of mineral resources already found in the Andes, South Africa, India and Australia. It was calculated by the US Geological Survey that over 900 economic mineral deposits exist on the continent, although only twenty-one of these are likely to occur in ice free areas. Similarly the hydrocarbon deposits, already discovered in southern continents, are likely to be mirrored in Antarctica. Known resources include large quantities of mineral ores, particularly iron and copper. Gold and silver have also been discovered, and the coal deposits are enormous.

The Antarctic Treaty created a moratorium on mineral exploitation. Intensified exploration would have a major impact on the environment, so consequently the full extent of the South Atlantic's natural resources remain largely a matter of speculation.

The potential of icebergs as a source of water is also well known. Ice forms 98 per cent of the earth's fresh water resources.

Antarctica contains 90 per cent of the world's ice, and therefore 88 per cent of the world's fresh water. The annual iceberg production by ice shelves and glaciers fringing the continent is vast. Although it is considered impractical to tow icebergs to continents in the southern hemisphere, it is possible, even plausible, that ice could become an economic resource for water and energy.

It is equally well known that active and dormant volcanoes are associated with sulphur deposits. There is considerable fumarolic activity in the South Sandwich Islands. As yet there has been no study made of the quantity of available sulphur.

Within the South-West Atlantic the main life resources could be categorized as whales, seals, birds, fish, krill and squid. The harvesting of whales began a century ago, peaked in the mid-1930s, then diminished. Seal stocks were not seriously reduced during the early part of this century, and are not exploited today. Penguins were taken for oil on some islands but there is little likelihood of future exploitation.

Krill, a prawn-like plankton, is the cornerstone of the eco-system. The squid industry has already progressed from just a few ships to large fleets from Spain, the Far East and Argentina. Fishing has been heavy in some areas, with krill fished experimentally since the early 1960s. More recently the Russians and Japanese have been harvesting krill on a limited commercial basis. In 1980 the squid had hardly been exploited, but catches have risen steadily. In Lord Shackleton's second (1992) report it was noted that Antarctic krill appeared to be the world's biggest known source of animal protein. 15 per cent of krill weight is protein, a similar value to fillet steak.

The Antarctic Survey had at the time completed a number of studies which estimated the potential annual sustainable yield at between 100 and 150 million tonnes. A very substantial proportion of this appears to occur within a 200-mile band between South Georgia and the Antarctic Peninsula. The swarms contain about 500 individuals per cubic foot of water. This density makes them look from the air like a red oil slick. Catching krill, as we found in *Endurance*, was relatively simple. The major difficulty is in avoiding crushing them as the catch is hauled onto the deck. Krill looks and tastes like prawn, but once caught must be processed within four hours. They cannot simply be frozen because digestive enzymes within the krill work at very low temperatures. This means first boiling, then removing the shells. The shelf life of krill processed in this way is three to four months. To make harvesting economic the quantities taken must be large, and the sale and distribution swift. The remoteness of the fishing grounds mitigate against this, but the developing demand (particularly in the Far East and Spain) makes it likely that the days of large-scale harvesting are not far away.

Commercial exploitation of Antarctic fish is a relatively recent activity. Notofinia probably makes up about three quarters of the coastal catch. Sample scoops include eels and sea-snails, rat-tailed fish, cod-like specimens and skate. These once existed in larger quantities off South Georgia and the South Sandwich Islands, but were largely fished out by the former Eastern Block countries. There are still reasonable stocks of blue whiting and Patagonian hake.

But since 1982 it is the squid industry that has brought a measure of prosperity to the Falklands. Until recent years the prospect of the Argentines exploiting these fisheries was very small. They are not a nation of great fish eaters, and most of the stock demand is taken from the River Plate and northern coastal areas of Argentina. But the market is such that the Argentines do now fish for squid outside the 150 mile (latterly 200 mile) Falkland zone. They also follow the available data on squid stocks and take an active part in international discussions on stocking levels.

An additional resource for the future may be the larger algae. It is possible to extract the Giant Seaweed (kelp) and to produce a wide range of products used mainly in the food, drink, textile, rubber and paper industries. However, synthetic substitutes have in many cases been so efficient that the alginate industry has not prospered. But the position could change. One company has approached the Falklands Islands Government on the subject of seaweed harvesting. It is estimated that this business could be worth £40,000 a year.

But even the limited data available in 1980 made it clear that the live resources were plentiful in the area around the islands and this gave considerable scope for the improvement of the Falklands economy. These prospects are being investigated. But, at the time of the Conflict, the total GNP of the Falklands was less than £4 million a year. The islands were simply not tooled up for the job. They did not have the right kind of fishing vessels, shore facilities, or the necessary air and sea connections. With the exploitation of the fin fish industry, and revenue from squid fishing licences, the islands' income had risen to more than £30 million by 1985. Through this burgeoning of offshore activity, not anticipated even by the Shackleton reports, the political and strategic value of the islands has become considerably enhanced.

There had also been some difference of opinion in the past among the islanders themselves about what the thrust of development strategy should be. In general terms the expatriate British were against further exploitation; Falkland islanders of longer standing believed some development was essential for the survival of the islands' economy. Lord Shackleton believed that development should begin with those island-based projects that had the most potential. Later initiatives, such as exploiting living resources and hydrocarbons offshore, could use the islands as a resources base.

During the last 15 years Antarctica has become targeted by the tourist industry, to the extent that ships from Argentina and Australia travel to areas that are navigationally unsafe. Charts, very much part of the rôle of HMS *Endurance*, remain few and far between. Surveys are made around large tabular icebergs, but if the iceberg is firmly aground the survey will not be completed until the iceberg breaks up or moves. It is not rare for ships to become impaled on rock pinnacles. The mapping of the area is of paramount importance for the safety of tourist vessels and the supply ships which support research.

A significant level of Falklands tourism began with an awareness created by the Conflict. In 1980 onshore tourist facilities amounted to one hotel and one guest house. The small cruise ships, *World Discoverer* and *World Explorer*, called fairly regularly at Stanley, and occasionally there were short-haul passenger vessels from Argentina and Chile.

The failure of successive governments to match the economic aspirations of Argentine society was high on the nation's political agenda in the early 1980s. The Junta was well aware of the propaganda as well as practical value of a firm foothold in the South Atlantic. And the Argentine claim to the islands should not only be seen in terms of disputed historical precedents. Several generations of Argentines had been brought up to believe that the Malvinas were their property. Negotiations had repeatedly failed to find any satisfactory solutions. The 1982 Conflict hardened the attitude of the British government. It was difficult to discuss sovereignty before 1982: it is almost impossible now.

Before the 1961 treaty was ratified Britain claimed an Antarctic sector of some 60 degrees, roughly south of Cape Horn round to an area south of South Georgia and the South Sandwich Islands. A similar area was claimed by Argentina, and Chile also had a claim within the sector. To the east there was a large sector claimed by Norway and another by Australia, who also claimed a second smaller sector. New Zealand and France also had claims to smaller sectors. The New Zealand sector ice shelf has since become important as the staging base for US exploration.

Much of the continent is covered by an ever-mobile ice sheet up to four kilometres thick. The main areas worth considering in an exploitation context are the continental margin and the area beneath the ice shelves. A 1978 study of world oil resources suggested that Antarctica was likely to hold oil fields of more than 700 million tonnes. Equally it was clear that, because of the harsh Antarctic environment, nothing less than these giant deposits would be economically viable. There was also evidence to suggest that large fields were most likely to be found in the West Antarctic continental margin. Perhaps most promising of all was the Weddell Sea area. Significantly, this is within transport aircraft range of South America. Thought was also given to the logistics of an oil operation using the deep water harbours of the Falklands and South Georgia.

The treaty powers began in the early 70s to anticipate the day when mineral exploration and exploitation would begin. One political dimension of this was the OPEC oil crisis, and the subsequent rationing imposed in many western countries. This, in turn, raised the question of what mineral exploitation may do to the environment.

There was also reciprocal fear and distrust. No country wanted to break the Treaty, but neither could they afford to be left at the starting post. The moratorium agreed in 1975 was essentially an expression of status quo until such time as the tactical, political and environmental problems could be resolved.

The conclusion, as quoted by Quill in *A Pole Apart* was: 'To urge their nationals and other states to refrain from all exploration and exploitation of Antarctic mineral resources while making progress towards the timely adoption of an agreed régime concerning Antarctic mineral resources. They will thus endeavour to ensure that, pending the timely adoption of agreed solutions pertaining to exploitation and exploration, no activity will be conducted to explore or exploit such resources. They will keep these matters under continuing examination.'

One response concerned the discordant voices sounding from several of the treaty countries. A widely held view in the US was that the moratorium achieved little but the delay of important decisions.

A number of companies put up the cash for a circum-polar seismic study to operate throughout the deep south. In 1978 Gulf Oil sought official US blessing for a consortium to begin the work. The proposal was turned down because Washington did not want to be caught with dirty hands. But, since that date, a number of countries have made geophysical surveys of their own.

Many of the treaty powers have become more hawkish in what they see as the pursuit of national interest. It is significant that this hardening of attitude comes largely from the energy-dependent countries. It has been said that nothing makes nations as covetous as oil.

Even though the extraction of hard rock minerals now seems distant this eventuality must be seriously considered. The claimant states must therefore devise some tangible benefit from mineral extraction on their territory over and above what others may gain. This could be disguised in a variety of ways, perhaps even as a contribution to environmental protection.

The thoroughness of my briefing from the British Antarctic Survey in 1980 made me at least reasonably informed about what to expect at the Antarctic bases. But this was not just to enable me to take an intelligent part in the conversation. One of my jobs would be to report on the progress of projects undertaken by the various nations established in 'the British Sector.'

More emotive at the time were the prospects that faced the Falklands. In 1976 Lord Shackleton led a report on the economic value and prospects of the islands. The report commented that the geological knowledge of the area to the east of Argentina had increased steadily, though much of the knowledge had been obtained from areas up to 100 miles from the Argentine coast, and not in the area to the north and west of the Falklands. Opinions therefore varied about the prospects for the oil in the South West Atlantic.

The Malvinas Basin was seismically surveyed by BP in 1979 and test drilling had taken place near the vicinity of Rio Gallegos off the Argentine coast. This had been done under contractual arrangements with the Argentine oil company YBF and had so far yielded seven hydrocarbon finds, of which about half were believed to be natural gas.

A US geological survey was anything but conclusive. But they did estimate that the area to the north and to the west of the Falklands could provide nine times the oil deposits of the North Sea. If this was so, it would be the largest untapped source of oil in the world. Even if this US optimism is combined with the guarded pessimism of the British and Argentine oil companies, the area would still be of great economic significance. Shackleton also believed that oil would have to be found in considerable quantity throughout the Malvinas Basin.

Despite an increasing weight of evidence suggesting that it was only a matter of time before competing nations joined the world's greatest oil rush, the Ministry of Defence did not consider the Falklands to be of any strategic importance. The British government held a similar view. Even in 1982 the resource potential of the South Atlantic was not a reason for going to war. It has often been said since that the reason Mrs Thatcher's decision to take on the Argentines had much to do with the known resources of the area. This is categorically and utterly untrue.

As part of my briefing I was told that the South Atlantic's mineral and hydrocarbon resources were far less likely to be exploited in the short term than the living marine resources. Indeed in the years running up to the Conflict one of the main sources of onshore income was the sale of stamps. In 1980 this amounted to £700,000 – more than 20 per cent of the GNP.

There was always the scope for agriculture and diversification, but an equal reluctance to develop beef farming beyond the needs of local consumption. 20,000 sheep carcasses were disposed of annually. The cost of butchering and cold storage has been prohibitive. This could change if the sheep meat industry shared its freezing and shipping facilities with a significant fishing industry. For the time being, however, wool is likely to remain the mainstay of the economy. The yearly clip amounts to over 2000 tonnes, taken from 650,000 sheep which are mainly of the Polward or Corriedale type with a mixture of Romney and Merino blood. The fact that each animal grazed (in 1982) approximately four acres indicated the scope for improvement. There were various schemes, such as the Grassland Trials Unit, that were seeking to improve the quality of grazing. Wool output has been falling since 1975 and revenue from this has not been reinvested. It is also probably true to say that new attitudes need to be established before a proper infrastructure can be maintained.

There were also only forty-one Falkland Farms ranging from 5000 to 400,000 acres. The twenty-three smallest farms owned just 13 per cent of the sheep. The five largest owned 43 per cent. The Falkland Island Company, then owned by Coalite, had seven farms and 45 per cent. Shackleton believed some of these 'monopoly' farms should be divided and owned by existing islanders, or people interested in settling on a long-term basis. In effect this meant transferring ownership from absentee landlords to people with a truly local interest. He recommended that the 'new' farms should be units of 12 to 15 thousand acres.

But it was recognized that it would be difficult to establish new farm buildings and access roads, and to find suitable owner occupiers.

The lack of roads and tracks is a major problem. The islands of Lewis and Harris in the Outer Hebrides are probably most comparable, although the infrastructure was rather more civilized and developed. The Falkland Islanders relied on tracks rather than roads. These networked the farms before leading inexorably to Port Stanley. There was a road of sorts leading from the capital to Stanley airport. Mount Pleasant did not exist at that stage.

The islands' population was then approximately 2000. The view of many local pundits was that significant development could only come through enhanced infrastructure.

The major role of HMS *Endurance* was as the guardship to the Falkland Islands and British interests in the Antarctic. In effect this made her an important diplomatic tool in the Southern Hemisphere. This may have been considered fairly insignificant in terms of our wider defence commitments in 1981. The decision of John Nott to withdraw the guardship appeared to give carte blanche to Argentina. In turn this made the *Endurance* pivotal in what followed.

From Denis Healey in 1966 to John Nott in 1981 financial pressures appeared from all sides. Successive reviews and studies were carried out, always with the primary objective of cutting expense, but not commitments.

It is generally fairly easy for a Secretary of State to determine the rôle of the other services. Political exigencies almost predetermine what this should be. The RAF are usually deployed primarily as air support to the Army. It is rather more difficult to establish a tangible rôle for the Navy: politicians are less inclined to invest in 'contingency scenarios'. Partly because of this, there was never much doubt that John Nott's 'rationalization' of defence policy would hit the Navy hardest. He followed the NATO minimalist line on strategy and had no difficulty in accepting that the long-standing commitments of the Army and Air Force should remain. He was far less convinced by the Navy's (necessarily) more convoluted reasoning. But he accepted advice that the emphasis of anti-submarine effort (by which the Navy set much store) should shift to nuclear-powered submarines and shore-based aircraft. He appeared to discount the importance of the amphibious rôle.

In May, 1980, Keith Speed, Minister for the Navy, resigned in protest at the decisions he saw as inevitable. The ensuing document: 'Defence Policy: the Way Forward' imposed a severe cut in the Royal Navy force level. Only two carriers were to remain, specialized amphibious ships were to be reduced, destroyers and frigates were to be heavily cut and manpower was to be commensurably diminished. In effect the Royal Navy was to become 'a contribution to NATO'. Anything beyond the NATO area was discounted or not seen as a significant threat.

Admiral Hill, summed up the situation: 'Admiral Leach had the unenviable task of trying to explain the policy to the men and women of the Royal Navy and to keep up morale.'

Another problem we faced was implicit in the nature of Whitehall. A ship, or a squadron of ships, may work for a number of different ministries all of whom are equally keen to defray costs elsewhere. The ensuing paper chase inevitably makes life more difficult and slows down the process of decision making. Later, for instance, when I became Captain Fishery Protection the main political battle was to maintain Ministry of Agriculture and Fisheries funding for what was a Naval commitment. And, when the Fishery Protection Squadron was involved with oil platform protection, or helping the Customs in their battle against imported drugs, this became a Home Office problem. At times I found myself involved in circuitous arguments and discussions with half a dozen departments represented around the table.

Much of the same applied to *Endurance*. She was a Naval ship employed on Foreign Office, Ministry of Education and MOD tasks. This later made arguing the case for her survival, and that of her successor, a minefield of fiscal complexities.

But there is no doubt that the sovereignty issue created most of the friction. At the heart of any sovereignty debate is the indisputable fact that the Falklands people are of British descent and do not wish to be part of Argentina. It was fundamentally on that basis that the Government of 1982 decided to deploy the Task Force.

All the claims and counter-claims are questionable and history is a poor advocate for any and all of the claimants. What matters is the status quo: the islanders are people of British descent who do not wish to be part of Argentina. But emotional flames were fanned by General Peron in the years following 1948. Even so, protests remained low key until the matter was brought to the United Nations in 1964.

Argentina's claims to the Falklands, and other disputed territories, tend to occur when the country's internal political situation is most unstable. Peron was the first to play the Falklands card. A long line of military dictators, all the way to Galtieri, have followed this lead. Peron arguably had the greatest impact on shaping Argentina for the second half of the 20th century. In 1946 this almost unknown army officer took advantage of his position within the Junta to introduce three new elements into Argentine politics. First, a well-organized trade union movement loyal to him alone. Secondly, an expansionist economic policy which produced hundreds of new jobs. Thirdly, he instilled a virulent spirit of anti-imperialism directed mainly at the United States. The formula was so successful that he managed to sustain his position for nine years. Even after his exile, Peronist policies gradually became indistinguishable from those of the powerful Radical Party. The legacy of the Peron movement is clearly evident in Argentina today. The man himself has become as much part of the national mythology as the 'fact' of the legitimate Argentine claim to the Malvinas, and the methods he used to seize and maintain power have become a model for a more subtle approach to dictatorship.

Following the Conflict a distinguished Argentine historian, Dr Carlos Escude, wrote: 'Myths in Argentina's political culture are taken to be unquestionable truths which lead to the implementation of self-defeating policies. When disaster befalls as a result of these policies the conviction that Argentina is a victim of fraud and conspiracy becomes even more deeply rooted.' Escude argues that Argentina's policy is less flexible than Britain's. He calls for realism and reconciliation. He warns his countrymen:

'Our outrage does not deserve to be taken seriously. When lack of realism engulfs not only the policy making, but also moral judgement, there can be little hope for a country's future.'

Britain had recognized the independence of the United Provinces as early as 1824. Neither that recognition nor the treaty of Amity, Trade and Navigation of 1825 made any mention of the Falklands.

Spain did not recognize the independence of her former colonies until 1859. This in turn was 48 years since the Royal Governor of Montevideo had withdrawn his garrison and settlers. This all adds to the weight of evidence against the Spanish inheritance claim. Argentina is hardly the sole heir to the inheritance and Spain could not legitimately bequeath any territory she did not possess.

The Buenos Aires Government was the most ambitious of the former colonial governments. Its boundaries with Bolivia, Paraguay and Uruguay were formed more by armed force than negotiation. This policy continued following the establishment of the Federal Republic of Argentina in 1853, 20 years after the British had re-established their Falkland settlement.

The United Nations Resolution of 1968 could have been a watershed in the sovereignty argument. Resolution 2065 called for Argentina and Britain to proceed without delay with a view to finding a peaceful solution to the dispute. But a succession of dogmatic Argentine governments and an equal amount of muddled thinking at Whitehall mitigated against any sort of solution.

During the seventeen years that followed six clear initiatives were taken. In each case there was little or no agreement. Inevitably further initiatives were stillborn. The clearest and most conciliatory communiqué of intent was issued in 1968. This statement was again highlighted by Lord Franks' enquiry following the Conflict. It said: 'The Government of the United Kingdom, as part of such a final settlement, will recognize Argentina's sovereignty over the islands from a date to be agreed. This date will be agreed as soon as possible after (1) the two governments have resolved the present divergence between them as to the criteria according to which the United Kingdom shall consider the interest of the islanders would be secured by the safeguards and guarantees to be offered by the Argentine Government. (2) the Government of the United Kingdom are then satisfied that those interests are also secured.'

Publication of the memorandum was to be accompanied by a unilateral statement making it clear that the Government would be willing to proceed to a final statement with Argentina that was acceptable to the islands' inhabitants.

Lord Chalfont visited the islands in September, 1968, to explain the policy. As Argentina would not accept the wishes of the islanders this visit was badly received in the Falklands, the Houses of Parliament and the British press. But even before the policy was laid to rest it was clear that the communiqué would come back to haunt the government. In fact the Government retraced their steps and substantial bilateral negotiations did follow, resulting in closer links between the Falklands and Argentina. A regular air link was established. Supplies and essential services including oil, an improved postal service and educational opportunities were all part of a Foreign Office strategy designed to woo the islanders towards a closer relationship with Argentina.

But in 1972 the Argentine stated that these improvements would only be allowed to progress if the British Government were willing to reopen discussions over sovereignty. The British negotiating position in the discussions that followed lacked clear guidelines. Improved trade and communications links were advantageous but the position on sovereignty was muddled.

British negotiators favoured a lease-back arrangement, but lacked either the will or the high-level support needed to implement the strategy. In 1973 Argentina ran out of patience and took the matter back to the United Nations. A special UN committee crafted Resolution 3160. This was very similar to the pronouncement of five years earlier. In essence the two countries were urged to accelerate negotiations on sovereignty.

Following the General Election of 1974 Harold Wilson was presented with a range of options. The decision was taken to initiate talks with Argentina on condominium. Again the islanders' response was that they would take no part in sovereignty talks, even if that sovereignty was to be shared. The initiative failed.

At this point a number of Argentine newspapers advocated invasion of the islands. Although the Argentine Government insisted it had done nothing to stimulate these threats, there is no doubt they were aware of the effect of this barrage of publicity on the islanders and in London.

The Joint Intelligence Committee in Whitehall advised the Cabinet that, although Argentine attitudes were hardening and that contingency plans may have been prepared for the occupation of the islands, military action remained unlikely.

What was partly anticipated were further adventurist attacks, similar to Operation Condor in which some Argentine civilians landed an aeroplane on Stanley Racecourse in 1966. But it was not until 1977 that the British resolve was tested. The Argentines occupied one of the South Sandwich Islands, Southern Thule. The response was to stand back and let them get on with it. This lack of commitment was noted.

Earlier, in 1976, the maritime research ship *Shackleton* was fired upon by an Argentine destroyer when she was 78 miles south of Port Stanley. An attempt was also made to arrest the *Shackleton*. The Captain called the Argentine bluff. He refused assistance and continued with his survey. This operation, which had been approved weeks earlier, marked a significant deterioration in the Anglo-Argentine relationship. In 1976 Argentina was subjected to another military coup. The Joint Intelligence Committee in Whitehall concluded that the Malvinas question would be high on the new Junta's agenda. It further concluded that Argentina may have high expectations of the success of their ongoing bilateral negotiations. However, they thought it was unlikely that the Junta would resort to force over the issue, although an aggressive response (within the United Nations) was anticipated. This conclusion was correct. President Videla did push for a solution through the UN.

In December, 1976, the Assembly passed Resolution 31/49. This approved a further report of the Special Committee by expressing gratitude for the continuing efforts made by Argentina to facilitate the process of decolonization and to promote the wellbeing of the population of the islands. The UN requested the Argentine and British governments to expedite negotiations and report progress to the Secretary General and General Assembly as soon as possible.

In terms of political signals received by the Junta the British stance must have seemed extremely confusing. While Lord Shackleton's earlier visit to the Falklands, and his subsequent (1976) report, gave credence to the idea that Britain might wish to make a go of the Falklands, everything else suggested that HM Government would slide this vexed problem under a shroud of indecision before moving towards an eventual handover to Argentina.

British and Argentine governments, then and now, have consistently failed to find a face-saving solution. This in turn has served to aggravate strongly held principles and to polarize opinion. Though Lord Shackleton produced his acclaimed report, and a series of progressive recommendations, the Labour Government announced that they were not willing to pay for most of these proposals. Only the least expensive proposal was activated; this was the encouragement of further links between the islands and Argentina. This could really only be read as a staging post to the time when a form of lease-back could be negotiated.

Although few would have believed it at the time, 1979 marked the beginning of one of the longest periods of one-party power in any democratic state in the world during the 20th century. Margaret Thatcher's government was certainly different, not least because there were very few representatives of the Conservative old guard in the new cabinet. Many of the incomers were little enough known in the UK; on the international stage many of them were debutantes.

One who quickly revealed his inexperience was Nicholas Ridley, the Foreign Office Minister handed the Falklands brief. One of his tasks was to canvass support of the islanders for the foundation of a lease-back arrangement with Argentina. His Falklands visit the following year was not a success. His dealings with the islanders were high-handed, bordering on the arrogant, and largely because of this he failed to put across the logical basis for a lease-back agreement. When he returned to the UK his report to parliament was equally badly received. He also found little support in the Defence Committee, and indeed the cabinet withdrew from supplying the kind of leadership that was so badly needed.

An opportunity had been lost. Opinion in the Falklands was divided at the time; a more circumspect approach may well have won the day. Instead his visit is remembered to this day with distaste, and his return to Westminster is seen as a turning point in the dispute.

Nicholas Ridley's failure to convey the lease-back scheme at home and abroad forced the Argentine Government, and through them their Foreign Office officials, into a more combative position. Further polarization took place when the Falkland Islanders called for a freeze on sovereignty negotiations.

Foreign Secretary Lord Carrington decided to accept the islanders' view. He stated that, 'Domestic and political constraints must at this stage continue to prevent us from taking any steps which might be interpreted either as putting pressure on the islanders or as overruling their wishes.'

The continued failure to reach any form of agreement, or even to set a timetable for further negotiation, caused only a minor reaction in Whitehall. However, the Ministry of Defence was asked to draw up a contingency plan for the defence of the islands. One of the assumptions for this plan was that approximately three weeks' warning time would be required before a task force could be deployed. To make this workable British Intelligence in Argentina would give a warning of staged escalation of any military build-up that could be interpreted as preparations for invasion.

In 1980 Rex Hunt was appointed Governor of the Falklands. His background was not that of the stereotypical career diplomat. He had served in the RAF during the War, latterly as a Spitfire pilot. Later he went up to Oxford before joining the Colonial Office. It was following the amalgamation with the Commonwealth Office that he became eligible for Foreign Office postings. He had served in Uganda as a District Commissioner, then largely in the Far East until 1972 when he returned to the Foreign Office in Whitehall. In 1974 he had been the Counsellor in Saigon when our Embassy was expelled. Before the Falklands appointment he had been the Counsellor in Kuala Lumpur. The great thing about Rex was that he was used to making decisions. This had been the way of things for him since working, largely unsupported, as a young District Commissioner in Uganda. Added to this he had a naturally purposeful manner which perhaps created divisions of opinion about him at Whitehall.

During my briefings I met Rex at the Commonwealth Institute in London. We both recognized immediately that we were tuned to the same network. That rapport, and the friendship that grew from it, has been maintained ever since.

As well as being Governor of the Falklands, his new job made him the area Commander in Chief of British Forces and High Commissioner of the British Antarctic Territory. In this latter rôle I would be obliged to take him, and his wife Mavis if she chose to go, to the Antarctic for one of our work periods in each season. In effect this meant one month on board. In time there would be very little that Rex Hunt did not know about the *Endurance* or her Captain.

It was also in 1980 that Britain established a full diplomatic mission in Buenos Aires. Before that we had only a Chargé d'Affaires. The new embassy was to be led by Anthony Williams, a diplomat with a distinguished career record. There he was to be supported by all the trappings of a Second Grade Embassy, and a team of people who proved later to be far from in touch with the activities of the Argentine government.

Anthony Williams, who was born in 1923, joined the Foreign Office in 1945. He had attended the former Imperial Defence College and served in Cairo, Geneva, Montevideo, Moscow, Prague, Rome, Washington and also, previously, in Buenos Aires. On the face of it, particularly because of his previous South American experience, it was an inspired appointment. His reports had always been noted for their intelligent wording and persuasiveness. When he did make a report from Argentina, right up to the time of his expulsion in April 1982, his words carried with them such a weight of credibility that this contributed to the exclusion perhaps of reports made by Rex Hunt.

John Ure and Robin Fearn, both senior Foreign Office officials, spoke highly of Anthony Williams. So did Dr John Heap, now with the Foreign Office, but previously a member of the British Antarctic Survey. The splendidly erudite Dr Heap had been very much the architect of the Antarctic Treaty. In his long experience of Antarctica and the Falklands he had regularly travelled through Argentina and Chile. I do not believe there was anyone at the Foreign Office at that time who had such a measured awareness of the region and the geo-political machinations it generated. He became the cornerstone of my understanding of the international presences in the Antarctic, and the treaties and agreements extant in 1980. And his Cambridge background ensured he was an invaluable source of information on recent scientific findings which often, in turn, anticipated future projects.

Nominally my ship belonged to the Third Flotilla, that is the flotilla of Naval ships that consisted of aircraft carriers, amphibious vessels and *Endurance*. The flotilla was led firmly and well by Vice Admiral John Cox who I came to admire enormously. He was a great ally in my crusade to keep *Endurance* in commission. He also passed on many of my views about maintaining a British military presence in the South Atlantic up the line to the First Sea Lord and the Government.

The briefing for the ship's rôle as the Falklands and South Atlantic Guard Ship had been shaped by the shots fired at *Shackleton* and the other adventurist incidents. Clearly we had to be capable of making an armed response, although according to the treaty we were not allowed to carry arms in the Antarctic. Our full outfit of missiles was therefore to be kept secret. Our AS 12s were air to surface missiles designed for helicopter delivery. They would be primarily effective against a smaller assailant such as a patrol boat. Anything larger would have the capability to shoot down the helicopter before it came within firing range. The Wasp helicopter that carried the AS 12s replaced the faithful Whirlwind. The price for this capability was a reduction in carrying capacity.

Later, when government spokesmen such as John Nott referred to *Endurance* as 'totally unarmed' they were not attempting to mislead. They had simply not been informed either that we carried missiles or that we were the first ship to fire them in anger during the Conflict.

In addition to the missiles and the helicopters capable of carrying them we had two of our three helicopters embarked at any one time. The 'Flight' (that is the personnel and equipment attached to *Endurance*) were based at Portland before joining the ship when it became operational.

Normally when joining a ship, especially in command, you need to be fully briefed on the weapon fit (the weapons system) and, most of all, how to employ the weapons tactically. In the event the main weaponry of Endurance was the people. It was their spirit and ability to work with limited facilities often under great pressure which earned the ship the reputation which she so richly deserved by the end of the Conflict.

Endurance joined the Royal Navy in 1968. Her previous name, the *Anita Dan*, betrayed her Viking origins. She had been built in Denmark in 1956 and had been employed largely as a Baltic trader. Her design was such that she coped well in waters where pack ice was a normal hazard. The frames were large and less than a foot apart: the plating forward was an inch thick. But she was not intended to be used as an ice breaker and was under-powered by an old Burmeister & Wayne diesel engine which produced just over 3,000 horsepower flat out. Although this engine unit was fairly venerable, it was reliable. Her maximum speed was 13.5 knots, at which she was able to run for long periods, and had a range, without refuelling, of 4,000 miles.

The *Red Plum*, as *Endurance* was called, was not an easy ship to control with just one propeller handling the limited power. In order to go astern you had to stop the engine and then re-engage the gear. Having commanded a fast frigate with 40,000 horse power, this was like coming down from a Porsche to a Morris Minor with all the implications for speed and manoeuvrability. Things got particularly interesting within the confines of the smaller harbours of South America, particularly when we were allocated a pilot who was as useful as a waterproof teabag.

The briefing process included a study of the machinery, the somewhat basic electrical system, the navigational equipment, and the remaining weapon fit. These included the machine guns that could be fitted to the helicopters and various light weapons carried by the Royal Marine detachment. This detachment consisted of one officer and fourteen marines, reinforced to make up platoon strength by some of the Falklands-based 8901 Naval Party (Royal Marines). They carried normal infantry weapons together with anti-tank mortars, Carl Gustavs and some other smaller arms. All this was of course designed to be used for an emergency landing party, not as a counter to an invasion.

It could be argued that the main armament of the ship was the listening suite. This was a small box parked on top of the hanger which contained a comprehensive set of monitoring equipment. It could also receive frequencies in most bands at sea or on station. Our communication technicians were Spanish linguists, which meant we were well informed whenever we went alongside in South America. Of course they were also skilled at seeking out valuable intelligence which allowed us to co-ordinate and review the situation as the political tension increased. In turn this meant they were invaluable during the Conflict.

The *Endurance* was, in effect, a listening station. The two senior ratings most concerned were known as 'The Spies' by the Ship's Company. It did not, of course, take the Argentines long to realize that the box added to the roof of the hangar contained something other than brooms for sweeping down the decks.

Our primary role was as guardship, but the survey function ran a close second. Our hydrographic team of nine could be subdivided into three smaller units each with qualified officers in charge. One would be landed in the Falklands, one in the Antarctic for a brief period, and the third one would normally remain on board charting areas designated for future seasons. Charts for areas off the Antarctic peninsula were, and to a considerable extent still are, sparse in terms of soundings, despite the burgeoning tourist industry and the number of scientific bases regularly serviced by sea. Apart from any international scheme of things that could determine the future use of the

Antarctic, there is an ongoing need for a reasonable set of charts for all navigable areas. This is complicated by the fact that these areas change from year to year depending on the state of the ice, the position of icebergs, etc. Our survey team therefore had a task that was as near impossible as it was essential, and they were consequently an important department within the ship.

Our 'assist' role for scientific projects would normally be led by the Director of the British Antarctic Survey, but we were also to provide support for projects initiated by, amongst others, the Scott Polar Institute at Cambridge and the University of Birmingham. This meant we always had rather more work than we could reasonably complete in a season.

Much of the British effort was co-ordinated by the Hydrographer, based variably in London and Taunton, who liaised with our own hydrographer Lieutenant Commander David Ives, who in turn was supported by his assistants Lieutenants Todhunter, Snaith and Ball.

For our first season the work was planned to follow a pattern that had been established over the past 15–20 years. The winter nights would coincide with our preparations in the UK and we would make the most of the Antarctic summer. The ship was to sail in late September and was due to return to Chatham the following May where repair work would certainly include damage to bottom plates and the bilge keels caused by ice and other underwater obstructions.

In our widest role, as guardship to the Antarctic, we were encouraged to visit the bases of the other nations. It was perhaps the only place in the world where you could have instant access to the Administrator of a Russian base. We also got to know the Poles, Chileans and Argentines within our operational area.

Within the Weddell Sea and Peninsula areas there were four British and an equal number of Argentine bases. There were also two Chilean bases, one each manned by the US, Russia and Poland, and several more temporary camps established by other nations. But projects of greatest scientific note were invariably inspired by the US or Britain. Alongside the US presence in other parts of Antarctica were the French, Australians, New Zealanders and, more recently, the Germans. The Argentines,

Chileans and Uruguayans also had a wider Antarctic presence which anticipates the day when the International Treaty breaks down. As any student of history knows exercising a territorial claim is largely about being there.

Chapter 2

ENDURANCE GOES SOUTH

Coming from a long line of Military and Diplomatic forebears it seemed inevitable that I should follow suit and join one of the armed services. My father had been killed in command of the destroyer *Ardent* on 8 June, 1940, whilst escorting the aircraft carrier *Glorious* off the Norwegian coast. It had been a brave action as the odds against two small destroyers sinking or damaging the German battle cruisers *Scharnhorst* and *Gneisenau* were long. But even so, and with appalling loss of life, the destroyers managed to inflict considerable damage by gunfire and torpedoes on the *Scharnhorst*. My mother had come from the Paget family who were steeped in traditions of service to the country, including commanding the cavalry at Waterloo. She died in 1943, so my paternal grandfather, Henry, a retired Naval Captain, decided to bring up my sister and myself. A strict disciplinarian, his clear intention was for me to follow the Naval tradition, but most of all for us both to enjoy our childhood at home in Cornwall.

In the circumstances of a war-scarred family (my father's brother had also been killed), my schooling had been pretty standard. I was sent off to a preparatory school at the age of 6 and then to Canford. It is fair to say that education during and shortly after the war was not good. In my own experience, schoolmasters were much more enthusiastic about their wartime exploits than passing on their classical or scientific know-how.

However, despite a much enjoyed but mediocre education, my enthusiasm to join the 'Family Firm', the Royal Navy, was not diminished and I entered the Naval Service (for National Service) in 1951. Following my initial training, I served as a Midshipman in HMS *Vengeance*, an aircraft carrier in the Far East, in the Rhine Flotilla as second-in-command of a landing craft and in HMS *Bermuda* as a dogsbody in the Mediterranean. In some respects this was a particularly impressionable period as we were closely involved in a major rescue operation during the floods of Southern Holland in 1953. Another but more unpleasant rescue operation followed an earthquake on the Greek island of Zante. In both instances it was death by large numbers, although the main differences were the climatic extremes. Having experienced the aftermath of the Plymouth blitz, these were situations where I could be of some assistance and deeply felt the anxieties of life-saving against a short time scale.

After training courses I served in a destroyer and was subsequently given my first command, a patrol boat as part of our Coastal Forces. It was a dream come true, which progressed into a command of a Squadron of three Patrol Craft with their associated ship's companies. However, in 1958 it was back to reality when I became the Navigating Officer of a new frigate HMS *Chichester* for a trip away from home lasting over a year when we circumnavigated the globe. More importantly I was married, in 1957, and met my elder son Henry, on return from the commission in *Chichester*, when he was already seven months old.

Later appointments as a Lieutenant included HMS *Jewel*, an Ocean Minesweeper attached to the Royal Naval College at Dartmouth where I was involved in teaching both Seamanship and Navigation to cadets, another navigating appointment in the Middle East-based Frigate, *Loch Fyne* and then two more Commands, HMS *Squirrel* and HMS *Brereton* in the Fishery Protection Squadron before being selected for the Staff College Course in 1966. This was followed by another training appointment at HMS *Ganges* and another small ship command, then a superb commission as second-in-command of the Tribal Class Frigate HMS *Nubian*, operating in the Middle and Far East Stations.

Putting this experience into practice, I was appointed to serve on the staff of Flag Officer Sea Training based at Portland. Going to sea each day in a different ship, including a variety of ships belonging to NATO Navies, was a hard task, after which I was promoted to Commander. Subsequently there was the reward of a shore job in Naval shipbuilding and ship acceptance from an office situated at Newcastle upon Tyne. It was also a time to get to know my family which by then had expanded to four children, all very close together in age.

In 1975 it was back to sea, in command of a new Type 21 Frigate HMS *Arrow*, a wonderful appointment with a tremendous team of officers and ship's company. Furthermore, and quite coincidentally there was a family continuity. My father had been serving in the previous HMS *Arrow*, based in Malta, when I was born. Indeed I was christened on board.

My next appointment was to the Ministry of Defence in Whitehall. I was to be the 'Appointer' – the person who allocates jobs to all seaman Commanders. Suddenly I had friends I had never heard of. People constantly came to see me about their career progression and prospects of promotion.

Part of my responsibility was to weed out those who had no chance of immediate promotion. There was no ulterior motive in this; it was simply to make the Captains' promotion lists more manageable. Only eight or nine Commanders would be promoted to Captain every six months, so the job was always likely to enhance my understanding of human nature.

There was an elite you rarely saw. They knew that promotion to top-class jobs would follow reasonably quickly. There were also some officers whose self-belief was not matched by ability and others who were more competent than confident. At the bottom of the class there were a few who were only ever going to be offered fringe appointments and whose chance of further promotion was as likely as Shergar making a winning return at Epsom.

But it was important to make everyone feel valued. An appointment to a missile or torpedo range in the Outer Hebrides may not be a mainstream career move, but with limited options I had to make it sound as attractive as possible.

'There will be plenty of fishing and shooting,' I would enthuse.

For each 'customer' I generally held half a dozen possible appointments. Having looked at the career pattern of each officer, I had a view of what was most appropriate. I would always push in that direction. The first card I played had to look like the winner. The 'customer' usually accepted that. But sometimes there would be objection on family grounds. If this seemed valid I would take the next card from the pack. Very rarely did I have to put all the cards on the table.

The job, which was fascinating, helped me develop skills in an area somewhere between PR and Personnel Management. But it also involved an Everest of paperwork. I worked more or less the standard office day, then late into the night at my lodgings. The plan was always to clear my desk by the middle of Friday afternoon and then beat the traffic as I travelled down to spend the weekends with my family in Dorset.

Two and a half years later, and rather before my time, I was promoted to Captain. I went to see the Naval Secretary who told me I had been selected to go back to sea in command of HMS *Southampton*. Predictably perhaps the new ship was delayed for a year because of labour disputes at Vosper Thornycrofts. This changed the course of my life. On my return visit to the Naval Secretary I was informed of my appointment to HMS *Endurance*.

I was disappointed. My recent insight did not encourage me to believe this was a main line job. HMS *Southampton* had represented a serious step up the ladder. HMS *Endurance* seemed to be uncomfortably close to an outward bound course. I was only consoled by a belief that I was not to be sidelined permanently. I cursed the dockyard unions.

Before I took up the new appointment I was to complete a series of specialist courses. These preparations meant a return to Portsmouth for six months. The courses included updates on administration, communications, engineering, navigation, supply and air warfare. And, because *Endurance* was quite unlike anything else in the Navy, there would be specialist briefings. This included input from the Foreign Office, the British Antarctic Survey, the Scott Polar Institute and the Security Services. The main thrust of it all was to understand the special conditions that apply to operating a ship in the South Atlantic.

Gradually I came to realize that the appointment to command *Endurance* was not altogether a bad thing. Officers with greater seniority had volunteered for this command. But I was not convinced. If I'd been offered the swap to a regular grey ship I'd have taken it. But the process of briefings completely changed my thinking. It was clearly going to be very different. I was particularly encouraged by the extent to which non-Naval Departments set such store by *Endurance* and her rôle in the South Atlantic.

I had always been interested in the remoter corners of the world. Parts of the Middle East, the North West Frontier in Pakistan and the deserts of Africa and Australia all captured my imagination. Perhaps the mystique of the Antarctic was even greater? This began by reawakening a boyhood interest in the history and heroism of Antarctic exploration. From there it did not seem too difficult to trace a line of descent to the scientific projects with which we were to assist. The Antarctic had been, and in many ways remained, the last terrestrial unknown. Even today we have hardly begun to learn the secrets of a continent that is half as large again as Australia.

I joined the ship in May, 1980, a few days after she returned from the Antarctic. There was a short handover from Captain James Lord and the next few months were spent generally getting to know my ship's company. This was mainly done through planning my first season in the South Atlantic. Most of this time I was living in Chatham barracks, or I was with the ship in her dry dock. My officers had to follow their own briefing schedules and specializations, mostly in the appropriate schools in Portsmouth.

During that summer of 1980 I also met members of the 'Antarctic Club'. In part this was seeking alliances with those who had a purposeful view of Falkland and Antarctic affairs. The most distinguished member was Lord Shackleton, a socialist peer who had served Harold Wilson's Government in a number of capacities. He was a great man, and the son of a man who was arguably even greater. Eddie Shackleton was much respected and admired by politicians of various colours and had proved himself as a formidable and resourceful statesman. During that summer he came to lunch with me in *Endurance*. I remember him sitting at the dining table in my cabin. With him were his daughter Alexandra (the ship's sponsor) and her husband Richard.

As we were chatting a pair of boots appeared at the window 40 feet above sea level. They were working boots suspended downwards from invisible ankles. This was towards the end of the lunch so the port had already been passed. I poured another glass, opened the window and handed it upwards. A hand reached down to take it and the boots disappeared. Eddie Shackleton noted what had happened and wryly observed that 'labour relations' with the workforce were not too bad in Chatham. What he didn't know was that there had been a similar incident during a working lunch the day before. On this occasion it had been a violent clattering on the deck above. I halted the meeting and went up to the bridge with the remains of the decanter and some glasses. The dockyard workers quietly polished off the port and we sat down to finish our meeting. The bush telegraph works rapidly in the dockyard. In the weeks that followed it was surprising how the port supplies diminished.

In fact the relationship between ship and dockyard was excellent. It was good to see junior sailors and ratings on first name terms with the dockyard workers. The spirit of co-operation was also fostered by cricket matches, and the local game of 'bat and trap' played on any number of pub runs. There was also a fair amount of on-board hospitality. All this added up to a special relationship with the dockyard which I have no doubt contributed to the quality of work.

Even so it was touch and go as to whether the refit would be finished on time. But they just made it. We sailed on Monday September 22, 1980, for sea trials in the Thames Estuary. The trials were successful, with the exception of the calibration of the logs; this was to do with the second log fitted as an addition as part of a fleet trial.

The flight joined us off Portland, and we were able to have families on board and to give our dockyard workers and their families a trip down the Medway and out to sea. There was also time to visit a UK port and I requested the opportunity to affirm my links with Sunderland. As a red and white ship we could hardly go to Newcastle, could we? A highlight of the visit was having the Sunderland footballers on board. They must have enjoyed themselves but I was a little surprised when they managed a one-nil win the following day. Before we left they had already arranged, with the ship's company, a similar visit to follow the 1981 refit.

On 13 October we sailed for an intensive period of sea training off Portland. There was also a special rededication ceremony for which we were delighted to have Sir Vivian Fuchs and Zaz Bergel, our sponsor and daughter of Lord Shackleton, as guests of honour.

On 30 October the ship sailed south, flying the flag of Rear Admiral John Cox, Flag Officer 3rd Flotilla, so he could see us operating at first hand.

On that long passage south we concentrated on flying training, missile firings and damage control exercises. Admiral Cox meanwhile had taken the opportunity to visit most departments and to meet the ship's company. He created such a positive impression that we were almost reluctant to land him at Funchal. Later we were disappointed that he was not eligible to lead the Falklands Task Force, particularly as we learned that he missed out on becoming Commander of the Group by retiring a few days too soon. It was natural that we should want our man, but any fears we had were misguided. Admiral Sandy Woodward proved to be an effective leader with an acute mind and sound tactical know-how.

In Madeira I gave a lunch party which a number of local dignitaries attended. After drinking a toast to the President of Portugal, the Deputy Military Governor, Carlos Lacerda, rose and raised his glass to Margaret Thatcher. I thanked him and waited for what seemed like a decent pause before toasting the Queen. This threw the Deputy Governor into confusion as he began to realize he had made a major gaffe. This probably explains why I was offered a car and driver to tour the island. Certainly his over-profuse apologies continued not only for the rest of the visit but for the next three years. Whenever our paths crossed he always brought up the subject before offering further recompense. This included an apartment on the island and the use of his private aeroplane.

On 24 November, 1980, we arrived in Rio. It is impossible not to be enchanted by the magnificent scenery at the harbour entrance. There are many spectacular ports in the world, which must include Cape Town and Hong Kong on any shortlist, but Rio would be my choice as the best. It has one of the most attractive harbours in the world. The Sugarloaf mountain dominates Guanabara Bay. Above everything is that giant statue of Christ, floodlit at night in a way that makes it seem suspended in the sky.

The city itself unfolds as you round the headland and enter the bay. On this occasion we were berthed in what seemed like the city centre. This was wonderful in terms of a good run ashore and I believe every one of the ship's company of 150 took full advantage. Someone later calculated they had spent around £12,000 between them.

One problem with being a Captain on this kind of visit is that you see rather more diplomats and dignitaries than night-clubs, but I could hardly complain that this was not a worthwhile compromise. On this kind of visit there is little that is accidental about the guest list for on-board entertainment. An RN ship represents an alternative extension of UK 'soil' to the more formal atmosphere of the Embassy. I was carefully instructed by the attaché, Captain Anthony Wheatley, as to who the Ambassador would like me to invite on board. A visiting RN ship is a magnet for local politicians and members of the military. The relaxed mood of these encounters means it is possible to learn a great deal.

From a UK standpoint the major difference between Brazil and Argentina is largely to do with cultural and historical links. Argentina had traditionally been close to Europe, and Britain in particular. Brazil is perhaps more like the USA: there is mutual respect and even affection, but sometimes the history and culture divides them as much as it brings them together. That sense of distance is perhaps accentuated in Brazil by the fact that the diplomatic missions are now all centred on the new capital,

Brasilia. This city is well detached from the main centres of population which include the extensive urban areas of Rio and Sao Paulo.

I was returning from a late party one night when a sense of disquiet began to grip me. It was the sort of feeling you get when you suddenly become sure that you forgot to lock your car and the world is illuminated by a burglar's moon. As I focused on the road I recognized the true source of my anxiety. My Brazilian driver was clearly intent on jumping all the red traffic lights along the Copacabana beach road. Although my Portuguese vocabulary is hardly better than my Cantonese I managed to convey my concern. Happily his English was adequate to put me at ease.

'If we stop,' he explained, 'we will be ambushed.'

'How would that be?' I asked.

'In the Copacabana there are many transvestites who never miss a chance to grab a wallet. And there are also gangs who operate in this area at night. It is not safe to stop.'

I found this explanation oddly reassuring, but was less convinced when he turned off the Copacabana towards Botofogo. The car was now coming to a halt at the green traffic lights. He anticipated my question. 'This is because,' he explained, 'there will be many coming through the red traffic lights the other way.'

It was the kind of logic that I later came to apply myself when thinking about the way South Americans approach a problem: the simple rule of thumb is that their thinking will be consistently 180 degrees opposite from our own.

The next port of call was to be Buenos Aires. We navigated very carefully up the River Plate: I remembered the problems I had previously experienced there only too well. We anchored off Buenos Aires overnight, then took a pilot into the port. Once again we were berthed close to the heart of the city. I was obliged to call on the Chief of Naval Staff, a man who later played an important part in our lives, Admiral Anaya.

I did not call on the President, but I did meet a number of senior politicians. In true Argentine style these gentlemen were all either military or dual-hatted. Equally correctly I was always shepherded by either the Ambassador or the Naval Attaché. The Ambassador knew all the key players in the Argentine game of political chess very well. His Spanish was excellent and his interpretation included the gift of picking up the nuances that can all too easily be drowned in the river of protocol.

The first day of any visit by an RN ship is invariably taken up by calls on local dignitaries. At lunch or the ship's cocktail party reciprocal visits are arranged. In Buenos Aires this meant organizing a flight deck cocktail party for two hundred visitors. These were essentially representatives of the Argentine military and political hierarchy, and a more modest number of influential British expatriates. The Argentine military had assimilated aspects of British culture through the expatriate influence. This included a taste for the finer fruits of Scottish distilleries with which we were necessarily well stocked.

A routine procedure for a captain on these occasions is to stand, booted, spurred and telescoped, in the vicinity of the gangway. By his side will be the Naval Attaché introducing each of the guests as they arrive. For the Captain this then becomes a memory game made as tricky as possible because of the similarity of the uniforms. It can also be a fairly drawn-out process: in South America punctuality is treated no more seriously than bribery. This meant that almost as soon as the last guest arrived it was back to the gangway station to acknowledge the farewells.

We had a special little sunset ceremony which we performed with the Royal Marine Guard and bugler. At the same time we closed the bar to provide a second heavy hint that the party was over. This was interpreted in two ways. The visiting dignitaries reluctantly downed their whiskies and said their goodbyes. Meanwhile the wardroom scooped up the most attractive females and took them down to the mess.

In contrast to Rio the cost of a run ashore was prohibitive. Added to this there were wild fluctuations of currency and the Shylockian instincts of local traders. This meant we had to rely on local invitations and the round of sporting events to create a break from sea time.

For some reason, lost in the miasmal mists of seagoing

folklore, the best shore option was known as a 'grippo'. This is not perhaps what the uninitiated imagine. A 'grippo' is simply an invitation of hospitality. 'Great grippo' is therefore an approbation. It ensures that the run ashore is enjoyable and, best of all, free. The first grippo for myself and my officers was a visit to the Argentine Naval Hydrographic and Oceanic Establishment. This meant a guided tour, lecture, drinks and lunch. The next was a lunch on board the Argentine square-rigged sail training ship *Libertad*. This was also an opportunity to really get to know the Ambassador, Anthony Williams, his Number Two, John Chick, Naval Attaché Ben Neave and other junior members of the Embassy.

When I later said that I knew a great deal about the thinking within the Embassy, both then and during the build-up to the conflict, it is in part because I was receiving information from sources close to the Ambassador himself, and equally from people who had the ear of the Anglo/Argentine community. In the event they were fortuitously placed with a number of influential friends.

Through them, and through other Embassy sources, I learned a great deal about the Argentine administration. It was clear that corruption was rife at every level and the strongest characteristic of political life was feathering your own nest. It was a desperate administration lurching from one crisis to another and failing to solve anything.

Those with left-wing or even humanitarian instincts were labelled reactionary. The likeliest fate of someone who dared question the Government was to be taken for a helicopter ride, weighted round the feet and dropped into a remote lake. Even by South American standards it was a brutal and cynical administration. The British community knew what was going on, but equally they knew that their good health depended on silence. What I learned was always 'in confidence'. Some of the stories, which I believe to be broadly true, were harrowing.

The Ambassador and his wife, Hedwig, were hospitable and charming, though they had very fixed views about 'the locals'. But Ben Neave, the Naval Attaché, was particularly sound. If he had remained in post beyond the spring of 1981 it may have been that the Embassy's perception of events in Argentina would have been different.

John Chick, the Commercial Attaché, was largely preoccupied with oiling the wheels of the business machine. In Argentina the machine was decidedly rusty. I remember asking him what he actually did.

'Oh, we introduce British business men to the locals and vice versa and arrange meetings and put them in touch,' he said.

'What sort of results have come about from these meetings?'

He did his best to put a positive interpretation on it: 'Oh, there's lots of British activity in Argentina. Unfortunately this is an agricultural country and the Argentines buy their equipment from almost anywhere other than Britain.'

I formed the impression that he was out of tune with commercial reality. But it was also clear that commercial links between the two nations at that time were hardly encouraged by the Argentine administration. Oddly enough I do not recall any of the Embassy hierarchy even hinting there could be something worrying in that.

Some time earlier the Argentine had bought two Type 42 destroyers, one built in the UK, the other in Argentina. Other than that the volume of British exports to Argentina was pitched somewhere between poor and derisory. It would also be true to say, however, that the state of the Argentine economy was such that potential exporters must have been concerned about when, and even if, they would be paid.

The tune that echoed round the Embassy was that everything was fine. But I heard the hollow notes. That Embassy orchestra may have included competent soloists but they lacked the direction of a strong conductor and the overall effect was less than harmonious. I could not have guessed it then, but in the months that ran up to the conflict it was going to become a symphony of errors.

Chapter 3

'PLANET EARTH'

We arrived at our Falklands station on 16 December. Although we could not get alongside at Port Stanley, I exchanged calls with HE the Governor and it was the first time I experienced the extraordinary hospitality of Sir Rex and Lady Hunt. We anchored in the harbour close to Stanley, which must be one of the world's tiniest capitals, even though a fair proportion of the colony's 2,000 population live there.

The ship was a piece of Britain floating in their harbour as far as the islanders were concerned. They always looked forward to the times when the *Red Plum* made her way through the narrows and into the lagoon-like harbour off Stanley. This event provoked sentiment and ceremonial. There was also a very practical reason why they should welcome our visits: we carried stores and supplies. These included the seemingly insignificant, such as a set of books or some preserves. There were also small items of furniture and some tools. Many of the items are the kind of thing we take for granted but to the islanders they were hard-earned luxuries. We were generally told what we had carried after it had been collected; in fact we never really knew what was inside the crates and never had cause to check.

During our short visits to Stanley, apart from my calls on the Governor, we would refuel, embark mail and people who were going to assist with scientific projects, and sometimes land project personnel returning to South America or the UK.

On this, my first Falklands visit, we landed a survey team at Fitzroy which was virtually uncharted at the time. The fifteen members of the team were to complete hydrographic work and soundings, and to make maps of Fitzroy Sound and Bluff Cove. They were to stay in a farm building which served both as work-place and dormitory. They would have to rely on the farmer and the other members of a sparse community for some of their food and supplies.

We were also to embark David Attenborough and his team. This was part of his 'Planet Earth' project which was to feature some of the Antarctic islands and the Antarctic itself.

However, on arrival in Stanley, we encountered one of the British Antarctic ships, the *John Biscoe*. She had sheared two blades of her propeller and had managed to make a very slow passage from the Antarctic on her bow thruster. The problem was doubly unfortunate because rectification could not be carried out underwater. She needed to be docked for her propeller to be replaced. Worse still, towing did not seem to be an option because of the expense. Following a flurry of signals, it was finally agreed that I could undertake the tow of over 1,000 miles – probably one of the longest tows since the war by a warship, from Port Stanley to Montevideo where the *John Biscoe* could be properly repaired.

That meant an almost immediate about turn for the *Endurance*. We met only briefly the people who we were to serve as guardship. We set off with a long string of plaited nylon tow-rope behind and several shackles of cable veered from the *John Biscoe*. The journey also meant that we were to spend Christmas at sea, not at South Georgia as planned. Even though we managed to make nine knots on the tow north it also meant the Antarctic programme was to be delayed by a fortnight.

The weather was kind to us. The main problem was flattening the tow to ensure that the plaited nylon tow-rope rose almost to the surface. The alternative was to risk dredging up the *Graf Spee* or any of the considerable number of wrecks that lie off Montevideo. If nothing else this was a good PR job which knocked on the head the British Antarctic Survey's nickname for *Endurance* – 'HMS *Encumbrance*'.

We ran straight to South Georgia from Montevideo. On the way we met up with the British Antarctic Ship, the *Bransfield*, and transferred David Attenborough and his film crew. At Stanley we had also embarked a team from the Scott Polar Institute at Cambridge. They were to do some experimental work on the movement and flexibility of icebergs.

One of the most satisfying aspects of life in *Endurance* was the relaxed and friendly working environment. This was in part created by the Antarctic itself. To be successful working in the waters around the cold continent meant that, by design, the *Endurance* was different. Our bridge was both driving centre and Operations Room. It therefore became a place where the sailors could come and speak to the Captain or First Lieutenant on a purely social basis. In turn this created opportunities for officers to get to know the men to a degree that is almost impossible in a regular warship. The dividend of this unique relationship was paid in full in those dark days when we needed it most.

Our arrival at South Georgia heralded the start of nearly two years of a growing interest in the background, sounds and climate of the area. It was impossible not to be overwhelmed by the Antarctic scenery. South Georgia is an extraordinary place. It's like taking a ridge of the Alps and parking it in the middle of the ocean. Grytviken, Stromness and Husvik border the shores of Cumberland Bay, the focus of former whaling activities. I found myself increasingly fascinated by the history of this, particularly when I encountered some of the old characters who had experienced the full hardship of life in the whalers.

Grytviken, probably the largest of the old whaling stations, had by 1980–81 become the base from which mostly biological work was done by the British Antarctic Survey. Close to the station is the monument and last resting place of Sir Ernest Shackleton. Sir Ernest is buried in a small cemetery amongst sailors of many nations, particularly Norwegians, who led the way when it came to fortitude. Right next to the small cemetery is a penguin colony, the remains of two veteran whaling ships, and the flensing pans – slipways where whales were drawn up and dissected. Nearby is the church where we held a number of services during the Conflict.

It was at Grytviken that David Attenborough and his team

48

were now based. This reunion was quite special and reminded us all of what a joy it had been to have them on board. In addition to filming his epic series 'Planet Earth', they were also putting together some footage for children's programmes.

At Husvik I was determined to carry out a small investigation of my own. It was rumoured that the local duck were particularly tasty so I took my shotgun ashore. I perched myself behind an old whaling shed and waited for a prime specimen to come within range. After a while the icy silence was broken by a human voice. A peer round the edge of the shed revealed David Attenborough. His clipped and deliberate voice to camera was setting the scene. I was distracted as a flight of duck winged into view. The repeated roar of the shotgun echoed around the bay and a South Georgia Pintail fell to the ground. As I set off to retrieve it I was aware of the Attenborough monologue continuing:

'Man has not been here since 1963. (Bang, bang) He left these bases like the *Mary Celeste* (bang, bang) waiting for phantom crews to travel once again to the whaling grounds . . .'

I understand that when the programme was broadcast a number of phone calls suggested that the echoing shotgun blasts had done little to complement the dialogue. Indeed the idea that man had not set foot in this place for almost 20 years was quite literally blown away. And this slight lapse in the Attenborough credibility was all because of one modestly sized duck which, when prepared for the table, tasted of seaweed and salt.

On the night of 6/7 January we tried to find an island which had been reported by an American research ship 30 miles to the north of the South Sandwich Group. After hours of frustration we determined that it had either disappeared or their navigation was faulty. We did, however, visit most of the South Sandwich Islands. These have the appearance of little ice-clad Gibraltars running in a line running roughly NE–SW. The most south-westerly of these, Southern Thule, was the island the Argentines had claimed in 1977. The Foreign Office response to that had been predictably weak-kneed. They reasoned that the island was in an international area and therefore there was no need to interfere. I am not alone in believing that the lack of formal protest sent signals to the Argentine that were later to prove costly.

The first island we visited was Zavodovski, a desolate volcano at the northern end of the group, populated according to David Attenborough by 9 million chinstrap penguins. The smell of the island, in part created by countless tons of guano, gave credence to this claim. To make matters worse the fumaroles at the side of the volcano were pumping out sulphuric smoke. The smell was bad enough on board. On shore it was like living close confined with a group of people who ate only baked beans and boiled cabbage. This had given the mapmakers a chance to be creative. The names of various coves, inlets and headlands included Pungent Bay, Mount Asphyxia and Acrid Cove.

David Attenborough loved the place. Predictably he positioned himself among several thousand penguins and prepared to tell the world all about them.

'Here we have the distinctive strap of black feathers under the chin. This is why they are called chinstrap penguins . . .'

He paused and grinned at me.

'That's a touch obvious, isn't it Nick? Perhaps you can help me to come up with something better when we get back on board?'

His natural humility, which I noticed again and again, surely comes from the confidence of having nothing to prove. David is quite simply the best at what he does and is a constant inspiration to those who work alongside him. The sailors thought he was wonderful. Here was a national figure who enjoyed a joke at his own expense and was always keen to hear what others had to say. Only when strongly encouraged would he become 'the star' and then his fund of excellent stories seemed inexhaustible. He once told us about filming a snake on the side of the Mombasa to Nairobi road. He wanted the pictures to appear as if this was the desert. Meanwhile the sound man became increasingly frustrated each time a truck went past.

Towards the end of this tortuous day a Cadillac full of 'orange-haired American ladies on Safari' stopped to enquire what was going on.

'I am studying the artificial insemination of an elephant,' he said.

'How are you doing that?'

'With this black thing I have in my hand [his elongated microphone] with a knob on the end.'

After that, when he was going ashore, the sailors always asked him if he had his artificial inseminator with him.

'Are you going to stuff it up the arse of a penguin?' they asked.

Another purpose of our visit was to investigate the political situation on Southern Thule. My exchanges with Whitehall and the Foreign Office made it clear that I was not to upset the diplomatic apple-cart by doing something as provocative as landing at the base the Argentines had subsequently created there. I did however win permission to overfly. Naturally this was purely on the basis of 'vital scientific research'. David wanted to have a close look at some more penguins. By sheer coincidence of course the low-level flying that was required to monitor the colonies gave us the opportunity to tune into every frequency we could and to note the numbers of people on the base. We were not surprised to find they were Naval personnel. At that time there were around forty-five of them on the base which was being supplied by the Argentine ship *Bahia Paraiso*. These little bits of information were to prove invaluable when, 18 months later, I was to return in very different circumstances.

On 11 January we found the right sort of tabular iceberg. This specimen, about 50 metres high, with perhaps half a dozen times as much sitting below the surface, was ideal for the Scott Polar Research Institute experiment. Three scientists, together with six helpers from the ship's company, were ferried by helicopter to the top of the iceberg complete with the impedimenta of scientific instruments to establish a semi-permanent automatic satellite transmitting station. The ship also launched a waverider buoy that was to give an indication of the sea state at any time. This berg was wedge-shaped, roughly one and a half miles long and a mile wide at the base of the wedge. It was also heavily crevassed at the apex, so those who jumped from the helicopter experienced the dubious pleasure of a snow bath up to their necks.

The plan was to dig a large hole in the surface to install a fleximeter. This instrument would provide an indication of how the iceberg flexed, and through that to form a judgement of what would happen if it was pushed to the north-east by the weather and sea. The idea was to try and predict whether these forces would cause the iceberg to break up. A transmitter, also mounted at the top, would provide satellite communication data that included position, course and speed. Ultimately it was hoped that the experiment would successfully monitor the life cycle of the iceberg during the course of a year.

Another scientific project was to explore what happens to the krill during the winter months. It was known that penguins tend to disappear in the colder months and whales and seals are also pretty scarce. One possible conclusion was that they followed the krill. But it was the view of some scientists that large tabular icebergs are concave underneath and swarms of krill could use these areas as their winter home. This research was at least part-funded by Arab money. The other side of the research coin was to consider ways in which icebergs could be transported to warmer climes as a source of fresh water and energy.

Although the Sandwich Islands are bleak and inhospitable, they abound with marine wild life and feature unusual rock formations and associated flora. As another part of our scientific programmes on behalf of the British Antarctic Survey we were to assess variations in microbe-flora for comparison with other places in similar latitudes. This work was to dovetail with the Attenborough filming projects. Aerial photographs were taken of all the seal and penguin colonies for an ecological study. One problem here was that high-level photography, valuable equally for ecological and for cartographic purposes, was going to be difficult, sometimes impossible, because of the low cloud and poor weather.

Visibility in the Antarctic can reduce very quickly. On the occasion when we had the Scott Polar team on top of the iceberg visibility suddenly reduced to below 100 yards. The ship remained within the vicinity for some hours waiting for an improvement. As daylight began to fail we edged to within 50 yards of the iceberg. It was brown trouser time when we caught a glimpse of the massive ice shelf mistily towering above us. Without being able to get an horizon it was too dangerous to fly the helicopters. All we could do was to remain in radio contact and wait. Fortunately the marines and scientists on the iceberg had emergency equipment and rations. They dug a snow hole and stuck it out overnight.

One of the Scott Polar team, the Norwegian explorer Monica Kristianson, was a natural morale booster. Indeed any lady who is as resourceful and gorgeous as Monica should probably be categorized as a secret weapon. Some years later she tried a solo run behind a dog team to the South Pole. She didn't make it but did make her reputation. But I sometimes think about that night on the iceberg. They all had to snuggle up together. I wondered which hardy lad had the special responsibility of keeping Monica warm.

It was at this time that we received an SOS signal from the BAS base on the South Orkney Islands to say that the base was running dangerously low on food and essential supplies. The problem had arisen because the *Bransfield* could not make it into the base because she had been caught in the pack. We were forced to mount a rescue in deteriorating weather. This was my first view of pack ice. It was the radar that first picked up what looked like a coastline. In the daylight we saw a fog bank rolling towards us. This proved to be a northern extremity of the winter ice that had not yet melted. It had to be negotiated. It was still heavy pack, some 8–9 feet thick, but separating. The *Endurance* made necessarily slow progress. We rose up on the pack then down again. The bow rose and dipped like the nose of a veteran steeplechaser. On each fall there was a crunch like trampled bones as the ice split and shattered. For those of us who were in the Antarctic for the first time it was a memorable experience. Camera teams hung almost over the ice-breaking bow as we made best use of our ice-strengthened plating. This was not a time for reminding anyone that we were not truly an ice-breaker or that we were seriously underpowered for the task of ploughing through fast ice.

After thirty-six hours of this slow progress we landed the emergency supplies at Signy. The Attenborough team also came ashore to take advantage of a rare filming opportunity. They managed to capture some remarkable marine life footage.

Our next destination was Beauchene Island, south of the Falklands and right in the weather course of low pressure areas tracking round from Cape Horn. This is a severe area when the weather is bad but David wanted to take the opportunity to land if possible. I was concerned. There could be a problem getting them back if the weather worsened. It would be tricky setting a course for the helicopters and the rough sea added to the risk. We just got away with it by using the lee of the island to provide a modest amount of shelter.

David was thrilled to bits with the island. They filmed albatrosses taking off along grassy paths as if they were 747s on runways, and he also filmed skuas and a variety of petrels.

Our side of the operation began with the problems of getting the helicopters and personnel ashore, and ended with some rather fraught moments as we retrieved the team in the late afternoon. At one point I had visions of acres of newsprint carrying the obituary of a very distinguished film maker, not to mention a gallant aircrew.

This first work period ended when we returned to Port Stanley. Following the long Antarctic silence the small town seemed both lively and welcoming. Now it was back to playing guardship. We said goodbye to David and his lively lieutenants, Hugh Maynard, Ned Kelly, and Dickie Bird. We also said goodbye to Peter Wadhams and his iceberg research team which included the eminent glaciologist Olaf Orheim and the delectable Monica Kristianson. Our sailors were particularly sad to see her go.

'And I'm so sad to say goodbye to my boys,' she said and meant it.

I accepted an invitation to inspect the resident Royal Marine detachment, Party 8901, commanded by my old friend from HMS *Nubian*, Major Robin Gilding. This was a deservedly popular detachment which had become utterly integrated into island life. But in numbers the detachment was utterly inadequate as a serious deterrent to an invasion force. They had a tactical plan for defending the islands, but this was primarily planned as a response to the kind of incidents that had already occurred. Indeed, they did an excellent job in dealing with an incursion on West Falkland.

For the next work period we were to embark HE the Governor and his wife, Mavis. This was to be Rex Hunt's first visit to the Antarctic. We also welcomed a Pebble Mill documentary crew led by the production experts John Smith and Peter Hercombe and presenter Bob Langley. This team, which was steered by Marion Foster and Carol Morgan from Birmingham, had already built an excellent reputation for location work.

The plan was to make a series of six programmes in the Antarctic, the Falklands and Argentina. The outcome was extraordinary not just in terms of enlightening and entertaining television but also in the parts that proved to be prophetic. The greatest drama occurred with an unintentional re-enactment. The *Endurance* was stuck fast in the ice for a couple of days in the Weddell Sea. The irony of being very close to where Shackleton's *Endurance* became fast was not lost on the documentary makers. Happily we managed to escape rather more quickly.

During my briefing I was warned about the possibility of being stuck in the pack and fast ice; when it happened my concern was not so much for safety, but how to do our work. The longest period that any British Antarctic Survey ship has been stuck in recent years is fifty-four days. If something similar happened to us it would end the season with a great deal of work uncompleted.

While the wardroom and the TV team were enjoying themselves at a Burns supper I was on the bridge trying to work out how to break free. Our options seemed limited to trying to blast our way out with demolition charges, or to wait for a change in wind to push a large sheet of flat ice in a direction that would open up a channel for *Endurance* to back out of. The sailors were massively entertained by the predicament; they played football on the pack ice. The TV team were equally delighted; here was real Shackleton-style adventure.

My main anxiety was possible damage beneath the waterline. We were listing slightly to port which, although not worrying in itself, could be an indicator of something more sinister. Happily the ice opened up for us naturally and we continued our passage southwards with increasing certainty of no significant damage.

James Ross Island, our next stop, was to be the site of some geological work for the British Antarctic Survey. It was a place almost unknown and therefore greatly in need of preliminary hydrographic survey. After three days of trouble-free steaming it may have been easy to be lulled into a false sense of security. But the Antarctic has a way of reminding you to take it seriously. Without warning the depth of water suddenly reduced from about 30 fathoms to three in the space of a few hundred yards. We went full astern then paused to assess the situation. Our instruments suggested an underwater pinnacle of some size. We avoided becoming impaled by no more than a few seconds. This rocky pinnacle has since been named Barker Bank. It has been suggested that I earned an appropriate kind of marine immortality by giving my name to a serious hazard to shipping.

These moments of anxiety were captured on the Pebble Mill film. They always astonished me with their ability to whip out camera at the first hint of drama, or when things were at their most fraught. This perhaps begins to explain why no movie producer has ever approached Nick Barker to play the Kenneth More style of stiff upper lip hero.

On the deck immediately beneath the bridge the Governor and his wife had a special double cabin. On the same deck there were two smaller cabins housing the Flight Commander, Lieutenant Commander Tony Ellerbeck, and the Navigating Officer, Lieutenant Commander Bill Hurst. On the starboard side was my day cabin, sleeping cabin, and a small bathroom. Aft was the wireless office, the main communications centre, which became the Operations Room during the Conflict.

The other room on that deck was a pantry used by my leading steward, Deacon, whose misfortune it was to take care of me for almost three years. He did an outstanding job, particularly as his duties extended to looking after our star guests. During the first work period he looked after David Attenborough who also took his meals in my cabin. For the second work period Rex and Mavis Hunt followed the same arrangement, except of course when they accepted hospitality ashore. This meant three meals a day at the Captain's table, an arrangement that may be delightful on a cruise ship, but which could become culturally claustrophobic on board *Endurance*.

In order to save our honoured guests from continuous helpings of Barker anecdotes I invariably asked other officers to join us for dinner. Apart from adding much-needed stimulation to the conversation it also gave the Governor and his wife the chance to get to know all the officers in the ship. And just in case this routine began to pall I also invited senior ratings for dinner or drinks. As the weeks went by Rex got to know every face on board. And when we finally left our Falklands station thirty months later most of the ship's company had enjoyed reciprocal hospitality at Government House in Port Stanley.

We had planned to do geological work on James Ross Island with Dr Mike Thompson of the British Antarctic Survey. It had been a season of troublesome transport for them and typically Mike was marooned on one of the British Antarctic bases on the Peninsula. The plan had been that he would fly up to the area in a Twin Otter aircraft but the plane had been grounded due to poor weather and minor mechanical problems. In the end he was forced to supervise the geological work from a distance. I spoke to him twice a day on the radio and we exchanged information on fossil collection and earth and rock samples. I relayed his instructions from the bridge and our sailors and Royal Marines were deployed to collect the samples from the areas he designated. The island was divided into a grid and each day we would go to a selected square either by boat or helicopter. It was a strange feeling to be working in areas where man had never even stood before. It was certainly true to say that parts of the island were completely unknown territory.

Despite working in this unusual way we managed to complete nearly all the geological and palaeontological work and a significant amount of the survey. To accomplish this both our helicopters were flying almost constantly. This was not without risk as the Wasp has one engine. If it fails, and the helicopter goes down, the only real chance of rescue is by the other helicopter. Because of this there were restrictions on the range from the ship that a solo helicopter was allowed to operate. Whilst the safety implications were obvious, it was also a limiting factor in the ground we could cover.

The Wasp is not the ideal aircraft for the Antarctic. Because of the single engine and the possible need for a quick exit, they normally flew with the doors off. This might have been OK in the Mediterranean, but in an already cold climate the added airborne chill factor made it a pretty uncomfortable ride. The air crew were plugged into their heated suits, but passengers had to rely on a bulk of clothing that made them look like competitors in a Paddington Bear lookalike contest. Despite these precautions, at the end of longer trips exposed skin was tinged with blackness. I experienced this most days, either flying to one of the international bases or to a work area. Despite the discomfort it was thrilling to be airborne in this ice-clad corner of the world.

The Pebble Mill team were now concentrating on a film recreation of Ernest Shackleton's epic trip from the Weddell Sea to Elephant Island. For the latter part of this re-enactment the ship's company became instant movie extras as 'Shackleton's intrepid crew'. This filming took place on the same beach where Shackleton's crew had been marooned. It is a forbidding place, but it was impossible to recapture the essence of Shackleton's epic voyage of in a small boat from Elephant Island to South Georgia. Despite this heroism, it was almost a year before the crew were rescued. They had created shelters from the inverted hulls of the *Endurance*'s other two boats.

Much later, during the run up to the conflict, when contact with home was sparse, the Pebbles kept us in touch with letters and news videos. This made an enormous difference. The extraordinary thing is that Bob Langley maintains to this day that it was just a matter of routine courtesy. For 'courtesy' of that order I am eternally grateful.

Another member of the team, John Smith, later joined forces with Lords Buxton and Shackleton, Sir Vivian Fuchs and others, to set up SWAG – the South West Atlantic Group. This was a kind of 'Friends of *Endurance*' with a fair amount of political clout.

The Pebble Mill 'South Atlantic' series proved to be more than perceptive, particularly in terms of the politics. It is perhaps rare for media people to have such a thorough grasp of issues as convoluted as the Argentine claim to the Falklands. I have no doubt that Rex and Mavis Hunt, their co-hosts for many dinners, had a great deal to do with that. The 'Pebbles' were primarily concerned about the future sovereignty of the islands because of the potential threat to living resources and the management of scientific projects. They were also ahead of the game when it came to painting probable political scenarios. The programmes made it abundantly clear that the Argentine threat should be taken seriously.

Even without a military threat the dangers of sailing in Antarctic waters are real enough. Night orders for the Officer of the Watch invariably included an instruction to keep a lookout for bergy bits and growlers. These are colloquial names for types of small icebergs. At 10 or 12 knots they could make quite a dent in the hull of even the relatively well-protected *Endurance*. They could easily pierce the side of a modern thin-skinned ship. Infra-red binoculars are needed to pick them out.

Coastal navigation in those waters is full of hazards. Two large icebergs can create a temporary channel through which the water is funnelled fast. If this causes you to lose steerage way the tidal stream is sufficient to slew the ship across an ice-made channel. This happened to us once when we glanced an iceberg quite hard. The damage was minimal only because we were making way slowly. The Officer of the Watch recovered a thin strip of red-painted metal which was later to be taken home and mounted on a commemorative plaque. I have no doubt that even 15 years later this conversation piece evokes the moment.

The *Endurance* also called on the Argentine, British and American bases in the area. Rex Hunt was particularly impressed with the atmospheric science projects in progress at the British Faraday Base and the biological work on penguins and seals at the American Palmer Base. For reasons that can only be described as political, Rex was not permitted to visit the Argentine bases. Wherever possible I did my best to represent him. Unlike other bases, where serious scientific work was in progress, the feeling was that the Argentine purpose was primarily to create political precedent. Two such bases were on Seymour Island and at Hope Bay where Argentine families were accommodated. There were also temporary bases in the Lemaire Channel, known as the Kodak Gap because of the fjord-like scenery. The Antarctic has a trick of making the most spectacular places most difficult navigationally. Here there are icebergs great and small, pack and fast ice, and a chill blast of weather funnelling down from the high peaks on either side of the channel. While a stint on the bridge demanded the ultimate in concentration, the ship's company clicked away with their cameras from the upper deck.

The American base that had been established close to the western side of the Le Maire Channel was primarily to investigate the possibility of copper. One of the mountains is called Copper Peak because of its green-stained rock. Whatever the explanation of this phenomenon it is a misnomer. Plenty of mineral resources have been identified in the area but there appears to be little or no copper.

Towards the end of that work period we visited Deception Island to the north-west of the Peninsula and just to the south of Cape Horn. The island is a volcanic crater with a recent history of activity. The shore line is covered in a mixture of lava and ice. These warm pools are a kind of health farm for seals and penguins. To get into the bay the ship had to enter through a narrow passage where the water is relatively shallow, then on to the crater area itself where the water is very deep. This made anchoring rather tricky.

We were surprised to find company in the form of the German research ship, *Meteor*. I invited some of the scientific team and the Captain over for dinner. I think we made an impression on the Germans largely because of Britain's long-standing commitment to the Antarctic. We learned that this was really a fact-finding mission. There were plans to replace the *Meteor* with a modern ice-breaking research ship, and to establish a base on the edge of the Weddell Sea. The scientists had already agreed that this was both feasible and desirable. There was also something of an historical precedent. During the period of the Third

Reich there had been a base at Bellinghausen; it was likely that the new base would be nearby.

The enthusiasm of everyone we met from the *Meteor* was infectious. I recalled this during the summer of 1981 when it was decided to withdraw the British military presence from the South Atlantic. There were already bases representing perhaps a dozen nations in the vicinity. The scientists worked in an atmosphere of co-operation and camaraderie that transcended politics.

Maritime infrastructures were quietly supported by a military presence; that was the way the Antarctic game was played, and it seemed as if the British were to take no further part in it. We, who had stolen a march in some key areas of research, were going to pull out. It was almost unbelievable.

The presence of *Endurance* gave us the Falklands as a staging post for exploration, and South Georgia as a forward operating base. They were stepping stones to potentially the most valuable land mass on earth. To throw it all away seemed to me to be imprudent almost to the point of stupidity. These kind of issues provided a constant source of discussion between the Pebbles, the Hunts and myself. Of course I was committed, but I have not yet met anyone who has visited and understood something of Antarctica who does not feel as passionately.

It is the Peninsula area itself that has greatest impact on visitors. The great peaks running sheer down to the water are unforgettable. The icebergs along with coastline abound with wildlife. There are seals taking a nap and penguins sliding in and out of the water. There are also the leopard seals which bring to mind mythical sea serpents. They never tire of their fresh penguin diet. Indeed they are one of the most efficient murder machines on the planet: they can take and kill a penguin within a matter of seconds. The prey is taken and shaken on the surface and then the carcass is dragged beneath the waves for a swift silent dinner.

Rex Hunt later acknowledged how 'perceptive' it was of the television companies to send their crews to the Antarctic just a year before the conflict. Until then there had been very little British media coverage. Both films 'Langley South' and 'More British than the British' reflected Islander opinion and accurately predicted the result of the October General Election. It is hard to say to what extent these factors influenced events but there can be little doubt they did. Until the films were broadcast the Falkland Islands were hardly part of British consciousness; afterwards there was at least some awareness of these tiny parts of Britain in the South Atlantic.

After taking Rex and Mavis back to Stanley we set off north. The intention was to give the sailors a fortnight's rest. Our destination was Mar del Plata. Following the unsullied condition of the Antarctic, this visit to Argentina's Blackpool was perhaps something of an eye-opener. Not that we heard many complaints, apart from the prices. Later reports indicated that our men had taken full advantage of the local culture.

The officers were offered something more sedate. We were to stay at a farm run by Anglo-Argentines Duncan and Bridget Cameron. There was a tradition of hospitality here: several generations of *Endurance* officers had stayed with the Camerons. There was riding and shooting, as well as insight into the way a large beef estate operated. Included in my itinerary was a trip to Buenos Aires to renew contacts at the Embassy and a swift trip in Uruguay. These visits were really an update on political thinking.

From Mar del Plata we went down to the southern part of Argentina to lie off Rio Gallegos. The purpose was to fly one of our helicopters to pick up some helicopter parts. As it happened I flew into the airfield later used extensively for the Falklands invasion and for the deployment of strike aircraft. Early in 1981 it was a base for Mirage and Super Etendards, ostensibly in the front line against Chile. We watched them operate. The pilots, who wore large red scarves and grey overalls, looked uncannily like Second World War Spitfire pilots. No doubt this was the influence of the movies. It certainly had the desired effect on the opposite sex, who regarded them, even before a mission was flown in anger, as heroes. We also watched a helicopter come in from one of the oil rigs. The South African pilot had been trained alongside our own Tony Ellerbeck in the UK. This contact led to insights into Argentine oil exploration off the Straits of Magellan which pushed out approximately 100 miles towards the Falklands. The residual gap was now down to 300 miles.

Most of March was spent off the Peninsula and the vicinity of Rothera Base which was used for life and earth science studies by the British Antarctic Survey. This was the first time I had been so far south. Our main purpose was to survey an area where a ship had run aground two years earlier. There was also the opportunity for some life science work. One morning I took the helicopter to a rock where Emperor penguins had been sighted. This was slightly unusual because these penguins usually disappeared during the summer months. In the event the population seemed to amount to one Emperor. The instruction had been not to land in case we disturbed nesting arrangements. Under the circumstances I felt this could be safely ignored. I went in with the aircrew and ship's photographer to try to get a close-up view of this enormous penguin. The idea was to place a copy of *Moby Dick* and a Penguin chocolate bar close enough to him to help capture the scale. We were just about to complete the task when Nigel Bonner, the Head of Life Sciences at Cambridge, hove into sight over the rocks.

'Good morning Nick,' he called out, 'what are you doing here?'

When he reached us I was forced to explain that the plan had been to photograph the penguin with a book and a Penguin bar.

'But haven't you read my instructions?' he asked.

I admitted I had, but at the same time had felt safe enough from the Director on this desolate Antarctic rock. How wrong I was.

We returned to Stanley at the end of March, and then it was briefly up to Montevideo to collect the latest detachment of marines who would serve in the Falklands through the winter. It was then plain sailing via Santos and Tenerife for Portsmouth where we arrived on 12 May.

Chapter 4

ENDURANCE VERSUS WHITEHALL

I was to report to the Ministry of Defence and the Commander-in-Chief Fleet. This I believed would be a complete affirmation of our presence in the South Atlantic. But the debate beginning elsewhere would come to a very different conclusion.

In the summary to my 'Report of Proceedings' [July 31, 1981] I wrote:

> It was a valuable and thoroughly enjoyable season. I am convinced that both the Antarctic continent, and the continental shelf, will offer immense mineral wealth in the not too distant future. Her Majesty's Government would be very unwise to give up the British Military presence in both the Antarctic and Falkland areas.

The Defence cuts had been announced on 25 June. *Endurance* had been placed on the disposal list and Chatham dockyard was to close. Those of us who cared about these things were immensely saddened. It was the kind of unity that comes from mutual pain that let our Chatham refit continue without any form of industrial disruption.

This was to be a summer of mixed emotions for me. The euphoria I felt on returning to the UK had quickly evaporated. It took a while to prepare my case. In part this included taking advice from other RN captains. It was clear that the balancing act would be tricky. Whilst it would be understood that a captain would fight for his ship it would have to be done in a measured and objective way. The principal argument would certainly be that £3.5 million was excellent value when the many roles of the ship were considered. Steadily I put together a portfolio of evidence and made ready for calls on the Commander-in-Chief Fleet, my own boss (Admiral Sir John Cox) and the relevant sections in the MOD. I particularly remember calling on the Director of Naval Plans, Captain (later Admiral Sir) John Kerr. He yawned throughout our meeting at his Whitehall office. Either I wasn't putting my case concisely enough or he simply wasn't interested in the Antarctic. After about 15 minutes he yawned theatrically and announced that Admiral George was waiting to see him about a dockyard problem. His attitude had angered me.

'Bugger Admiral George,' I said, 'he can wait a bit longer.'

I knew Tony George and was sure he would agree that the safety of one of our colonies took priority over a dockyard dispute.

'I will conclude this briefing as quickly as possible and then I shall go.' I said.

This may have been less than diplomatic but it did capture his attention. By the time I left his office I think he understood that the rights of two thousand British subjects should be considered and that withdrawing *Endurance* would be seen as a green light in Argentina. He noted my comments without enthusiasm.

Getting his attention was like getting in one good punch at a boxing contest. But it was already clear that I was up against heavyweight opponents whose combined strength was perhaps more than enough to camouflage a lack of strategic awareness.

Already the Royal Marines based on the islands had been informed that they were not going to get new accommodation. The Islanders were also now aware that they were not going to get British citizenship. All these indications were absorbed by the Argentine Junta and would later be used as propaganda. The argument continued through the Summer of 1981. The crux of the whole thing now was – if *Endurance* was to be saved who was going to pay?

I knew it was pointless going back to John Kerr, or even over his head to Rear Admiral (later Admiral Sir) Derek Reffell. His view, I had every reason to believe, was that decisions had to be made in line with priorities and £3.5 million for the South Atlantic was not his main priority. Later, as Barker's luck would have it, he later became my boss; our differences over *Endurance* were not the best foundation for a working relationship, particularly as by then he had been proved to be wrong.

I also called on an old friend, Captain Brian Outhwhaite, then Director of Naval Operations and Trade. In contrast to John Kerr, he listened most intently and immediately became the most supportive of all the Divisional Heads. Later he wrote a summary of events and some of the discussions to which he was privy:

I consider the course of the fate of *Endurance* was the principal signaller of our intentions to the Argentines. It is therefore important to appreciate the emotions she generated within the FCO and MOD and to realize that, subconsciously at least, Nick Barker's name was a dirty word to some and therefore to be discredited or, at the very least, discounted.

My reason for saying this is because our intentions with regard to the *Endurance* was read by the Argentines as evidence of our military will because every time her future was raised in the Commons, and in the national press, the reply was negative. The most that was admitted was that a frigate would visit the Falklands from time to time.

The Naval Staff had put up a long list of cuts that included *Endurance*. The original saving was to be in the region of £2 million, later increased to £4.5 million. Nick thereupon started a valiant campaign. He was even caught in the House of Lords itself, lobbying. [This last remark was untrue but it no doubt reflected the nature of the response to my campaign.]

Nick also called on Assistant Under-secretary of Naval Staff, Mike Power, and Nigel Nicholls, and had a stand-up row. [Again, an understandable elaboration of the facts.]

My own thoughts were very clear about the idiocy of scrapping the ship. But the First Sea Lord and Vice Chief of Naval Staff had other priorities, perhaps understandably.

Nick continued to lobby forcibly and in the early part of this year Michael Shersby (a Conservative MP) went to Lord Carrington and said that the Foreign Secretary had misled the house on the subject of the number of Argentines on Southern Thule. Somewhat naturally Lord Carrington was cross and asked how he came by this information. Michael Shersby replied that Captain Barker had showed him one of his reports before he sailed. The FCO had in fact been sent the report by DI4 [an intelligence section] and had not taken note of it. DS5 sent a signal to Nick, without discussing it with me, for which they subsequently apologized. In this they asked for his reasons.

In the latter part of 1981 a large number of Conservatives signed an Early Day Motion on the Falklands. Part of this was an expression of concern about the future of *Endurance*. The Foreign Secretary sent a note to John Nott saying that, on balance, he thought it wiser for the ship to be kept. The latter replied, somewhat curtly, suggesting that unless the FCO could fund the *Endurance* he had rather more important priorities for the defence vote.

There were a number of times when either the First Sea Lord or the Commander-in-Chief Fleet wanted to make sensible precautionary dispositions and their proposals were treated harshly. The abiding impression I have is of diplomatists who had no wish to see delicate negotiations upset by heavy-handed sailors.

By the time I left DNOT I can honestly say that I was worried more than usual by the Falklands. The Foreign Office had firmly indicated by thought, word and deed that a military encounter was not an option. I had considered British Military engagement but had recoiled from the effort and risk involved. Was I wrong to be cautious? DI4, when we visited, did not even mention the Falklands and did not remember the early scrap merchants' diplomatic telegrams pointing to armed action.

Brian Outhwhaite also let me see some of the inter-departmental and inter-divisional correspondence. This made it clear that I was losing the battle for *Endurance*.

A change of tactics was required which must now include making representations at the highest Government level. What if Lord Carrington, the Foreign Secretary, could be won over? Would he perhaps bring a little pressure to bear on John Nott? To this end I went to see Robin Fearn in the Foreign Office. After a whole day's discussion, we put together a short, but strongly worded document that set out the main arguments. This was submitted through Robin's boss, John Ure, to the Foreign Secretary.

Much later I found out what had happened to our brief. Lord Carrington had indeed made representations to John Nott, but by then our case had been diluted to a single paragraph of a wide-ranging document which was more concerned with the future of Hong Kong and Gibraltar. I sought other support from within the MOD. I knew that my old friend Captain Tony Collins, then Director of Navy Publicity, had the ear of the Vice-Chief of Staff and the First Sea Lord. I also called on Admiral Fieldhouse who was Commander-in-Chief Fleet, and Admiral Anson who was Chief of Staff. Both of them gave me a fair hearing, and, at a later stage, Admiral Fieldhouse called for a contingency plan for the defence of the Falklands to be discussed. In essence this was putting the question: 'What do we have in mind as a response to a possible invasion?' The answer was inadequate but a contingency plan of sorts was discussed. In the event it was not put into practice.

I was certainly not without allies. My own boss, John Cox, supported me wholeheartedly. This caused him no end of trouble, but to his great credit he was not to be deflected from putting the argument across. He did his best to convince Admiral Reffell. He also took up my cause with Admiral Staveley, the Vice-Chief of Naval Staff. I hoped this might be a fruitful course to steer. Admiral Staveley had a family association with the Falklands: his grandfather (also an Admiral) had won the first Battle of the Falklands. Sadly, in keeping with the opinion of his senior colleagues, he saw the Falklands as insignificant, out of area, and nothing to do with the mainstream of a defence strategy which was focused almost entirely on the Soviets. The Falklands was an unwanted legacy, the bin end of an empire. The indecisions made in Whitehall were against the best judgement, not just of myself, but of others well placed to perceive the threat. As the announced cuts were likely to include the aircraft carrier *Invincible*, and a number of destroyers and frigates, the fate of *Endurance* did not feature on the list of priorities.

John Nott's view was that the concept of global reach for the

Royal Navy (implicit in the idea of a balanced Naval Task Force) was something we could no longer afford. It was supported only by those whose aspirations were driven by nostalgia. He also believed that the balanced Naval Task Force was in itself an anachronism that should have been buried when the last fixed wing aircraft carriers, *Ark Royal* and *Eagle*, were decommissioned. All we had now were anti-submarine helicopters and a handful of Harriers. The strike aircraft, Buccaneers and Phantoms, were fast becoming redundant, and in any event were operated by the RAF.

If a global rôle was no longer a reality, this 'achievement' was by no means the property of one Government. As far back as 1966 Denis Healey had announced that the Navy would never again operate fixed-wing aircraft.

But the simple truth is that we would not have won the Falkland Conflict if the Review of 1981 had been put into effect. The Government was spared this embarrassment only by a coincidence of time-scale. If the Argentines had delayed their invasion by no more than a few months our capacity to respond would have been irretrievably reduced. HMS *Invincible* would have been sold to the Australians and we would have only had two other carriers available, one of which would almost certainly have been in the process of a refit. One carrier could not have been the basis of a feasible force to combat the Argentine shore-based aeroplanes.

There is no doubt that John Nott had been appointed as Margaret Thatcher's hatchet man. His brief was not only to cut Defence expenditure but to cut it quickly. In turn this meant that his Defence Review contained sharper cuts for the Navy than the other services. We believed that this had more than a little to do with a personal crusade to dismantle the last vestiges of empire. The logic, such as it was, was of imperial and naval retrenchment. This was not new. It had been the undertow of British policy for many years.

It was also strange and dishonest that swingeing cuts implicit in the Review of 1981 came from a Conservative Government politically pledged to strong defence. In fact these proposals were more draconian than those of any previous administration. Even

Denis Healey had held back from going so far. The Review caused alarm within the Services and created conflicts of emotion and reason for some senior Conservatives.

Navy Minister Keith Speed had a Dartmouth education and had served as a Naval officer. He was also a friend of Sir Henry Leach, the First Sea Lord. There can be little doubt that he felt divided loyalties and voiced his disquiet at the highest level. It was therefore less than surprising when he was sacked from his ministerial post at the Ministry of Defence.

In the wider scale of things my dispute was really little more than a flanking operation. Sir Henry Leach was battling for the survival of the Navy vanguard. Indeed what was at stake was nothing less than the Navy as we knew it. But now the battle lines were drawn within the establishment itself. Though fought by memo and inter-departmental discussion the principal protagonists were clearly lined up behind John Nott and Henry Leach. Admiral Leach later summed up the strength of feeling when he said: 'John Nott's view was ill-conducted and ill-conceived. It was a vindictive attack on the Royal Navy.'

It was supremely ironic that John Nott was soon to have the opportunity to prove that a truly balanced Naval force was the requirement for the Falklands. This was what Henry Leach fought so determinedly for, and because the cuts had not yet been implemented, had managed to achieve.

In his book *The Little Platoon* Michael Charlton refers to a conversation with Henry Leach. This concerned the withdrawal from the Simonstown base in the 1960s and the retirement of the resident South Atlantic Squadron. This, in the Admiral's view had removed the credible deterrent to full-scale Argentine invasion. Since then the Islands had only remained in British hands by inculcating in Argentine minds the belief that the Falklands could not be held against a serious attempt by the British to repossess them.

In this dangerous game the joker in the propaganda pack was HMS *Endurance*. She was at least a tripwire for the Argentines. This is Michael Charlton's analogy which he developed further: 'Both the tripwire and the Task Force were going to melt away. Following these declared intentions of 1981 what was there to forestall the Argentines taking military action if their ambition was not satisfied by negotiation?'

And Admiral Leach said: 'In theory deterrence rested on the forty Royal Marines who formed the Falkland Island Garrison. As part of that Defence Review, *Endurance* the Ice Patrol ship, which is only normally deployed there for half the year, would have been withdrawn and disposed of without relief.'

Since the 70s the Chiefs of Staff had made it clear that a large Task Force, including aircraft carriers, would be required for this purpose. John Nott did not dispute this, but remained rooted in the insistence that Britain could no longer afford the resources for its commitments. One consequence of this was a need to end the Task Force mentality.

The Chief of Defence Staff was Admiral (now Lord) Sir Terence Lewin. As a Naval officer, who had served with great distinction, it must have been particularly difficult for him to remain restrained and impartial.

In June Lord Shackleton asked me to come and see him at his London Office. He was about to speak in the House of Lords and wanted to check some facts. He invited me to stay for lunch and began by talking about relatively minor matters. Suddenly he asked, 'Has the ship been axed?' I told him I couldn't answer that question.

'Do you mean you're not going to tell me?'

'I cannot answer,' I repeated, 'but if you want an answer you're in a very good position to find out by putting the question in the House of Lords.'

This meeting led to a subsequent confrontation with Michael Power in the Ministry of Defence.

On the same afternoon I had been to see Captain (later Rear Admiral) Patrick Rowe. I stressed the importance of convincing those in the corridors of power that we should have another look at the question of our military presence in the South Atlantic. He wholly agreed and brought Nigel Nicholls, then Head of DS5, into the discussion. What began to emerge from that meeting was a strategy aimed at convincing the Assistant and Vice Chiefs of Naval Staff, and the First Sea Lord, of the perils implicit in the Defence cuts. During these discussions Michael Power, then an

Under-secretary in the MOD, entered the office. He was the 'buffer state' between the Naval Staff and other ministries and therefore a very important cog in the wheel, particularly in terms of discussions between the Foreign Office and Ministry of Defence.

'I hear you've been briefing a socialist peer,' he said.

'That's not so,' I told him. 'In fact I refused to give any answer to the main question asked.'

'If one of my senior civil servants was found to be briefing a member of the opposition I'd have him sacked,' he said.

'If that's the way you feel,' I replied, 'why not take this up with Admiral Leach? Perhaps you will get me sacked. But if I go, it will be with honour. What I have been able to talk about within the confines of the MOD has not been discussed with any politician.'

What followed was forty minutes of diatribe in which I was accused of multitudinous misdemeanours. I hardly made a response, other than at some stage to point to a White Paper (about Hong Kong) of which he was very possibly the author. The paper, I suggested, could well be considered for a major fiction award. This did not endear me to him. And standing my ground only served to make the veins in his neck and face stand out as his mood changed from poisoned civility to outrage.

I repeated that I had not, in any way, briefed anybody outside the Naval and Civil Service circuit. 'I was perfectly capable of doing so,' I said, 'but to date have kept my own counsel.'

He didn't believe me. By the next day he had informed Admiral Cox, various members of the Naval staff, and possibly the First Sea Lord that I had been behaving in a way that was totally unacceptable for a serving Captain. He had also been free with his opinion that appropriate disciplinary action should be taken.

But the ripples of my run-in with Michael Power were to spread further than this. When I sent my warning signals later in the year, and early the following year, the information was either filed in the waste paper bin or dismissed as 'that fellow Barker trying to keep his ship alive'. I have no doubt he was one of those primarily responsible.

That evening I went to the House of Lords to listen to the debate. The question of the possible scrapping of *Endurance* was raised. It was, inevitably, Michael Power and the Naval Staff who would have to provide the Ministerial answer to their Lordships' enquiries. It was some small consolation that he should be presented with this difficulty. *Hansard* records how the debate had been conducted. During the course of his speech Lord Buxton said:

> I outlined this whole problem of the British Antarctic Survey in a debate last June and pleaded that we cannot be the only nation to pull out of the Antarctic. Through the British Antarctic Survey we have been a leading influence for nearly 50 years. Would the Minister kindly tell us what is the intention regarding the Royal Navy vessels and HMS *Endurance* in particular? And is he aware that the British presence and influence in the Falklands and dependencies, and in the Antarctic Peninsula – and therefore our longterm interest in the resources of the South Atlantic – would be placed in serious jeopardy if the intention towards *Endurance* and BAS has any foundation? I trust that it cannot possibly come about.

Aubrey Buxton covered most of the key Antarctic issues in his speech. His words were reinforced by Lord Shackleton who also added:

> Obviously HMS *Endurance* is not a very powerful force although I believe she did send her helicopters when the Royal Research vessel *Shackleton* was pursued into the Falklands. Nevertheless, the fact is that *Endurance* is a proper ice patrol ship of a kind that has been used in keeping Danish bases in Greenland. It is therefore not only suitable but a very cheap operation. This really is a folly because we know that a frigate with its thin skin would not be able to penetrate the ice. Such a ship would not be able to visit Faraday, Halley or Signy, or many of the bases. They would have to rely on the British Antarctic Survey ships *Bransfield* and *John Biscoe*. These are civilian ships. They are not a Naval presence. And this we are doing at a time when the Germans are building a big icebreaker and the Argentines have a big icebreaker. I shall not even talk about the Americans and Russians.

Furthermore, HMS *Endurance* practically earned her keep last year when she towed the *Biscoe* after she had damaged a propeller in the ice. Towing the *Biscoe* into Montevideo, a distance of over 100 miles, saved enormous cost and probably paid for HMS *Endurance* for that season.

The debate continued through the evening. Eventually the Parliamentary Under Secretary of State for the Department of Trade, Lord Trefgarne, responded. Following the more predictable platitudes he added:

My noble friend, Lord Buxton, also asked how the views of the Falkland Islanders on any solution to the dispute would be determined. This would be for the Falkland Islanders for themselves to decide, whether by a referendum or some other means. In effectively judging the views of the people the noble Lords Buxton and Shackleton, and also Lord Mottistone, also referred to the decision in respect of HMS *Endurance*. I can confirm that HMS *Endurance* will be paid off in 1982 on her return to the United Kingdom following her deployment in the South Atlantic and the Antarctic region later this year. There are no plans to replace her. However, the Royal Marines Garrison in the Falkland Islands will be maintained at its present strength and from time to time Her Majesty's ships will be deployed in the region.

Although we had known all this for some time, this was the first time it was officially confirmed by a Government spokesman.

It was a sad team that retired to the bar in the House of Lords at the conclusion of the debate. I remember commenting to Robin Fearn that I was dismayed that the brief we had prepared for Lord Carrington had apparently had no effect whatever. Robin saw this as the end of the line: 'When one Secretary of State has rejected the views of another [in this case John Nott rejecting Lord Shackleton] there is nothing more that an ordinary member of either of those Departments can do.'

'Unless of course,' I pointed out, 'the Prime Minister can be brought into the discussion.'

'Yes,' he said, 'I suppose that is one option. But so far as we are concerned there is nothing more we can do.

74

We were not surprised when it was formally announced that *Endurance* would be taken out of service in March, 1982, and not replaced. This was seen in Argentina as a deliberate political gesture, a calculated diminishment of British interest in the Falklands. It was for this reason that the decision to dispose of this minimal deterrent was opposed by the Foreign Office.

But despite Lord Carrington's protests the decision was confirmed in Parliament in the summer of 1981. Behind the scenes the debate continued but John Nott formally declined to reverse his decision later in the year and again shortly before the Conflict.

In the Ministry of Defence the argument had focused on the relative merits of *Endurance* and a frigate which could visit the Islands from time to time. I pointed out many times that a frigate was not a tenable option. Apart from *Endurance*'s ability to survive in the ice pack, and her authentic multi-rôle identity, her running costs were likely to be no more than one weapons system in a frigate. If the cutbacks were about saving money, the best case for *Endurance* was that she was cost-effective. The decision was made, at least in part, on the 'fact' that *Endurance* had little or no defence capability. This too was an inadequate assessment. Apart from *Endurance*'s useful intelligence fit, she had sixteen air to surface missiles. She also had two (possibly three) gunship helicopters. But the politics of economics frequently defy financial logic. It became clear that the choice Admiral Leach had to make was between *Endurance* and a frigate. He chose the frigate, no doubt on the advice of John Kerr and his boss, Derek Reffell. And that, it seemed, was the end of the matter.

Chapter 5

THE BATTLE CONTINUES

The British decision was discussed at some length in Argentina. Indeed their two leading newspapers *Le Clarin* and *La Prensa* ran articles and editorials on the Falklands in general, and *Endurance* in particular. The *Buenos Aires Herald* (the English language paper) was also concerned with the subject. The conclusion of all this newsprint speculation was that the British were relaxing their hold on the Falkland Islands, and this was a clear signal that sovereignty would be handed over in due course.

Between 1976 and 1981 Argentina was ruled by a Junta of the armed services. This was headed initially by General George Videla. Whatever else could be said of the Junta it was true that the tough economic policies had brought the annual rate of inflation down to 100 per cent. Under the previous President, Isabelita Peron (second wife of the late President Juan Peron) the rate had been 400 per cent. But this success was accompanied by rigid controls. Political self-expression was ruthlessly suppressed by the secret police employing every inhuman method and tactic available. More than nine thousand people are known to have 'disappeared' during those years. Many were interrogated and eliminated by serving officers of the armed forces.

Roger Perkins, author of *Operation Paraquat*, describes the political manoeuvres in Argentina in 1981 like this:

In March Videla reached military retirement age and the Junta elected as his replacement another soldier, General Viola. He came to power in a cloud of rhetoric. He spoke of an early return to democracy and free elections. Unfortunately for him inflation once again soared to 400 per cent per annum and his swift removal was engineered by three men of the Junta – General Leopoldo Galtieri, Galtieri's good friend Admiral Anaya and Brigadier Lamidozo of the Argentine Air Force.

They used the winter and spring months to plot the downfall of the President and in December, 1981, Viola was forced to resign on the grounds of ill health, and the new leader emerging from these manoeuvres was Leopoldo Galtieri. Galtieri was ambitious but unsophisticated in the sphere of international politics and diplomacy.

But Galtieri did have many contacts in Washington where he was courted by the State Department: the Americans viewed him as a new anti-Communist ally, easily manipulated, so his succession to power could be exploited to bolster US influence over South and Central American affairs. The State Department sought to extract a commitment from Galtieri that he would send some of his counter-insurgency specialists (with long experience of fighting Argentina's own home-grown guerrilla movement) to serve in Central America. They appealed to his intense national pride and held out the offer of elevating the status of Argentina from the Third World category to a significant world power.

The offer was overwhelmingly attractive. President Reagan's National Security Adviser Richard Allen publicly hailed Galtieri as possessed of a majestic personality. It was all very heady stuff for an army officer with no previous exposure to American hospitality and good fellowship. Galtieri's ego became dangerously inflated in a very short period of time.

It is alleged that Galtieri was advised by the Americans to keep control of the army after his succession to power, but to cover himself by ensuring the total support of at least one other member of the Junta.

Admiral Anaya was the obvious candidate but he had ambitions of his own and these centred upon his determination to advance the interests of the Argentine Navy. A service which had never carried the same clout as the Army with Argentina's closed ruling military circle. Anaya was an energetic man of high professional competence. He did not like the British. He had served as a Naval Attaché in the Argentine Embassy in London between January, 1975 and January, 1976. He had found it an unhappy experience and it seems to have left a residual resentment. Those

77

who knew him believe he was the one man who possessed the ability and personal commitment to mastermind a seizure of the Falkland Islands.

This assessment was reported in detail by the British Embassy to the Foreign and Commonwealth Office in December, 1981, and Naval Intelligence Departments in February, 1982. Evidence now suggests that Anaya was setting the wheels in motion at the end of 1981 for direct action against the Falkland Islands but had not, at that stage, informed Galtieri and Lamidozo. There was no immediate need to show his hand. The target date was January, 1983 – the 150th anniversary of British settlement.

Being a seaborne operation, it would be directed by the Navy and would therefore reflect greatest credit on that service. With 12 months in hand Anaya could lay his plans quietly and thoroughly. It is unlikely that the island of South Georgia came within the orbit of the scheme, or if it did that was no more than peripheral interest.

In my view Anaya was certainly the nasty bastard of the three. I had called on him in Buenos Aires and I can't say I was particularly impressed or unimpressed. But I knew from his demeanour that he did not like the British. I also knew that he had written (at some stage of his London appointment) a contingency plan for capturing the Malvinas.

So, with this gang of pirates in charge of Argentine fortunes, little encouragement was needed to think about exploiting a situation. One distinct possibility was an invasion of Chile which would perhaps resolve another territorial ambition, the disputed islands in the Beagle Channel.

But the decommissioning of *Endurance* must have looked like the removal of the last significant obstacle to 'recapturing' the Malvinas. Pressure to move quickly came from an urgent need to divert attention within Argentina from a disastrous economy. The Malvinas operation, when compared to an attack on Chile, must have seemed a low-risk strategy guaranteed to win enormous popular support.

I kept in touch with the developing situation in Buenos Aires. The Anglo-Argentines were particularly interested in the reaction to the *Endurance* decision. Through them I received many

1. The Author

2. '*Red Plum*, as *Endurance* was called, was not an easy ship to control' (p.30). On station in the South Atlantic.

3. 'The new embassy was to be led by Anthony Williams, a diplomat with a distinguished career record' (p.28). Here he is returning my call at Buenos Aires.

4. Royal Marine guard of honour commanded by Lt Keith Mills being inspected by His Excellency the Governor and Commander in Chief Falkland Islands, Mr Rex Hunt.

5. I welcome Captain Moya, CO of the submarine base at Mar del Plata on board *Endurance*. (see p.62).He was soon to lose one of his main assets, the *Santa Fe*, at the hands of the helicopter in the rear of this picture.

6. Life on board *Endurance*, Christmas, 1980. The youngest sailor swaps roles with the Captain for the day....

7. ....David Attenborough (see p.47) and A B 'Taff' Jones would like to do the same.

8. 'The idea was to place of a copy of *Moby Dick* and a Penguin chocolate bar close enough to him to help capture the scale' (p.63).

9. 'The plan was to dig a large hole in the surface to install a fleximeter' (p.52). Assisting the Scott-Polar Institute in measuring the movement of icebergs.

10. 'The helicopter hit the ground with violent forward momentum at speed and tipped up on its nose'. (p.102)

11. '... and most of all Sir Ernest Shackleton... as always, we had duly paid our respects at his Grytviken graveside' (p.105). Left to right: Lt Cdr Mike Green, Mrs Hunt, Lt Cdr Andy Lockett, Rex Hunt, Lt Cdr Arthur Ainsley, the author.

12. 'The hut is tiny, but superbly neat and tidy' (p.132). Lord and Lady Buxton on South Georgia.

13. Annie and Cindy come on board. Seen here with the author and Surgeon-Lieutenant Neil Munro (see p.132).

14. '...surveying the area around the British Atlantic Survey Base at Rothera' (p.129).

15. *Guerrico* and *Bahia Paraiso* off Leith, South Georgia (see p.168).

16. HMS *Antrim* (right) and RAF *Tidespring* in Cumberland Bay (see p.175).

17. HMS *Plymouth* (see p.175).

18. The author countersigning Captain Astiz's surrender document on board HMS *Plymouth* at Leith, South Georgia, watched by Captain David Pentreath and selected members of his ship's company (see p.196).

19. Left to right: *Blue Rover* (Captain J. D. Roddis), *Saxonia* (Captain H. Evans) and *Endurance* (see p.202).

20. HMS *Endurance*'s main armament!

21. Royal Marines boarding a Wessex 3 on *Endurance* prior to the recapture of Southern Thule.

22. The *QE2* unloading stores and men in South Georgia. (Note low cloudbase at right background.)

23. The surrender of Southern Thule aboard HMS *Endurance* (see p.212). Right to left: Captain A. P. Overbury (RFA *Olmeda*); Commander A. Morton RN (*Yarmouth*); Captain Nick Barker; Captain Chris Nunn (OC 'M' Coy, 42 Commando, RM), Captain Alan Stockwell *(Salvageman)* and members of the ship's company.

24. HMS *Endurance* detachment back in business on Southern Thule.

25. United Towing's tug *Salvageman* (Captain Alan Stockwell) alongside ARA
Santa Fe (see p.216).

26. The *Red Plum* and those who sailed in her.

27. A day at the Palace.

28. Goodbye old friend.

29. Retreat to the sticks

translated newsprint cuttings and tapped the changing mood of the Anglo-Argentine community. It was one of high anxiety and alienation. The early years of the Conservative Government had demonstrated that budgetary controls for a wide range of Government Departments had become progressively more stringent. Added to that, the trend was increasingly towards more but smaller departments and inevitably departments within departments.

The annual budget round was described by one commentator as 'The Rats' Birthday Party'. Each year the cake becomes progressively smaller and the most tenacious rodents grab the larger portions and hide as many crumbs as they can. The impact of this is twofold. The weaker rats, or those who cannot adequately defend their position, are faced by starvation. Driven in this way, ultimately nobody understands or even cares about the purpose of the game any more. They know only how to play it.

This loss of a strategic overview, and a long-term strategy based upon it, made it very difficult to fight the battle for *Endurance*. Only those at the very top could even speak in that sort of language and we were denied access to them. The Foreign Office had put the case for maintaining a presence in the South Atlantic and this had been bluntly refused by John Nott. There were therefore no more cogs that could be purposefully turned in the Whitehall machine without direct access to the Prime Minister. Lord Shackleton had come to the same conclusion.

'It will have to be a letter to the Prime Minister,' he said, 'and would be better coming from a Conservative peer.'

We agreed that Lord Buxton would be the ideal choice. Could he be persuaded to write to the Prime Minister? Mrs Thatcher, of course, was the only person in a position to take hold of the FCO and the MOD and, if necessary, the Dept. of Education, and shake out of them a method for paying for the ship.

Lord Buxton was wonderful. He suggested that I put together a draft which he could use as the basis of his letter. This I was more than happy to do. After kicking around the text between us for some time the final letter was despatched.

Dear Prime Minister,

I opened a debate recently on the Falkland Islands in which I broadly supported the Government's line in holding discussions with Argentina, but I was disturbed to get confirmation from the Minister that HMS *Endurance*, the only ice patrol ship possessed by the Royal Navy, which protects all British interest in the Antarctic and the South Atlantic, is to be paid off in 1982. The purpose, apparently, is to save £4 million a year whereas the consequence could be the loss of literally billions of oil revenue for this and future generations in Britain.

Through the British Antarctic Survey Britain has for long been a leading influence in the Antarctic and the South Atlantic. This internationally recognized status gives Britain an option on future opportunities in the last undeveloped part of the globe. It would seem incomprehensible if we meekly fade out whilst most other nations are openly increasing their scientific and military presence.

The work of BAS is supported by two unarmed scientific vessels, the *John Biscoe* and *Bransfield*, and these are under continuous threat of reduction. But the important fact is the work and role of BAS cannot be sustained and protected without the presence and the service of HMS *Endurance*.

It is known that spectacular hydrocarbon prospects are likely to be realized in that part of the world. Can we really be the only nation in the world to throw away these prospects when we are already established there, effectively if slimly, sustained by HMS *Endurance* for which at present we have no substitute?

With regard to the Falklands, the British discussions with Argentina are strengthened by our Naval presence; so without it we will have few, if any, cards left in our hand. It so happens that at this particular juncture, the Argentine political and economic situation is becoming progressively more critical. Providing Britain negotiates with some semblance of confidence and strength, there is a chance of our reaching an acceptable solution to the Falklands problem. But if we announce the withdrawal of *Endurance*, with no prospect of an immediate replacement, the British position would be weakened.

I believe that the electorate would not take kindly to the international humiliation which could well be possible if the Argentines see there is nothing to hinder their bullying of the Falklanders. In the debate, the Minister stated that the marines would remain in the Falkland Islands. Being familiar with the situation at first hand, I must ask you to believe that this is probably impossible without *Endurance*, or without a Naval presence of a specialized nature.

It has been stated that the role of *Endurance* will be fulfilled by other Naval units, but rare and occasional visits by other Naval vessels will not solve the problems to which I have referred above in any way. All the risks and dangers will remain; a continuous Naval, specialized presence is paramount.

A vital role which *Endurance* fulfils is the inspection of British Bases in the Antarctic, but she also keeps an eye on foreign bases within the Antarctic treaty area. As a converted merchant ship, painted in the accustomed Antarctic red, *Endurance* is not warlike in appearance and consequently attracts little diplomatic reaction when visiting South American ports; the appearance of grey warships, (which in any case cannot play the necessary role in ice areas) would create a different image and have many disadvantages.

I expect it would be ambitious to ask that the decision to scrap *Endurance* should be reversed, though I feel sure that the consequences could not possibly have been understood by people who have not been to that part of the world but I do implore you to decide that *Endurance* must remain in service until she is replaced by a modern and better equipped successor. A stay of execution is absolutely vital for this nation. It is vital if we are not to surrender our prospects to other countries and be left out of the rich prizes that must lie ahead for Britain if we stay.

I cannot contemplate that this Government, which I support, should be the one that scrapped Britain's prospects in the Antarctic and the birthright of future generations.

Yours sincerely,

Buxton

The letter was dated 21 July, 1981, and at the same time Lord Buxton asked for agreement with several other people including Admiral of the Fleet Lord Hill Norton who sent him a letter agreeing with his assessment. I wrote to Lord Shackleton endorsing Lord Buxton's letter.

81

On 19 August the Prime Minister replied to Lord Buxton:

Dear Lord Buxton,

HMS *Endurance*, like *Protector* before her, has been a familiar sight in the South Atlantic and Antarctic for many years and her annual deployments have allowed her to perform a number of useful functions.

It would be surprising therefore if the news that she is to be withdrawn from service in 1982, on her return from her next deployment, was not met with some disappointment. This said, it is important not to overestimate the ship's rôle both in actual and potential defence of our national interests. She has only a limited military capacity being armed with two 20 millimetre Oerlikon guns and equipped with two Wasp helicopters.

She is not essential to our defence commitment to the Falkland Islands of which the Royal Marine Garrison provides, and will continue to provide, a tangible demonstration. The withdrawal of HMS *Endurance* from service will not impair our ability to maintain the operational effectiveness of the garrison.

I accept that the presence of HMS *Endurance* in this region for six months of the year helps to underline our commitment to the defence of the Falkland Islands but in re-appraising future Defence Programmes in order to insure that the several rôles that our forces undertake are carried out to best and most economic effect it has been necessary to take some hard decisions including a reduction in the number of service warships.

Against that background we have reluctantly to conclude that HMS *Endurance*'s primary task, when deploying in Antarctic waters, has been to conduct hydrographic surveys, and in this capacity she has been able to assist the British Antarctic Survey with their scientific and research programmes. To this extent her withdrawal from service will have some effect on the work of the British Antarctic Survey. It is, however, not the case that the rôle and work of BAS cannot be sustained without the presence of *Endurance*. BAS operate their own ships and are not dependent on HMS *Endurance* for maintenance and supplies.

You imply that BAS activities are in need of protection but, as I have said, *Endurance*'s ability to provide defence against a determined assault is limited, especially bearing in mind that for much of her six months' deployment outside the UK she is at considerable distance from the BAS area of operation. In any case the scientific and research programmes being conducted by various countries in the Antarctic region have hitherto been undertaken in an atmosphere of friendly and peaceful co-operation and within the terms of the Antarctic Treaty. This as you know expressly excludes any measures of a military nature in an area south of latitude 60 south.

You were concerned that HMS *Endurance*'s withdrawal would prejudice our ability to secure maximum economic benefit from any possible mineral exploitation in Antarctica. A number of countries, as signatories to the Antarctic Treaty like us, lay claim to certain areas of Antarctica. It is in an avowed attempt to avoid military conflict in defence of such claims, and so to provide for the continued demilitarization of the region, that all the treaty partners are about to engage in negotiating a régime for the exploitation of mineral resources of the area within the framework of the treaty itself.

It is in our best interests that exploitation should proceed on an agreed basis rather than for individual countries to press their separate claims and so risk a breakdown of co-operation. Even if, despite our efforts, this were to happen and certain countries were to resort to the use of force for the furtherance of their objectives, it is not easy to see what significant role HMS *Endurance* could play in defence of our national interests.

As for our negotiations with Argentina our position is clear. We are in no doubt about the legitimacy of our sovereignty over the Falkland Islands and we are determined to ensure that the Islands' territorial integrity is preserved. We shall continue to preserve the permanent Royal Marines Garrison at its present strength on the islands as a demonstration of our commitment. The *Endurance* on the other hand, has spent on average only some 30 days in Falkland waters each year.

I would not like you to think that the decision about HMS *Endurance*'s future was taken lightly. The annual visits by HMS *Endurance* are a feature of long-standing and I know that she will be missed but I hope what I have said will help you to put the decision in perspective and also to indicate the Government's determination both to see to it that the interests of the Falkland Islanders continue to be upheld and to ensure that our important economic interests in Antarctica are successfully pursued.

Yours sincerely,

Margaret Thatcher

Lord Buxton wrote a short letter with a copy of his reply from the Prime Minister.

Dear Nick,

I regard it as the usual departmental stuff, but I am not discouraged because, either by accident or design, the letter makes no mention of my main request which was that an axing of *Endurance* should be deferred pending an appropriate replacement. I intend to send a robust reply as soon as possible but would be very grateful for your comments and I could perhaps come and see you briefly to get your guidance.

Aubrey Buxton

On 3 September I responded:

Dear Lord Buxton,

Thank you so much for your letter and indeed for all your help in this most important crusade. I could not be more grateful and I hope that one day some of those distinguished but faceless people in Whitehall will realize the potential of the Antarctic before it is too late.

It confounds me that the FCO, DTI and Energy Ministries have not supported the cause. As you say the response from the Prime Minister is departmental claptrap, poorly staffed in my view. This may be because of the summer leave period.

Several points emerge from her letter. I will summarize them as follows.

Nobody has ever considered that *Endurance* is completely adequate for her several rôles in the Falklands and Antarctic

84

waters. Indeed, far from being withdrawn for the service, she should be replaced.

The Prime Minister states that it is Government policy to ensure that our important economic interests in Antarctica are 'successfully pursued'. Why does she therefore decide to withdraw our very cheap Naval presence when the other signatories are increasing their scientific and military presence?

It is possible that South Georgia could assume great importance as a forward base for oil exploration. If *Endurance* is withdrawn it is very possible that the Argentines will establish a base there first as they have already established a base on Southern Thule in the South Sandwich Islands.

Furthermore the Russians are presently using the sheltered waters of South Georgia for fish factory ship operation. I suggest that it is less likely that these countries will take the law into their own hands in either the remaining South Sandwich Islands, or South Georgia if they are regularly patrolled by the 'poorly armed' *Endurance*.

The British Antarctic Survey place great reliance on the presence of *Endurance*. Much of their geological work during last season was carried out by *Endurance*, not to mention the tow by *Endurance* to one of the BAS ships from Port Stanley to Montevideo which saved a large sum of money. I do not imply that BAS needs military protection but it does need support, and generally gets support when *Endurance* is carrying out marine surveys in an adjacent area.

The exploration of Antarctica has been a joint effort between scientists and the Royal Navy for many years and when some of this exploration is coming to fruition it would seem to be very unwise to give it up.

One further point has arisen since I last wrote to you. There is the possibility of a South Atlantic Treaty Organization: I am aware that the USA is interested in such a project and it would seem that we ought to keep a membership card in this area and in any projected treaty.

I have stated that the Royal Marines in the Falklands need to be complemented by a Naval ship equipped with radar, aircraft, and good communications, if they are to fulfil their role efficiently. To say that *Endurance* spends no more than 21 days in the Falklands is hardly relevant. I would suggest that she is within four days' steaming from the Falklands at any stage of the

South Atlantic Season. She does not operate in the area for five months a year because the ice edges too far north, and, furthermore the British Antarctic Survey also operate on a seasonal basis.

I have spelt out many of the assets provided by *Endurance*. Once again I do ask you to consider a stay of execution for the season following 1981 so that the whole situation can be considered in detail and with full consultation between Government departments.

I am told that the only way to save the ship is to canvass other Cabinet Ministers and Secretaries of State. I can therefore only suggest that Foreign Affairs, Trade and Industry, and Energy are the only people left to lobby.

I am continuing the fight and would appreciate a very low profile on the personal front. Thank you once again.

Yours sincerely,

Nick Barker

During the course of this correspondence another possible route to the Prime Minister, through her greatly respected PPS, Ian Gow, was attempted. Aubrey Buxton invited him, and his wife Jane, to dinner at his London flat. Ian Gow was kind enough to give me a few minutes to state my case. We could only hope that he would take the matter up with the Prime Minister. He wrote to me the next day:

> Jane and I very much enjoyed meeting you last evening and I valued our talk. Here is just a line to say I've written to John Nott, giving him your address. I'm not sure whether protocol would permit him to see you, but I hope that it will. In any event the ball is now in his court.
>
> Yours sincerely,
>
> Ian Gow

I believe his intention was honourable, but he probably already knew that it was highly unlikely that John Nott would wish to see me.

I knew there was nothing more I could do directly, and there was now a real danger of my personal influence being misinterpreted. It would now be up to distinguished peers and MPs to make whatever case they might out of the information provided by Lords Buxton and Shackleton.

Two MPs in particular, Michael Shersby (Conservative) and Eric Ogden (Labour, later SDP) had taken a special interest in the Falklands. They were about to go on a fact-finding mission to the area and let it be known they would welcome an invitation to lunch on board *Endurance*. This created a particular difficulty. Of course I could not just invite two MPs on board without clearing it first. Equally, these MPs had decided that I was the person to brief them and I could hardly prevent them travelling to Chatham. Despite my early application on their behalf when Admiral George Brewer finally became aware of their plans, he made it clear they must not be invited on board for lunch.

'I understand the position,' I told him, 'but they're arriving at Chatham station at 12.15. Do you want me to put them on the next train back to London?'

'I wish to Christ I'd known about this earlier.'

I explained that I had informed him of my dilemma, but obviously a bureaucratic cock-up had prevented the letter reaching him on time.

They came to lunch and we found we had an immediate rapport. Their interest in the islands was already considerable. Later they were to become members of the South West Atlantic Group, and we have been in regular contact ever since. Nothing 'sensitive', however, was discussed at that meeting.

On 17 September I also had a letter from Dr John Heap in the Foreign Office:

Dear Nick,

Just a line to thank you very much indeed for lunch in *Endurance* last week.

It was sad for me to think of such a fine ship coming towards the end of her days. I hope I am wrong for there seems so little straw about for making the necessary bricks.

It must be particularly sad for you. No commanding officer has made more of his command of *Endurance* than you have, and there is irony in the likelihood that you should have the ship's last days in your hands. I have much admired the fight you have put up. Nobody could have done more.

All the very best in the South this year. My warmest thanks for all your interest and help with our Southern problems.

Yours ever,

John

Following the announcement of the scrapping of *Endurance* I also received many similarly unsolicited offers of support. These included letters from a number of important media influences, not least the Pebble Mill production team who had already decided that their series about Argentina, the Falklands and the Antarctic were to be shown again. I was asked if there was anything else they could do. Anglia TV, presumably encouraged by Lord Buxton, were also keen to do something. David Attenborough's producer, Ned Kelly, wrote to say that John Nott must be out of his mind. Even in my most altruistic mood I may have had difficulty in disagreeing with that.

Chapter 6

BACK SOUTH

At the end of August, 1981, I had one further opportunity to call on the First Sea Lord, Sir Henry Leach. I knew that whatever I asked he would try to achieve, but because of John Nott's proposals for the Navy he had a much larger problem. He pointed out that it was not the business of Armed Forces to decide how much money should be spent on national defence. That was a political matter to be determined by the Cabinet of the day. The heads of the three services would advise the Secretary of State for Defence on what the effects of the budget would be on the nation's defence capability.

For the Navy the cuts were twice as great as those affecting the Army and seven times greater than those to be imposed on the Royal Air Force. Additionally it had been decided that virtually the entire cost of the new strategic nuclear deterrent, Trident, would be financed from the Naval budget.

Admiral Leach told me that he would have been happy to see *Endurance* continuing her usual rôle, particularly as her running costs were so low. He also explained that the reason why the Navy was to take the lion's share of the cuts was because, according to the Secretary of State, they had expanded their programme beyond all proportion to the sums of money available to sustain it. This, John Nott believed, had been largely a matter of tactics in an attempt to acquire a larger slice of the budget. That may well have been true. Once something was agreed and fixed within the programme it was a political embarrassment to take it out. In John Nott's view, therefore, the Royal Navy was treated as fairly as the other services.

But it was also clear that the relationship between the First Sea Lord and John Nott was now so strained that any insistence could well have led to losing some other, perhaps more valuable, asset. The Admiral was his usual courteous self, but he admitted there was little or no hope for *Endurance*.

But there were a few shots left in the locker. One was a letter to *The Times* signed by many interested parties, all of whom became founder members of SWAG – the South West Atlantic Group. Among them was the producer of 'Langley South'. An extra programme had been devised to update the original five. Bob Langley, the presenter, approached Lord Shackleton to ask him to take part in this, a special television debate. He not only agreed to appear he also decided to use his political experience and personal prestige to back the Pebble Mill campaign.

The *Endurance* was now in the final stages of refit. Indeed the Chatham dockyard had been so efficient that it was possible to bring forward the completion date. We sailed for sea trials on 7 September. After a successful week of trials the ship spent a weekend in Sunderland. This repeated the precedent begun the previous year: the red and white ship re-established links with the red and white football club, and renewed acquaintances with local friends and dignitaries.

During the refit a hall porter in the Chatham Barracks had been particularly good to us. He was Bob Scott, a former CPO and renowned Geordie. I took him as a VIP to Sunderland and gave him the Governor's Cabin. When we arrived at Sunderland he noted that we had no flowers for the cocktail party and were obviously poorly equipped as we did not have a greenhouse on board. I suggested he could make up for this Admiralty oversight by collecting some flowers from the town. He returned with armfuls.

I said, 'That's a bit over the top, Bob. Where did you get them?'

'I've been round every cemetery in Sunderland,' he said.

Of course he hadn't, but the gesture was hugely appreciated. During the Conflict I received a large scroll from him. It honoured me as 'President of the Flower Nickers Association,

Sunderland Branch'. It has been a treasured possession ever since.

After the initial trials there was a short period of defect rectification and the ship sailed on 21 September for a trip down the river, taking many of those who had worked on the ship for a day at sea. Then it was Portsmouth for stores and ammunition and on to Portland for a work-up where the ship was yet again thoroughly checked out by the staff of Flag Officer Sea Training. A busy exercise period followed with an emphasis on flight deck operations, fire fighting and damage control. Finally we returned to Portsmouth for a short period before sailing to the South Atlantic on 13 October.

Sailing from your home port for a longish period away – in this case it was planned that we would not return until May – is always quite a traumatic event. There were girlfriends, wives and families there to see us off. Their faces captured the rainbow of emotions felt by many of us on board. They then moved from the jetty to Sallyport, a bastion at the harbour entrance. This is as close as families can get to the ship as she slides out of the harbour into Spithead. The last thing we saw was the waving arms growing smaller and smaller before disappearing into the dark background.

We called at Gibraltar and embarked our boss, Flag Officer of the Third Flotilla, the much loved Vice Admiral Sir John Cox. When we arrived at Madeira we prepared for the farewell to Admiral Cox at the customary ship's cocktail party.

There was a married woman on the island who managed to invite herself to the party. We had been warned that her passion for Naval Officers was incremental to their rank. She also had friends in Funchal and later the same evening we all ended up at a rather splendid residence for more drinks. We noticed that the Admiral and the lady were engrossed in deep conversation on a sofa. One by one we quietly slid out leaving them to it. We retreated to my cabin for a nightcap. Half an hour later the Admiral entered. We could tell by the doubts he expressed on subjects such as our parentage and sexual predilections that we had stitched him up rather well. His escape from the good wife of Kent had exercised his resourcefulness to the limit. But, by morning our crimes had been forgotten. He departed after wishing us all the very best of fortune for the season ahead.

We arrived in Rio on 9 November. It was a week packed with pomp, social and sporting events. Indeed the ship's company were royally entertained by the British and Anglo-Brazilian communities. We also re-established links with the Brazilian Navy, particularly the Hydrographic Service. There I shared some important conversation with the excellent Ambassador, Mr Harding. The contrast between our missions Rio and Buenos Aires was most marked. The service personnel in Brazil were thoroughly on-the-ball and untiringly efficient. Mr Harding was a true expert on South America and it was most refreshing to hear his views.

There was a kind of hidden agenda. If, as seemed likely, the *Endurance* was sold, Brazil might be one of the few countries who may wish to buy her. At least there was every chance she would be employed in much the same way; there was even the possibility of a lease-back arrangement if a changing situation warranted it. It was clutching at straws, but even the remotest possibility that our work could continue was worth considering. With all this in mind, some weeks later I wrote to my boss:

The Ambassador, Mr Harding, has been in his present post for less than a year. Before that he was the Superintending Under-Secretary for the South American Department in Whitehall. It follows therefore that the Falklands debate, and indeed some of the Antarctic problems, were well known to him.

I outlined the case for a British presence in the Antarctic, talked about the potential, and also about the political, scientific, and military activities of other interested nations. He asked my views about the Falklands and we found much common ground. He is a most impressive diplomat with an authoritative ambience about him, a quick and incisive mind, and few qualms about asking Brazilians direct questions. He said that whether the British liked it or not the Brazilians had insufficient oil and they intended to be part of the Antarctic bonanza.

However, they need to look at the area in more detail. They need careful guidance to select a base and support before becoming full members of the Treaty; hence their need for

92

Endurance. We took our party line into any discussions with the Brazilians. The sale of the ship was not a matter for Diplomats or Naval Officers. Our Governments would talk about the matter when the time came. However, the Brazilians did express a deep interest; we apologized for not being able to take some of them to the Antarctic this season.

It is believed that if we do not influence the Brazilians over the Antarctic, someone else will. This could be another lever towards keeping the ship going next year.

The Ambassador, together with his Naval Attaché, Captain Anthony Wheatley, put a brief together. The Ambassador was going to London the following week. It had become clear that if we could take Brazilians to the Antarctic periodically (over the next few years) we could exert the kind of influence that could set up their aspirations and could provide a counter to the Argentines. It could even become a peripheral consideration in the Falklands debate.

The more we talked through the problem the more attractive the proposition became. We agreed on all the significant details. I have since learnt from Anthony Williams that Mr Harding's brief was not greeted with much enthusiasm in London. Perhaps I should have expected this. Acting on Williams' advice the FCO strongly countered any proposal to sell the *Endurance* to Brazil. Anthony Williams also argued that if Britain was seen to be actively influencing Brazil over the Antarctic it could be interpreted as an insult to the Argentine.

I later spoke to Anthony Williams at Bahia Blanca and told him I understood the decision not to sell the *Endurance* to Brazil, but the question of who else might influence Brazil remained. He eventually agreed that Brazil could be a useful ally in exerting pressures on Argentina in the event of the Falklands or Antarctic becoming a more vicious impasse between our Governments. He even said there was merit in this alternative view. Whether or not he does anything about it I cannot say, but it smacks of the usual problem where insufficient homework has been done. However, despite these diplomatic moves we seem to be no further on the question of the future of *Endurance*. No disposal instructions or drafting indications have yet been received.

I understand that the impact of the television series together with several letters to *The Times* has been considerable. I gather too that more pressure has been put on Mr Nott to change his mind. But as Admiral Eberle said: 'The pressure would be more effective if it came from within the Navy and from Admiral Reffell in particular who has taken, as far as I can see, a totally passive view throughout.

As that seems unlikely I can only assume there has been no change of plan. No doubt the disposal notice will be posted before long.

We left Rio to take passage south to Montevideo. On the afternoon of our planned arrival the port was closed due to a force nine gale blowing across the entrance. This was potentially very dangerous. The water in the entrance is shallow, approximately 10 metres, with banks of six to seven metres. There was always the fear that strong winds would reduce the depth further and the silting of the banks would cause us to be hard and fast if our line was anything but plumb centre of the channel. The sea was also too rough for the Pilot to come out. The weather forecast was for another three or four days of the same. We asked for four tugs and the best pilot to meet us as we crabbed our way up the entrance channel. This was a true test of seamanship; there were so many things to consider at the same time. But like juggling jelly whilst riding a unicycle it concentrated the mind. I noticed one ship, in the outer harbour, with a heavy list to starboard and apparently aground. This was not a good omen.

As we headed up the inner harbour a pilot did eventually embark. His first comment was: 'Captain, turn the ship round. No tugs.'

I explained that this was now impossible. Turning round would have meant playing dodgems with the merchant shipping. I ignored him and continued on up the harbour. He became increasingly wild-eyed and wound up as his repeated requests to abandon any attempt to berth were ignored. My plan now was to use the anchor as a brake and let the gale blow me slowly onto the berth. Shortly before we reached position, three tugs arrived and the pilot miraculously regained his cool. We berthed gently alongside without the help of the tugs. It had been an interesting hour. The pilot had been useless and the absence of tugs had done little for morale.

But the ship's company had been magnificent with actions and reactions of the cut-throat razor variety. It was the kind of experience that cannot be reproduced as an exercise; if there was a moment when the ship's company truly became a team this was it. With the benefit of hindsight it was probably ideal training for what was to come.

Visiting Montevideo before or after visiting Argentina is always useful because you get an entirely different perspective. Uruguay is in many ways a poor relation and the people are particularly scathing about their 'neighbour'. The Ambassador, Patricia Hutchinson, was particularly well informed and quite often Uruguayans were first to the post over Falklands matters. After the fall of the Falklands the Embassy played a major part in the repatriation of prisoners.

We also embarked a Uruguayan officer, Mario Fontanot, who was to join us for experience in the Antarctic. He soon became a lively addition to the mess.

Bahia Blanca, our next port of call, is largely devoted to the Argentine Navy. We were met there by Julian Mitchell and Anthony Williams. In my report of proceedings I said of Anthony Williams:

> He was less positive than his colleague, Mr Harding. He knows the Argentine extremely well but is always at great pains to avoid offending them rather than taking a more definite approach. However, he was extremely diplomatic during our round of calls, particularly so as the Argentine President Videla had suddenly resigned and there was considerable unrest amongst senior officers and officials while his successor is chosen. This is not an easy period on the military or political front.

During that visit I flew up to Buenos Aires for special briefings and to meet the Argentine Antarctic team led by Commodore Cesar Trombetta. We each followed our prepared programmes at a special meeting where, in a friendly atmosphere, areas of co-operation were agreed. These included daily communication schedules and opportunities for cross-operating helicopters. As things turned out this programme of co-operation was stillborn.

I can only conclude that Trombetta received a directive that encouraged him to be increasingly elusive.

It had also been decided that we were unlikely to visit Mar Del Plata. This was because of a South African entry in the Whitbread Round the World Race. Diplomatically we could not possibly have our break there at the same time. The risk was, of course, that one of us might be reckless enough to have a chat with a South African. It was another example of the muddled thinking that can sometimes emanate from Whitehall.

Our visit to Bahia Blanca was something of a watershed. I had to climb in my white uniform up a tarry pile on the jetty side to reach the car that was to take me to my call on Admiral Lombardo, the Argentine Fleet Commander. The Naval Attaché had forgotten to order a gangway.

Bahia Blanca is primarily a wheat exporting port, but included in its environs is Puerto Belgrano – the main Naval port. Admiral Lombardo, as it turned out, was later to lead the Argentine Falkland Campaign. Our host ship was the cruiser *Belgrano*. On behalf of Admiral Lombardo I was well looked after by Captain Zaratiegui with whom I struck up an immediate rapport. We had several evenings together. I learnt he was waiting to be promoted to Rear Admiral together with a special posting to be in charge of what amounted to the operational base from which a Falklands Campaign could be launched. I told him we were to visit the base, Ushuaia, at the beginning of the following year. In the event when we arrived there Captain Zaratiegui was conspicuous by his absence. I later learned that he had been prevented from seeing me. However, we made many friends among the officers and ship's company of the *Belgrano*. To this day I do not know how many of them survived.

I was also able to further discuss the demise of *Endurance* directly with Anthony Williams. I placed emphasis on the message this would send to the Argentines. I am sure he thought my fears were overstated. But I did learn from him something extremely useful. It appeared that the two old school friends, Galtieri and Anaya, were creating a power base within the Junta. I have already labelled Anaya as the 'nasty bastard' of the emerging triumvirate. He was more politely described by a brother officer as a 'solitary, severe and self-disciplined person'. Martin Middlebrook offered a very similar assessment in his book *Fight for the Malvinas*.

I was beginning to form a picture of the likely main players in the new political régime. Of course I had met Anaya the year before and found little to like. Lombardo, however, was much more approachable. According to Martin Middlebrook it was not long after (on 15 December) that Anaya called for a contingency plan for a Falklands invasion strategy. This was to be used perhaps as a lever within the negotiations scheduled for February, 1982. If talks remained deadlocked the plan would be put into action before January, 1983.

But at this stage it is unlikely that Anaya's plans were known to anyone other than Lombardo and, to a lesser extent, Galtieri. If the British became aware of the Argentine agenda the plan could be scuppered by the deployment of a nuclear submarine. This had happened previously in 1977 when Anaya was Fleet Commander. Ambassador Williams was in regular contact with John Ure, the Assistant Under-Secretary of State at the Foreign Office, who had been dispatched on a visit to the Falklands and Buenos Aires in June, 1981. His mission in Port Stanley was to review the dispute (with the Islanders) in preparation for the policy reappraisal. This had become necessary following the collapse of Nicholas Ridley's lease-back proposal. John Ure said that he formed the impression that opinion among the Islanders had not hardened irrevocably against lease-back. This was very different from the mood I had encountered. And wouldn't this have hardened since the news of the scrapping of *Endurance*? He recommended that a genuine effort would have to be made to educate Islander and UK opinion about the danger of inaction and the safeguards on which the Government would insist. His Argentine brief was to reassure the Junta that Britain's intention was to secure a peaceful solution to the Falklands question. Part of the strategy was an attempt to dissuade Argentina from forcing the pace. His conclusion was that the Argentine Foreign Office was reasonably relaxed about progress, and still well disposed towards a lease-back arrangement. He warned, however, that the Military leadership was more hawkish and might demand a more forward policy. He warned that there was a risk of Argentina using Britain as a scapegoat for its domestic problems. It was now less possible to depend on continued Argentine patience and understanding. He also argued that the British Government had to be more visible in the support of a negotiated settlement.

Nicholas Ridley decided that the immediate aim should be to play for time. Rex Hunt referred to this approach as an example of 'Better Notting'. Certainly it was a model of diplomatic procrastination. The Secretary of State also made no recommendation that lease-back should be reviewed. But John Ure must have encouraged Nicholas Ridley in his view that it remained a negotiating option. Certainly he made a special effort to re-enlist Lord Carrington's support for the scheme. Meeting the Foreign Secretary earlier in the year, he argued there was really no alternative to lease-back. Whilst he recognized the strength of Island opposition, he calculated that it might only be possible to stall Argentina for one more round of talks.

Meanwhile, back home the campaign to save *Endurance* was gathering momentum. The Pebble Mill repeats had helped. Groups of MPs and Peers were forming ranks behind the cause and *The Times* was publishing a steady flow of supportive correspondence. All this was putting renewed pressure on John Nott.

We sailed from Bahia Blanca on 1 December, and at sea there was time to reflect. It seemed to me that the ball was beginning to roll in the right direction. Now I could devote my entire attention to operational tasks. I was particularly looking forward to the visit to Port Stanley.

We arrived in Berkeley Sound on 4 December and disembarked a survey party. They were to set up their season's camp at Green Patch Farm. On 5 December we sailed round the corner to Port Stanley. 8 December is an important day in the Falkland Islands calendar: it is a national holiday which marks the celebration of the (First World War) Battle of the Falklands.

I called immediately on Rex Hunt. I brought him up to date with what I had done, and learned, and asked him to spell out the present mood of the Islanders. It was not quite that portrayed by John Ure.

After the visit of the Assistant Under-Secretary of State, Rex and Mavis had been home on leave. He later described how Nicholas Ridley took the chair at a meeting of FCO officials which included Head of the Foreign Office, Sir Michael Palliser, Anthony Williams and John Ure. Anthony Williams was still maintaining that Argentine Foreign Affairs Ministers and Officials were reasonably relaxed. Nicholas Ridley emphasized the point about doing more to educate opinion and pointed to the safeguards that the Government would insist on when lease-back returned to the diplomatic agenda. He identified a number of measures to assist the 'education campaign'. These included assurances to the Islanders on access to the UK, and a resettlement scheme for those dissatisfied with any arrangement reached. There were also further land distribution schemes.

Rex said that, as the day wore on, he listened to the discussions with mounting incredulity. The Islanders under discussion were clearly not the same people that he had come to know so well. His colleagues talked as if the Falkland Islanders could be manipulated (or persuaded or educated) into doing something that they had made perfectly plain they had no wish to do. There was an air of unreality in the meeting far removed from the true situation in the islands. His only contribution was to make clear his own belief that the Islanders wanted nothing whatsoever to do with the Argentines. He did not believe, under any terms, that they could ever be given the guarantees they would require. Rex went on to explain how Michael Shersby and Eric Ogden (the two MPs, who had travelled south with him) had been struck by the tone of the islands newspaper, *The Penguin News*. The paper had reported a deepening crisis with Argentina and commented indignantly on an Argentine note which had stated that Islanders' wishes could not be considered as there was a considerable lack of knowledge in the Islands as to the friendly intentions of Argentina which could only improve life on the islands.

'In other words,' said *The Penguin News*, 'Falkland Islanders are not wise enough to determine their own future.'

Talks between the Governments had been scheduled for Geneva in December, but because of the change in the Junta leadership that month the Argentines had requested a post-ponement until January. In the event the talks were further postponed until the end of February and the venue was changed to New York because Mr Luce (who had by then taken Nicholas Ridley's place at the FCO) had other commitments in January.

Chapter 7

SOUTH GEORGIA AND CAPE HORN

Rex and Mavis Hunt embarked on 9 December to sail with us for the first work period. We were to visit South Georgia and Signy, British Antarctic Survey bases. It would be a foreshortened work period. The ice had not yet retreated far enough from the Antarctic Peninsula for us to do any meaningful work in that area. The plan was to return to Stanley for Christmas.

It was a great pleasure to have Rex and Mavis on board once more. The extra stimulus of conversation they brought added a little warmth to the cold windy passage to South Georgia. We had also embarked a BBC film crew and sixteen members of a Joint Services Expedition to South Georgia. We stopped several times to collect plankton samples for the Marine Biological Association of Plymouth. And, as always, we enjoyed the wildlife. We had a Wandering Albatross following the ship, and, as we got closer to South Georgia, there were seals and penguins aplenty. Throughout my time in the Antarctic I never grew tired of watching them from vantage points on the upper deck.

Rex and I were encouraged by the accelerating campaign to save *Endurance* back in London. We decided, at this range, that there was nothing we could, or should do to add to the momentum. But I had already promised myself that *Endurance* would again prove her value through the course of the season.

We were to disembark the Joint Services Expedition and their stores at Royal Bay. The weather prevented anchoring off the beach as planned and disembarkation was begun by helicopter with the ship under way. The katabatic wind funnelled between

101

two mountains made this very difficult; at one stage the winds accelerated to over 50 knots inside the bay. It was not unexpected. High winds in South Georgia are an absolute fact of life. However, the two Wasps managed to offload the Joint Services team of sixteen and their eight tons of equipment safely. The TV crew were similarly landed with three of the ship's company on the Ross and Hindle Glaciers. The purpose was to get additional location shots for a forthcoming BBC film about Ernest Shackleton's epic journey.

Rex and Mavis had planned to drop in on Annie Price and Cindy Buxton who were filming for Anglia's 'Survival' series at St Andrew's Bay. These remarkably courageous ladies had already spent the winter in their tiny beach hut and were now looking forward to pushing on with their project during the warmer season.

Rex himself filmed out of the open-doored helicopter as it flew into the bay. Tim Finding, the pilot, brought them down over Cook Glacier towards the tiny hut on the beach. As the helicopter closed in, Cindy Buxton, also a qualified pilot, hung out a large Union Jack to indicate the wind direction. For some unknown reason Tim approached downwind, although it was probably his intention to turn into the wind at the final stage of descent. But he was descending rapidly, or, as Rex later wrote, 'too rapidly'. The helicopter hit the ground with violent forward momentum at speed and tipped up on its nose.

'For a moment,' said Rex, I thought we were going right over, but the rotor blades saved a complete capsize by hitting the ground. The aircrew and pilots were thrown to the side.'

It was a very nasty incident for those in the helicopter. For those of us on board *Endurance* there were several very long minutes of worry. We did not honestly expect to find anyone in the helicopter who had not suffered horrendous injury. The relief when we heard they were not seriously injured was enormous.

Leading Airman Bob Nadin helped Mavis out of the stricken helicopter before climbing out himself. He also collected the camera from Rex who was grimly hanging onto it. Poor Tim, still in the front seat, was totally mystified as to why the camera should be so important. He was later to learn, as if further proof

102

was needed, that Rex was a passionate amateur photographer. Tim was equally unsure of the cause of the accident. At first he thought that the engine had failed to respond; he kept opening the throttle but the aircraft continued to descend. The answer, of course, was the unpredictable wind which had been blowing hard off shore 20 minutes earlier, but had veered 180 degrees by the time the helicopter approached the landing area. Quite simply they ran out of lift and were blown to the ground. Parts of the fuselage and rotor blades were flung more than 100 yards from the crash. The gearbox assembly whistled past Cindy's ear. Unfortunately for the pictorial record, but reassuringly for Rex and Mavis, Cindy and Annie had put the safety of those on board the helicopter first. They had rushed back to the hut to grab fire extinguishers. But as the Hunts emerged from the wreckage the girls were standing ready to douse them in foam. Happily the aircraft did not catch fire, and the extinguishers were rapidly replaced by large mugs of gin and tonic. Tim used the radio to report the accident to the other helicopter piloted by Tony Ellerbeck. He landed cautiously and surveyed the wreckage.

'I'm afraid it's a write-off,' he said. 'I suppose this means we cannot go south.'

He was well aware that we were not allowed to operate in the ice with only one aircraft. But Tony was as relieved as any of us to find everyone unscathed and in good heart. He returned to *Endurance* with Tim and Bob. Cindy and Annie took the Hunts between the groups of elephant seals and penguins across the beach. Mavis had already said she had no intention of returning to the ship by helicopter. Once the Hunts were back on board we returned to St Andrew's Bay to recover the salvageable parts of the aircraft. The fog became so dense by the late afternoon that we had to give up.

On 15 December the ship moved round to Grytviken for the Governor's visit to the British Antarctic Survey Base. We were also to carry out photographic work for the Survey in the vicinity of Bird Island. Although some helicopter runs were completed successfully we were again hampered by strong winds and poor visibility. As the forecast suggested we were to exchange poor weather for worse, the ship returned to Leith to allow the

Governor to visit the old whaling station. In particular he was keen to examine the scrap metal that the Argentines had contracted to remove.

We returned to St Andrew's on the 19th in an attempt to salvage more of the helicopter and to ditch the carcass, but bad weather again meant that this had to be abandoned.

Amidst all this there was considerable signal traffic from *Endurance* to Northwood and London.

At the time of the accident Mavis had been predictably resilient. She had suffered some symptoms of shock but, like her husband, had been determined to carry on the 'parish tour'.

We always intercepted the weather reports from Argentine Antarctic ships. This was the first time I began to have doubts about the integrity of Cesar Trombetta, the Commodore of the Argentine Antarctic Squadron. We had kept our part of the bargain, reporting positions and so on, but we were not getting the expected feedback. The weather reports had included details of his position, course and speed, so we knew pretty much where he was. In all probability it was when he heard the extent of signal traffic from *Endurance* that the weather reports ceased. This meant we lost touch with his movements for about a week. He also knew we had been delayed because of the loss of our helicopter.

According to the programme the Commodore was due to be heading for Southern Thule or the Antarctic. In fact he was on his way to South Georgia with Mr Davidoff, the scrap metal contractor, on board. Trombetta did not intend to land Davidoff while we were there, nor did he intend to let us know where he was.

Rex and I had assessed the position to be pretty much as it was. This was confirmed when we returned to the Falklands on 23 December when a member of the British Antarctic Survey reported the arrival of the ARA *Irizar* at South Georgia. It was also clear that people were landing, without permission, at Leith. The purpose it seems, was to allow Davidoff to compile an inventory of the scrap in order to plan a transport operation.

We intercepted a signal from Buenos Aires congratulating Trombetta on his 'successful operation'. It was all very odd. The

104

contract had been agreed with Salvessons, so why should Davidoff not go through the standard 'immigration procedures'? In fact he had not informed anyone, and both his landing and the way that Trombetta had facilitated it became a completely covert operation. It all looked unnecessarily furtive. According to Trombetta's programme he should have been in the Weddell Sea at the time. This was hardly the agreed spirit of co-operation. I concluded that the Argentine Navy had entered into a most convenient arrangement with Davidoff. It was nothing less than a test of British resolve over the sovereignty of South Georgia. It had been my stated opinion for some months that the Argentines would try to do something of this kind. I signalled my conclusions to C in C Fleet and the Ministry of Defence. Rex Hunt backed my judgement. The response of the Buenos Aires Embassy was equally predictable: they played it down in the interests of maintaining good relations with the Argentines.

The affection we all had for South Georgia made this intrusion particularly unwelcome. For those who have visited this remote British outpost it is not difficult to understand. Here is an island of spectacular scenery with the highest peak, Mount Paget, soaring to over 9,000 feet. The extraordinary variety of wildlife and ever-changing climatic moods also contribute to its unique character. And there are sturdy threads of history here too, particularly with the great Antarctic pioneers, and most of all Sir Ernest Shackleton. Indeed, as always on our visits, we had duly paid our respects at his Grytviken graveside. We had also had a look at the whaling stations of Husvik and Stromness. This had been partly political: Rex had not only wanted to check their condition but had wanted to find out if they were inhabited. The film team had wanted to film the bay area from which Sir Ernest Shackleton had completed his epic crossing of the island. In his book Rex discusses the Argentine 'visit' to Leith:

First there was a signal from Peter Whitty the Base Commander saying that the Argentines had made a clandestine night landing on December 20. The *Irizar* had been seen there by the crew of a visiting French yacht.

Peter had gone to Leith to investigate and found that the birds had flown but ample evidence that they had been ashore. Chalked on the Emergency Depot was a dated notice claiming possession of South Georgia in the name of Argentina.

The other pieces of the jigsaw came from our Embassy in Buenos Aires and from Salvessons in Edinburgh who Davidoff had also notified on the day of his departure from the mainland. In landing at Leith without reporting to Peter Whitty at Grytviken, Davidoff had not only broken the terms of his contract with Salvessons but also the law of the Dependencies with which he had pledged to comply.

More significantly Captain Trombetta had violated all the norms of international law by taking his vessel, a Naval ship, into British Territorial Waters without prior diplomatic clearance, ignoring the recognized port of entry, and sending a landing party ashore without permission. In my view he would not have done this without the approval of Admiral Anaya, the Commander-in-Chief of the Argentine Navy. My immediate reaction was that here was the beginning of another Southern Thule.

Anaya was clearly testing the water. If we allowed him to get away with it the Falkland Islanders would certainly be in a more vulnerable position. I recommended to the FCO that we should institute proceedings against Davidoff and make a suitably strong protest to the Argentine Government.

We had also intercepted a signal from the Naval Headquarters in Buenos Aires to the *Irizar*. It said effectively: 'Operation well completed.' If this had been a purely private deal with Davidoff the Navy would have been unlikely to be involved. It would certainly not have been an operation. But since it was, and because of the other innuendoes, there was only one conclusion to draw. The FCO sent instructions to Ambassador Williams to deliver the protest in the strongest terms, but instructed Rex not to institute proceedings against Davidoff under Falkland Islands Dependencies Law, because, as the telegram put it: 'This would risk provoking a most serious incident which could escalate and have an unforeseeable outcome'.

It seemed to me that the FCO hardly needed a crystal ball to see exactly what the future could be. This weak-kneed response was in fact giving Anaya exactly the encouragement he had hoped for. If there was a moment when invasion became inevitable, this was it.

The last day of 1981 was overcast with strong chill winds, violent hail squalls and the menace of worse to come. I was not the only one to feel this was ominous. 'It was an appropriate harbinger,' Rex wrote in his book *My Falkland Days*.

Our Christmas break in Stanley was brief. This was because we now had to go to Montevideo to collect a replacement helicopter. This had been boxed up and put into a Hercules and was due to arrive in Montevideo at the end of December. At 06.00 on Boxing Day we headed north. The timing was sufficiently accurate for us to arrive in Montevideo at the same time as the Hercules. In order to save as much time as possible the aircraft was unpacked and assembled at breakneck speed. Following a successful test flight on New Year's Eve the helicopter was embarked and we sailed for the Antarctic. This was a disappointment for some of us. If the test flight had been unsatisfactory we would have been able to enjoy the New Year in Montevideo. The irony was that soon after we left the ship's main engine suffered a major injector failure. We had to anchor just outside the harbour to carry out the repair. The Hercules had encountered similar problems. She suffered an engine failure on take-off and had to return to Montevideo. But whereas we were under way again in a few hours the Hercules had to wait for a new engine to be flown out from the UK in another Hercules. The RAF therefore had a further two weeks in Montevideo. We could have forgiven them their luck if only they had remembered to take our home-going mail out of the stricken aeroplane and put it on a commercial flight.

The storm was gathering, both literally and metaphorically, as we set off south. In the UK some 300 MPs had lent their support to the survival of *Endurance*, at least for another season. They were supported by an influential group of peers, newspaper articles and editorials, and media pressure from television and radio. Even John Nott was going to have to take notice. And certain people within the MOD must by now have realized that it was a mistake to axe the ship. Only those with the sensitivity of a bulldozer could have failed to recognize that the argument had been won and lost. If my involuntary protagonist Michael Power had climbed to the top of Ben Nevis and announced himself as the reincarnation of a poached egg I may have felt a measure of sympathy for him. As it was I had to believe that here was a perfectly rational man who had cemented himself into an utterly irrational position.

At one point, when we were in the Falklands, I received a message from the MOD accusing me of planting an article in *Lloyd's List*. I fired back quite a fierce signal suggesting that the accusation held as much substance as a colander. I had, however, little doubt about the source of this utterly scurrilous speculation.

Rex Hunt had written of the worsening situation, including unauthorized overflights by Argentine Airforce Hercules and the insensitivity of the Argentines in antagonizing the Islanders by reducing the flights out of the Islands from two to one per week. The only flights out of the Falklands were via Argentina. They could tighten the noose or slacken it according to the perceived political exigencies of the moment.

By this early stage of 1982 most of the effort, politically and ministerially, was in preparation for the 'talks about talks about sovereignty'. Subsequently Rex had wished 'God Speed' to Councillors Tim Blake and John Cheek bound for New York for the talks. The day before they left they had called at Government House and had met Lord and Lady Buxton who had flown in that day to sail south on board *Endurance*. Indeed Lord Buxton had also enjoyed a private conversation with Dr Costa Mendes, the Argentine Foreign Minister, before leaving Buenos Aires. Lord Buxton had formed the impressions that, although the Junta were putting Mendes under increasing pressure to produce a solution to the sovereignty issue, Mendes thought an invasion of the Falklands was unlikely, but that the Military might plan unopposed landings, probably in South Georgia. Dr Costa Mendes had also agreed that incidents such as 'Operation Condor' could not necessarily be prevented. He had told Aubrey Buxton that the sovereignty of the Islands was crucial to Argentina. This demonstrates not Lord Buxton's credulity, but the snakish style of Dr Costa Mendes.

Ambassador Williams was equally taken in. Indeed it was only two days before the actual landing on the islands that he acknowledged an invasion was under way. He later recognized his duplicity in an infamous signal: 'Dr Mendes,' he said, 'has been less than honest with me.'

Meanwhile a letter to *The Times* had a major impact:

Your columns have already carried correspondence regarding the retention in service of HMS *Endurance*, the Royal Navy's only vessel capable of carrying the White Ensign into the South Atlantic and ice-filled Antarctic seas thus maintaining both symbolically and practically Britain's traditional position in this potentially very important land and sea area.

Since the intention to pay off HMS *Endurance* at the end of the present southern season became known considerable public and parliamentary concern has been expressed.

We, the undersigned, who all have personal knowledge, or knowledge of the present and developing situation in the area, share these anxieties. While we appreciate the problems facing the Royal Navy in meeting essential Defence commitments in a climate of economy, the decision to axe HMS *Endurance* is tantamount to the withdrawal of the Royal Navy from hazardous waters that no other Naval vessel can undertake.

The saving will be greatly outweighed by the consequences to Britain's future interests in what is expected to become a vital resource area. With 21 nations from all corners of the world now moving fast to establish or enlarge an Antarctic presence, in many cases at expense considerably greater than this country seems willing to envisage, there is no time for Britain to pull back or to move along the path of retreat. The withdrawal of HMS *Endurance* will be seen as a step in this direction, thus Britain's influence will be diminished at a time when it will be greatly needed in a determination of conservation and the regulation of exploitation.

signed,

Lord Shackleton	Eric Ogden
Peter Scott	Jim Parker
Vivian Fuchs	Michael Shersby
Admiral Irving	Tom Woodfield
Lord Morris	

The sustained campaign can only have further irritated a now marginalized Secretary of State and certain Civil Servants and uniformed staff within the MOD.

During our time in Montevideo we had embarked a team from the Scott Institute led by Dr Vernon Squire. One of the team members was Monica Kristianson who had travelled south with us the previous season. The news that Monica was to join us once more had an uplifting effect on shipboard morale, particularly as off Montevideo she had taken the opportunity to show off her bikini in the sunshine. The team were to continue their work on the movement of tabular icebergs. The first large tabular iceberg appeared right on cue and it was possible to devote an entire day to the experiments conducted by the three scientists and their party of assistants from the ship's company. This iceberg was roughly diamond-shaped with sides some three-quarters of a mile long and with 50-foot sheer sides to sea level. The work went smoothly this time in reasonable weather. This was considered to be a little unfair by a certain senior rating who had determined, if the weather closed in, that it was his turn to huddle up closest to Monica. Such was the spirit of heroism in *Endurance* I believe every member of the ship's company would have volunteered.

We were a little surprised to see the Argentine ship *Bahia Paraiso* at Hope Bay. I invited the Captain on board but the offer was 'respectfully declined because of the urgent need to deal with matter of some importance'. Subsequently the same Captain (Cesar Trombetta) proved himself to be a less resourceful liar when he talked on the radio about the movements of the *Irizar*. He said the ship was making passage through the ice to Belgrano Base in the Antarctic Peninsula. I knew full well she was heading for Southern Thule.

The following day we spent in the vicinity of King George Island where a small team of us visited the Polish Base in the morning and the Russian and Chilean bases in the afternoon. The poor Poles were in a terrible state because of the lack of support from home, but they were battling with a little help from everyone except the Soviets. The Chileans were housed in a modern well-disciplined Airforce Transit Base. This was a centre for C130 (Hercules) operations throughout the Antarctic Peninsula. The next-door Soviet base was predictably dirty and the people were scruffy and apathetic; indeed only the KGB man who had arrived two days before had a spark of vivacity.

That night we anchored off the Russian Base and held a buffet supper for personnel from each of the bases. The several nationalities we already had on board helped to make this a truly international evening. After dinner we drank toasts to each of the countries represented. Because of a slight 'memory loss' I concluded by proposing a second toast to the Poles. It had been instructive to note the perfunctory way in which the Russians had acknowledged their Eastern Bloc neighbours the first time. This, at least, gave them a chance to make amends.

Before we went ashore we put food for the Poles into one boat and all our visitors into another. The boats beached simultaneously about a quarter of a mile inshore from our anchorage. When they reached the beach the coxswain of the boat carrying the stores leapt ashore and invited all the passengers in the other boat to help carry the food. I had the pleasurable vision of a KGB Officer carrying provisions to a dump at the head of the beach. Indeed I wanted to cherish the moment and took a flash photograph of him doing this and later sent it to Lech Walesa.

The better weather was a great boon to the second work period. The ice had also receded more than we had expected, and indeed more than most of the experienced Antarctic hands had experienced. The British Antarctic Survey geologists were pleased with what they had managed to accomplish, and the Scott Polar team had completed two successful iceberg experiments. Meanwhile, we had made better than anticipated headway with our hydrographic work and almost all the Northern Peninsula bases had been visited. In this context our Uruguayan Officer, Mario Fontanot, had been an invaluable interpreter. I made a special request for him to remain on board for the final work period. He told me that the South American Spanish spoken by the KGB Officer was absolutely perfect. It was only about 15 minutes into their dinner conversation that he had faltered on a couple of words. But for this he could easily have passed for an Argentine or Uruguayan. I had also noted how good his English had been. In the early part of the evening he told me he had never visited England, although half a bottle of scotch later he was able to describe Waterloo Station in some detail.

Towards the end of the work period my Second-in-Command, Mike Green, developed a grumbling appendix, but happily the symptoms never became too acute. Nevertheless for a few days he was in bed and in some discomfort. He struggled on for some time. Finally, at the doctor's insistence, we had to make arrangements to fly him home via Argentina.

We returned to Stanley on 17 January where my main task was to perform the annual inspection of the Royal Marines.

I enjoyed my leisurely call on Rex and Mavis, and had an equally relaxing schedule catching up with other old friends and acquaintances. The Falkland Islands is not a place where you are immediately seduced by the landscape or climate. But the warmth of the people more than makes up for that. We talk about a sense of community and being a good neighbour too easily in the UK. We have devalued the meaning. In the Falkland Islands, despite the isolation of many of the farms, there is a real sense of community and neighbourliness. In some ways it is like setting the clock back fifty years. For everything you lose in technological convenience you make up for with camaraderie. We were also joined by Colonel Love, the Military Attaché from our Buenos Aires Embassy. He and his wife had come to stay for a few days in the Falklands. Although we were very pleased to see him, I reported, 'I was disappointed at his lack of knowledge and, since he mentioned it, the special lack of knowledge at the Embassy of Argentine aspirations in the South Atlantic.' We lent him some videotapes to take back in an attempt to improve their understanding.

The next period of the ship's programme was in the Cape Horn area. This is where we were to perform our duties as a safety ship for the Round the World Yacht Race. I hoped I would not have to face an emergency if the South African yacht got into difficulties in our sector. A rescue would have exposed the ship to the possibility of holding a conversation with those rescued. But this was also an opportunity to visit the Beagle Channel area and later to make a low-key visit to Chile.

On 21 January we were pounding into heavy seas at Estrecho de le Maire which is an infamous stretch of water between the islands of Los Estados and the Cape of San Diego. The larger boats that were leading the race had already passed, and two of the smaller entrants passed during the day sliding down the steep slopes of a following sea. Late the same night *Endurance* succeeded in rounding Cape Horn, initially on a rescue mission to assist the British yacht *Bubblegum*. But the Chileans had the matter in hand so we entered the Beagle Channel and calmer waters. As we neared the disputed islands of Nelson and Picton we were joined first of all by an Argentine destroyer that was only slightly more communicative than a Trappist monk, and then by two small motor launches that kept a close station and followed us all the way up the channel.

We were equally surprised by the cool reception we received at Ushuaia. Our 21 gun salute was answered by the Argentine Naval Barracks, but the wind had increased and the cocktail party we were to give that evening had to be postponed. When conditions improved a little the party went ahead but very few Argentines attended. We thought perhaps this was because we were unable to get alongside and they had to come out by boat. In fact only one of their officers attended and he came as a private guest.

Later in the day the wind dropped to five knots and we were able to creep in alongside. But even this hardly encouraged an Argentine presence on board. They declined to play football against the ship and even refused the use of their ground for a match against a local civilian side. All this was completely against the pattern of cordiality we had experienced on previous visits to Argentine ports, even as recently as our visit to Puerto Belgrano two months earlier. There was a partial belief that this may have had something to do with the fact we were going on to Punta Arenas in Chile, but was this enough to explain such a complete snubbing? I did not think so and reported my misgivings in a signal.

When I went to call on Captain Russo, in the absence of Admiral Zaratiegui, I was informed that I was in the Malvinas War Zone. He was a large round fellow with seemingly cheerful disposition. I laughed and asked who the Argentines were going to fight.

'You,' he said without a flicker of emotion. Then he instantly changed the subject. 'I'm soon to go on my holidays to Mar del Plata,' he said, 'and believe it is in your programme to be there at the same time.'

'How fortunate,' I said, 'then we'll meet again. But when we are there you will be most welcome to come to our cocktail party with or without uniform. Or, failing that, please feel free to come on board at any time for a cup of coffee or a drink.'

'Thank you, I will,' he said.

'And when you come will you please tell me what this is all about?'

'I will,' he said.

And that is exactly what he did. I remember him cradling a large brandy glass in his hand and smiling a little as he cleared his throat.

'Captain,' he said, 'good health.'

'And good health to you too, Captain,' I echoed.

'I will tell you,' he said, 'there is to be war against the Malvinas. I do not know when, but I think quite soon. This is very good brandy Captain.'

'Then you must have some more.'

'I will,' he said.

Russo also admitted that he had orders not to fraternize with the British. He had also been told that in terms of the *Endurance* visit 'since the British Captain is acquainted with Admiral Zaratiegui, it would be better if they did not meet'. In fact Admiral Anaya insisted Zaratiegui should attend a meeting in Buenos Aires. All this I reported to London.

From Ushuaia we sailed west up the Beagle Channel. Our Argentine pilot also warned me that 'things were awry'. He confirmed that there had been rumblings over the Malvinas and in his view only the timing of the invasion was uncertain.

On our pilot exchange we picked up a 'plain clothes' Chilean submariner, Lieutenant-Commander Paul Ballaresque. His English was as perfect as his knowledge of the channels of Tierra del Fuego. The area, which brings the famous Darwin sketches to life, are very like the Norwegian fjords with towering mountains, occasional glaciers, and extensive birch forests. He too talked of the probability of a war over the Malvinas.

We were also briefly joined by an old friend, Commander Adolfo Cruz. Adolfo had been our next door neighbour in Tynemouth when he was second in command of a Chilean destroyer refitting at Swan Hunters. This was at a time when relations between the (then) Labour Government and the Chileans were at a low ebb and Prime Minister Wilson had instructed us not to fraternize. I had once said to him, 'We're going to the races today but I can't give you any tips. Remember we are not supposed to talk to each other.' He always played this story back to me. By this time he was Captain of the *Piloto Pardo*, the Chilean polar ship. He appeared in his small Bell helicopter and immediately following our reunion reminded me of 'the silent races'. He told me that the fishermen would visit us and that a bottle or two of 'old booze' or a joint of meat would ensure a most cordial reception. We were anchored at the southern end of the Canal Ballenero when the fishing boats came to meet us. We shouted exchanges of greetings and handed over some liqueurs. Indeed this encounter soon developed into a profitable exchange of goods.

As we looked along the shoreline we could see the cooking fires. They had already given us 120 Magellan crabs. At two o'clock in the morning they returned, already very much the worse for wear, wanting to exchange more booze for another consignment of crabs. The deal was done, and for some days there were crabs on the march around the ship. The sailors thought this was great fun. One or two of them woke to find he was sharing his bunk with a monster crab.

When we were short of food during the early part of the Conflict we found a 'loaf' of crabmeat – just about the only thing left – which was a reminder of that visit and the difficulty we had in cooking them. They had a leg-span of up to three feet which meant the standard Naval cooking pot could not cope. They had therefore to be part dissected at the preparation stage, a task which, though a lifesaver later, was not particularly welcomed at the time.

At Punta Arenas we fired another salute. This began a round of hospitality from the Chilean Navy that was in stark contrast to that we had received from their Argentine counterparts, in spite of the fact that this was a low key visit, and indeed the first Naval visit for many years. Our Royal Marines went off for some training with the Chilean Marine Corps whilst the rest of us enjoyed a number of social and sporting events.

Adolfo had parked his ship alongside us. There was also an historic link here. *Piloto Pardo* had been Captain of the Chilean tug *Yelcho* that had rescued the crew of Shackleton's *Endurance*.

The Chileans also warned us that Argentine intentions were hardly friendly. Whilst perhaps we might have expected them to say this – there was little love lost between the countries – there was an urgency in the tone of the warnings. In the event these warnings were sustained. Indeed the Chilean intelligence machine proved rather more useful to us than our own sources in Argentina. They were, for instance, the first to rumble Anaya's invasion plan.

By the time we sailed on 30 January I no longer had any real doubt that there would be an Argentine invasion of the Malvinas. Equally, however, there was only circumstantial evidence to suggest that it may be imminent.

We retraced our steps through the Straits of Magellan out into the Atlantic and wove our way through the oil rigs towards the Falklands. At Stanley we changed our survey party and made a patrol of the area. We had heard that an Argentine Lear jet had overflown some of the beaches. Indeed we later learned that these were the same beaches near Stanley Airport on which the invasion forces landed.

Chapter 8

TENSION MOUNTS

It was a quick turnaround of survey parties and a brief conference with Rex Hunt before a return to Mar del Plata for our fortnight's 'half term' break. For me this meant the usual round of calls and, refreshingly, a friendly reception for *Endurance*. Many of the Round the World yachts were berthed in the basin ahead of us. Anthony Williams was present, and Rear Admiral Charles Williams and other officials from the RNSA Committee were also there. The contrast in the attitude of the Argentines here was most marked. Here we were, close to their one and only submarine base, receiving some very traditional hospitality.

Following a short break in Buenos Aires, I joined some friends and drove across the border to the Uruguayan resort of Punta del Este. This resort had for a long time been popular with wealthier Argentines and Anglo-Argentines.

Before we left Mar del Plata we embarked another film team. This was headed by Mr Tippey, but in the charge of Commander Francis Ponsonby who was responsible to the Director of Public Relations Navy. Their task was to produce a Naval documentary on the ship's activities in Antarctica. In the light of the debate over *Endurance*'s future the scheduling of this programme was, to say the least, extraordinary.

We called at the Falklands on the way to the Antarctic where we were delighted to embark Lord and Lady Buxton. They were to be our guests throughout a third work period which was destined to end at South Georgia. Their daughter, Cindy, was still filming on the beach. I knew they were looking forward to seeing her at work. It was a special bonus to have Lord Buxton on board. I knew that during his three weeks in *Endurance* we would all learn a great deal about bird life; it would be an understatement to say he was an authority on the subject. I knew too that for Aubrey and Maria Buxton the opportunity to see the Antarctic at first hand would be a wonderful experience. I was determined to make sure they would enjoy it as much as possible. It was the least I could do.

Maria Buxton was also going to leave a lasting impression on us all. She was a lovely lady with a kindly word for, and a genuine interest in, everyone. She wrote to me later saying that her weeks on board *Endurance* had been one of the highlights of her life. A small book, a personal account of her trip, was later published for limited circulation. It was based on the letters she wrote at the time to her large family. It provides a uniquely gentle and humorous account of the Antarctic seen through the eyes of someone who truly knew how to observe. The copy I received contained the personalized inscription:

> With so many thanks, not only for your very charming 'comment' but for giving us both the holiday of a lifetime.
>
> With love,
>
> Maria.

In the light of what happened this 'diary' assumes a wider significance. A matter of days after the Buxtons left us to face a deeply worrying return trip through Argentina, en route to Rio, the Argentines invaded the Falkland Islands.

Six months after writing her account Maria Buxton died from stomach cancer. This shocked us all deeply. She had been on fine form during the trip, but her health deteriorated rapidly soon afterwards. We were all immensely saddened, but took some comfort from perhaps helping to make her 'Antarctic Adventure' memorable.

Maria's diary includes the following warming insights of her first few days aboard.

The welcome we had was unbelievable and we had a very nice cabin with two bunks, one above the other, a wardrobe and some drawers. What a lot of room sea boots take up. We also have a day cabin with a desk and chairs, a somewhat hard sofa, and a bath.

The motion of the ship is moderate and the ship's officers are charming. They look very smart in white shirts and black trousers and scarlet cummerbunds in the evening.

I am trying to take in as much as I can about the very involved goings on between Argentina and Britain, but Papa really has the picture much more clearly. There is more to this journey, and every other one that *Endurance* has made, than I ever imagined. There are also some rather interesting, but alarming, bits of information regarding the other country's activities. But it is all very confidential . . . .

We will be following the Captain's rounds, which always happens on a Saturday at sea. Papa and I were not looking forward to this but it turned out to be hilarious.

Endurance has no stabilizers so we are rolling in the swell. Boy are we rolling. Everyone grabs anything they can and holds on tight. Chairs shoot across the cabin and everything is stowed away.

The Captain emerged from his cabin. Whistles blew. We were all awaiting the start of the tour when the ship gave a tremendous roll. Papa lost his balance and put his hand out to save himself, managed to knock the guard off the fire extinguisher and his hand landed on the button. The foam flew out in a terrific gush like an oil strike and went straight onto my feet. I jumped back into the cabin and was, to my shame, convulsed with laughter. For one frozen second no one moved. The foam gushed out with increasing strength. I have never laughed so much. Poor Papa was marvellous and everyone else remained pokerfaced as a marine rushed forward with a small mop to deal with gallons of foam which was by now happily sloshing up and down the back corridor . . . .

When entering any particular room during the rounds you either flew rather uncontrollably if the roll was in the right direction, or were held bent at an angle against the roll before being jet propelled to the side as the roll started coming the other way. All in all this was an interesting experience which I doubt I shall ever repeat. At the end whistles blew, congratulations were given, and beer was awarded to the especially hardworking areas. But just then the ship gave an unexpectedly vicious roll and everyone flew forward some through open cabin doors, some through stairways, and the rest were forced to cling to whatever they could find.

Despite the shambles in the galley that had been caused by the rolling of the sea lunch was produced which we ate on our knees in chairs firmly wedged, mine in a doorway . . . .

We tried to have a few people in for drinks that evening but most of the drink was consumed when glasses went hurtling through the air. Papa had a nasty fall when the chair he was sitting in shot across the cabin and he fell half on my lap and half on the floor. He banged his shoulder very hard and I'm afraid his G and T landed in Francis Ponsonby's lap . . .

but never have I had such a wonderfully exciting day. After lunch we were all togged up in the most remarkable gear known as goon suits. These were orange rubber with welded seams. They have no shape except for two arms and two legs; they are rather like a rubberised baby-grow, and as difficult to put on because they go over your parka, fur-lined jacket and sea boots. A draw string pulls it tight round your neck. Over all this you wear a U-shape life jacket as hard as a horse's collar with straps between your legs. You can imagine what I looked like. Add to this a pair of metal ear muffs to deaden the sound and the mind boggles. Even the chopper pilots were convulsed with laughter and the photographer had a field day. Rather annoyingly for me Papa looked perfectly at home, if rather bewildered.

Getting into the chopper was equally hilarious. There are no doors and only two seats – one for the pilot and the one I had. It's about three feet from the ground and you all know how agile I am. Once I was strapped in, poor Papa and Nick were unceremoniously dumped on the floor. The navigator perched nonchalantly on the ledge opposite me, one foot dangling, trying to stifle his laughter. But I have never enjoyed a flight so much. It was breathtaking. There were snow-covered mountains and pack ice in the sea below us. A few minutes later we were put smoothly down on the snowy shore by the BAS station of Rothera on Marguerite Bay. This is the furthest south we'll ever get, a thousand miles from the pole itself and about a thousand miles south of the Falkland Islands.

Maria Buxton's account of the effect of bad weather in *Endurance* is very close to the mark. This was not a vessel built for comfort in high seas. My steward, Deacon, had very forthright views on this. Leading Steward Deacon, a salt of the earth character, looked after me for three years. He was normally a model of equanimity, whatever the weather, but his safety valve was the humour of exaggeration. He claimed that the *Endurance* would roll in a dry dock. His most frequent complaint was that the bridge never warned the sailors of approaching bad weather. This, he believed, was a plot to keep the men on their toes. He wrote this account of having to cope with dire weather and me at the same time:

> Working for the Captain, as I did, was the hardest job of all. He's a man who likes his home comforts. The problem is that home comforts liked to slide and crash about in rough seas and get broken. I'd lie awake in the mess till guilty conscience roused me.
>
> If the weather was really naughty the first thing I'd do was dodge the port decanter as it went whistling by my head. The Captain never noticed. He'd be too busy trying to save his effects. He always seemed to wear the same pyjamas in foul weather – the ones with the battle of Trafalgar murals printed on them. I got to know those murals well. I'd see them from practically every angle. That was because the Captain, likely as not, was turned upside down and sliding around with all the furniture and ornaments.
>
> My job was to lash things down with string or masking tape. He'd be sitting on a pile of magazines. His left hand would be holding a picture, his right arms and leg would be wrapped round a well-anchored chair, and his left leg pushed against the most valuable item of furniture – the booze cabinet. In that unlikely, and dare I say undignified posture, he would fearlessly direct operations. Once things were sorted out he went back to bed. I then repeated the rescue operation in the pantry and guest cabin. If I was lucky, I'd then be allowed to catch a couple of hours kip on the mess floor.

Deacon was equally perceptive when it came to describing the general dining arrangements in foul weather:

To be fair there wasn't a lot of work to do during the day. How can you work when you can't stand upright? The poor chefs would have a bad time of it. The ship's company were a demanding lot. They'd want feeding even in very unpleasant weather.

Breakfast was usually boiled eggs and maybe a grilled sausage if we were lucky. Lunch and dinner consisted of the age-old nautical delicacy – 'pot mess'. This was stew made up of anything edible scraped from tins. Handy with the can opener our chefs were.

But our lads loved it. Mind you most of them thought of pot mess as a gourmet meal. The crew would eat it from bowls, or even mugs. 'Pot mess' was not only spectacular, but hot. Plates were too dangerous. A serious spillage could easily ruin your next run ashore.

They ate it sitting on the deck, or in the dining hall where the chairs and tables were stowed or lashed down. If the ship had a really good roll those sitting down would slide right across the deck. The skill was to take your 'pot mess' with you rather than give it to somebody else to wear.

Those who didn't know the ways of the sea didn't usually do too well in *Endurance* in rough weather. Any ship in a Force Ten is bad. In *Endurance* it's hell. But I learnt a new trick. I could fall forwards without bending my knees, touch the floor, and then return to the vertical all in one movement. It's impossible on land, but easy on *Endurance*.

Not everything was light-hearted during that work period. Even in calmer waters I was finding life confusing. I had now been accused in absentia of stirring up further trouble that had been picked up by television. Until I received the videotape and checked with the Lords' *Hansard* I was unable to comment beyond telling the truth: I knew absolutely nothing about any further publicity. I later learnt that an attempt had been made to bring together a cross party group of MPs and Peers who shared the view that a Military presence in the Falklands should be maintained. I was delighted but could claim no part of the inspiration for this initiative. With this on my mind I wrote to Admiral Cox in an attempt to counteract wild accusations, and to restate part of my case for the retention of *Endurance* and also to inform him of the illegal landings on South Georgia.

Coincidentally, at almost exactly the same time, and for the first time in the history of the dispute, Argentina set a time limit for the resolving of the sovereignty question. On January 27 the Argentine Ministry of Foreign Affairs delivered a *Bout de Papier* to the British Ambassador in Buenos Aires. This set out in detail Argentina's claim. There was nothing surprising in this, apart from the conclusion that a Permanent Negotiating Commission should be established. This would, according to the Argentines, meet in the first weeks of each month alternating between London and Buenos Aires. Its remit would be to solve the dispute peacefully, definitely and rapidly. The Commission was to have a twelve-month duration and it would be open to denunciation by either side at any time and without prior warning to the other side.

This was the start of the process of escalation at the beginning of 1982 that led to the Argentine invasion. There was also corroborative evidence from other sources of a significant hardening of the Argentine position. General Galtieri, who had replaced Viola on 22 December, jested that 'the Junta had come to full agreement that a negotiating position had been agreed for a test period.' It remained to be seen, however, if negotiations got anywhere at all. At the same time Argentine Press comment at the beginning of the year indicated that relations between the two nations were in steep decline. Within the Joint Intelligence Centre at Whitehall these comments were seen only as an attempt to create more diplomatic pressure.

Jesus Iglesias Rucco, a columnist for *La Prensa* predicted, ahead of the Foreign Ministry's *Bout de Papier*, that the Argentine Government would specify strict conditions and time limits for the continuation of negotiations. This final olive branch, he suggested, would be withdrawn if the British failed to respond adequately. Rucco had close connections with the Argentine Navy and the Foreign Ministry. There were similar reports in the *Buenos Aires Herald* and the *Latin American Weekly*.

It should have been abundantly clear that Britain had less than 12 months to put forward an effective response. Ambassador

Williams suspected that the new Argentine timescale for negotiation might be related to the 150th anniversary of British Falkland rule. In this he was proved to be perfectly correct.

In the 1970s these kind of reports had been treated as a litmus test of the perceived threat. Indeed the Argentine Press Campaign in 1976 had been seen as quite an important indication of what may follow. By the early part of 1982 press warnings were quite specific. Unless the British moved promptly and purposefully towards an agreement an Argentine Military adventure was inevitable.

The *Bout de Papier* was analysed by the Foreign Office. 'Although toughly worded,' concluded Franks, 'little of the substance of the paper was regarded as new. The greater part of it was seen to be a reworking of the communiqué in July, 1981. The new element was the proposal for a Permanent Negotiating Commission working to a timetable of one year.'

Both countries quickly re-established their Falkland sovereignty intentions. The British Government reminded the Argentine that 'We wish to find by negotiation an early and peaceful solution to this dispute that can be accepted by all concerned, namely the British and Argentine Governments and the Government of the Falkland Islands.'

The British Ambassador in Buenos Aires delivered this message on 8 February. In a letter of 3 February Anthony Williams reported to the Foreign Office that 'all the indications were that Admiral Anaya, probably with President Galtieri's full agreement, had got into the driving seat and had ruled, in effect, that a test period should be allowed to see if negotiations got anywhere.' The Ambassador repeated that the period allowed may be up to the 150th Anniversary.

On 9 February an editorial in the English language *Buenos Aires Herald* drew attention to the apparent willingness of the new Argentine Government to accept the risks that any serious attempts to 'recover' the Falklands and the Beagle Channel Islands might entail. The Malvinas approach would certainly be far tougher than anything seen so far. The editorial also referred to talk about the pros and cons of simply invading the islands and informing the world that justice had belatedly been done.

The judgement was that an invasion would be unnecessary. However, unless the dispute was resolved in the only reasonable way (by transferring the islands to Argentina) a more messy and damaging solution would be found.

On the eve of the talks of 15 February Lord Carrington observed:

> In principal the idea of setting up working groups to look at particular aspects of the dispute had considerable appeal since it was in the Government's interests to maintain a dialogue in order to avoid the difficult and costly consequences of a breakdown. But it would be necessary to resist the unrealistic timetable of work proposed by Argentina. It would also be difficult to carry the Islanders since they would be most reluctant to agree to any discussion on sovereignty with the Argentines and Argentina would accept nothing less.
>
> The British Delegation would make it clear at the outset of talks that any future decision reached on the negotiation would be strictly ad referendum but the tougher attitude being shown by the new Argentine Government, together with the strong disinclination of the Islanders to envisage any change in the status quo, narrowed the options. I expect there will need to be a further discussion of the Falklands in the Defence Committee in March.

The Prime Minister commented, 'It must be made clear to the Argentines that the wishes of the Islanders are paramount.' This view was hardly consistent with the withdrawal of the Naval presence.

After each side had set out its position at the talks the British Delegation presented a working paper on the framework for a Permanent Negotiating Commission. Subsequent discussion was concerned with the detailed arrangements for the Commission. Meanwhile the Argentine Delegation pressed for a substantive response to its proposals within a month, and for the Commission to meet for the first time on 1 April. The talks concluded with the agreement of an informal working paper setting out the purpose of the Permanent Negotiating Commission and agreeing the issue of a brief general communiqué. The purpose of the Commission as stated in the working paper was:

> To be moving towards a peaceful and comprehensive solution of the dispute. It was to be presided over by Ministers who would direct its work and decide on the agenda. The paper also recognised that the British Delegation might include Islanders.

By agreement the joint communiqué gave no details of the informal working party. Its substance was that 'the meeting took place in a cordial and positive spirit. The two sides reaffirmed their resolve to find a solution to the sovereignty dispute and considered in detail an Argentine proposal for procedures to make better progress'. The respective Governments were to be informed accordingly.

Following the issue of the communiqué, the Argentine Delegation returned to Buenos Aires. The Argentine Ministry of Foreign Affairs immediately issued a unilateral communiqué which, contrary to what had been agreed in New York, disclosed the full scope of the discussions.

On 3 March Mr Luce sent a personal message to Enrico Ros referring to the agreement that the discussions should remain confidential until Governments had been consulted. He said that the communiqué and residual press comment had created more difficulty and an unhelpful climate for continuing the negotiation process. He added, 'I am deeply disturbed by what might be interpreted as threats and that it would be very difficult to make progress. There was a clear understanding that the issue could only be resolved through peaceful negotiation.'

So far as I could see the talks in New York were a flop. I found this frustrating because I had by now lost count of the times I had been told that this really was going to be the beginning of a permanent solution to the Falklands dispute. New York, it was now clear, was little more than another vehicle for procrastination.

The Joint Intelligence Committee was still demonstrating a lack of interest in the problem. I believe that this was a sad reflection on the sort of people who had been appointed to the JIC.

Their vision was simply not wide enough. I had taken the view for some time that key Civil and Military people with a track record of unblinkered thinking should have been drafted into this important area. The Franks Report blamed the JIC, but it was not entirely their fault. There can be little doubt that those responsible for putting out the alert were at least complacent, and at worst incompetent.

In *Endurance* we suspected that Argentina had two operation plans. 'Azul', renamed 'Losario', was under the control of Admiral Lombardo and under the orders of Admiral Anaya. This suggested a full amphibious assault on the Falklands in the Summer of 1982. We now know that detailed planning of 'Azul' commenced in December 1981 which was entirely consistent with the warnings we had despatched to London. The second plan, 'Alpha', was an incursion into South Georgia designed to test British resolve.

The latest communiqué from Buenos Aires had been an even clearer sign of trouble, even after Dr Costa Mendes had doctored it to avoid alerting British Intelligence. Indeed the increased volume of Argentine sabre rattling had been discussed in a Joint Intelligence Committee meeting assessment as early as July, 1981. The Foreign Office minute of their assessment clearly told Ministers that they now had either to negotiate in good faith on lease-back or fortify the Islands against likely invasion. Lord Carrington failed to get the message across. Could it be that a characteristically intransigent Margaret Thatcher had dissuaded John Nott and Lord Carrington from taking any positive action?

But on 3 March Mrs Thatcher annotated a note on the break-down of the New York talks, saying 'we must make contingency plans'. Five days later she asked John Nott about deployment. It would appear that nothing was done. But as nobody was pressing her, she can perhaps be forgiven for not pressing in return. In the event Lord Callaghan's later comment is hard to dispute. He said, 'This was a war that never needed to happen if proper precautions had been made.'

Following provocation from Rex Hunt and myself, the Buenos Aires Military Attaché, Colonel Love, had written a letter to London which was perhaps one of the clearest warnings yet to the Joint Intelligence Committee. In essence he told them that 'something might happen'. Again this was either ignored or dismissed.

By mid-March Joint Intelligence Committee assessment and Operation 'Azul' collapsed together. Anaya and Lombardo were at loggerheads following accusations of double dealing. Anaya had started the clock running on the second operational plan, 'Alpha'. Marines would be landed on South Georgia under the cover of Davidoff's scrap metal operation. It was, in effect, a backdoor invasion of the Falklands. When Lombardo was told to proceed with 'Azul' in January (this was the July invasion plan) he had asked Anaya to promise to cancel 'Alpha'. His thinking was that any incursion on South Georgia would force Britain to reinforce the Falklands and to deploy a submarine to forestall an invasion. The invasion, he reasoned, had to be blood-less in order to win international acceptance. It was, he said, 'Impossible to have South Georgia in April and the Falklands in July.'

In the end Anaya's self-confidence was his undoing. He allowed the South Georgia plans to go ahead. Throughout this sabre rattling it is difficult to believe that the MOD did not counter the invasion threat by the deployment of a nuclear submarine.

The film team we had embarked at Mar del Plata was well aware of the region's politics in general and of the escalation of the Falklands dispute. The team leader, John Tippey, also had considerable experience of Naval life and had served in the last war. When hostilities began it all seemed terribly familiar to him. His brief was to film the Navy in Antarctica. Indeed he did the job so well that the final edit, 40 minutes of 35 millimetre cellu-loid, won a number of prizes and considerable critical acclaim. Unusually, too, for a film that was essentially intended for Naval training, it broke through to limited general release and enjoyed something of a cult status on the cinema circuit. Certainly some of the scenes of *Endurance* in the ice were outstanding. The stills taken by Bob Mahoney, who is still very much a friend of the ship, have found pride of place in the homes of many Antarctic aficionados. His skill is such that he captures the ever-changing mood not just of the people, but of the extraordinary land and seascapes that surround them. He is one of the great photographic exponents of scale and perspective.

We did as much as possible to illustrate for the Buxtons the multi-rôle nature of *Endurance* as we ran along pre-planned lines and courses surveying the area around the British Atlantic Survey Base at Rothera. This included some tricky navigation in poor weather. It was also an opportunity for Aubrey and Maria to meet the assortment of characters that make up a ship's company. In the case of *Endurance*, in part perhaps because of her very nature, this was markedly diverse.

The humour from the senior ratings' mess was often up to music hall standards. This sustained us particularly in the dark days that followed the invasion of South Georgia. I am sure that if we had gone for an enforced swim in those icy waters one of them would have popped up with some well known one-liners. 'Scum always rises to the surface.' 'Now't like a cold dip before breakfast.' 'Will someone pass me the soap?'

My report of the approach to Rothera sums up the sort of varied experience we were having:

> In view of the excellent ice conditions it was decided to try to reach Rothera by the much shorter route passing inside Adelaide Island. On the morning of 6 March the ship entered Matha Strait and proceeded down towards Hanusse Bay. We encountered some pack ice which gradually became thicker. However, it was a beautiful sunny day and steady progress was maintained.
>
> The film crew enjoyed filming the ship working in the ice. Eventually a good clear lead was found inside Hanusse Bay and a helicopter recce was flown to investigate the narrows. The report was that they were blocked with thick fast ice.
>
> Our course had to be reversed and the pack ice renegotiated. As we took an outside route through an unsurveyed area the cry of 'Breakers Ahead' was heard. We had to go hard a' starboard to avoid an uncharted shoal.

This, as the Buxtons came to appreciate, was all part of the almost daily adventure of the Antarctic.

There followed a concentrated period of ship survey work in the approaches to Rothera. The idea was to provide a new route to the base inside Jenny Island. The ship covered the deep water while the survey boat coped with the more hazardous sections round the island. The RRS *Bransfield* had grounded on one of the shoals in 1980.

My report of 19 March continues:

The weather remained favourable and excellent progress was made. However, by Wednesday 10 March the time available had run out and the detached survey party had to return on board. As the ship started northwards the weather broke and the wind built up to force nine in the west. To avoid the heavy seas we took the inner route via the Pendleton Strait and the Le Maire Channel to the Eurlache Strait. In the Lemaire Channel winds were gusting up to 80 knots in the narrows. However, conditions eased overnight and I was able to visit at the Chilean base, Capitan Arturo Prat, on Greenwich Island.

Later the same day we made another visit to the main Chilean Base – Presidente Frei – on King George Island. Lord and Lady Buxton were able to accompany me on both visits.

The ice was beginning to set fast – our warning that time was getting short in the Antarctic Peninsula. The course was set north-east. Good speed was made with the assistance of the Weddell current and on Monday 15 March the ship was again off South Georgia.

During the morning personnel of the Joint Services Expedition were re-embarked with all their equipment. The men looked wild and dirty, but very fit after three months in the field.

In the afternoon the ship went round to St Andrew's Bay and the Flight were able to complete the salvage and the disposal of the carcass of the Wasp which had crashed on landing during the first work period. In addition Lord and Lady Buxton were able to go ashore and call on their daughter, Cindy, who together with her assistant, Miss Annie Price, have been filming the King Penguin Colony since November.

The ship spent the night at anchor off the Bay, going round to Grytviken the following morning to visit the British Antarctic Survey Base, and to deliver and collect mail and stores.

The third work period has been blighted by continual bad weather. In spite of this all major objectives were achieved. These include establishing a fully surveyed channel into Rothera west of Jenny Island, although (due to defects to the boat transponder) not as much of the boat work was achieved as had been hoped. The stores for the Joint Services Expedition to Brabant Island were not landed in the preferred location, but the Expedition Leader, Commander Chris Furze, was more than satisfied with their eventual positions. Although the poor weather caused some frustrations the film crew were pleased with the material they gathered. Most of the British and Foreign bases in the Antarctic have now been visited with the exception of those in the South Orkneys. Lord and Lady Buxton very much appreciated their visit and the Navy can now be assured of even greater support in the House of Lords.

Having returned to the Falkland Islands the Flight were disembarked as were the surveyors and the Royal Marine Detachment prior to the ship's planned passage up to Montevideo where the replacement Royal Marine Detachment is to be embarked.

This report concluded by referring again to my anxiety about the political situation and, predictably, to the campaign to save the ship, the impasses at Whitehall and the folly of Britain turning her back on the massive untapped potential of Antarctica. I added, 'It can only be hoped that it is not too late to secure our rightful advantage in an area which has been largely pioneered by British adventurers, British scientists, and the Royal Navy.'

On 25 March the Buxtons were reunited with their daughter, Cindy. Maria Buxton wrote:

The great day has dawned, sadly dull and damp. We were due to fly out at nine – that is from the ship to the beach – but the helo developed oil pressure troubles, so Daddy and I finally got off at 10.30. At 9.30 I spoke to Cindy on the radio. It was marvellous to hear her voice. We finally got off and it's only a short flight from Royal Bay to St Andrew's. On the way I took photographs of herds of reindeer on the mountains. And there they were; two tiny figures armed with cameras, a tiny hut and a huge Union

Jack doing its best to fly in the windless conditions. I had my camera out too, and photographed them as well. Hope the pictures come out.

We had a rapturous welcome; both girls looked wonderful. Cindy much better than usual and Annie her usual blooming self. Goodness, it was good to see them. We took our awful orange suits off to return them to the helo, which was going back to *Endurance* to fetch the film crew who tactfully left us alone and filmed us at a distance from the penguin colony and seals.

The hut – that's the hut the two girls are living in – is tiny, but superbly neat and tidy. Two bunk beds run the width of the end wall. Two windows opposite each other, a tiny table or shelf along the dividing wall, a chair, a stool and a door; that's their living quarters, bookshelves right up above the bunk. Heaven knows where their clothes are. Next comes the tiny kitchen, the shelves for perishable stores in use, through this to the lobby where coats are hung, cameras etc. and that's it. 12 feet by 7 foot 6 inches at the most. Outside the front door is a platform and on it the loo; built by *Endurance*'s carpenters a wooden throne with wooden cistern, a ball and chain hanging from it.

On the seaward side of the hut is a huge red tarpaulin where all the food – tins, of course, is kept; The tarpaulin weighted down by huge stones. Then round the end, opposite to the front door, a green tarpaulin where they keep heaven knows what. I think suitcases, skirts and shirts, and fuel, probably paraffin for the tilley and for the primus stove.

Penguins everywhere and very tame once the chopper had gone. They are madly inquisitive and poke their noses into everything, but the hut isn't among the main colony. Far too smelly. But there must be 20–30 thousand on the beach in the bay. King penguins are lovely birds, about 3 feet tall, with lovely yellow markings behind their ears, if they have any, and down their chest a little way with an orange red slash on the lower beak.

Whilst the Buxtons enthused about and recorded the flora, fauna, and wild life of South Georgia we got on with the embarking and sorting out of the Joint Services expedition. We lifted all their stores out from Royal Bay. The next day we went round to Grytviken, where Lord Buxton and his daughter discussed the progress of the film being made for Anglia TV's 'Survival' programme.

The Buxtons also visited the partly ruined small Norwegian chapel at Grytviken. The small organ is still there, and the hymn books are open at the appropriate page for a carol service that took place in 1960. There is also a Russian Orthodox prayer book and a Roman missal. This small church clearly served the various denominations of the whaling community. Perhaps the strangest thing of all is that the Christmas tree was still standing although now rather decorated with cobwebs. It is as if the Christmas worshippers walked from the church and vanished into the ether.

There were hugs and laughter as the Buxtons said their goodbyes. It was, after all, just five weeks to 20 April when they were scheduled to meet again. In the event it was a schedule that would be broken. The war had started by then.

On 19 March we arrived off Port Stanley on the kind of day that is all too rare in the Falklands. The sky was blue except for a few fluffy white clouds and the sea was a calm deep blue. At 11.30 that morning we picked up reports of an Argentine Lear jet 'in trouble' over Stanley. This was, of course, a reconnaissance flight. We also had news of overflights of South Georgia by a C130 Hercules aircraft. This too was unexceptional. Cindy had told us she had seen them many times.

In my report I mentioned the increasing crescendo of bellicose remarks being found in the Argentine press and my deepening suspicions about the combination of Constantine Davidoff, the scrap man, and the Argentine Navy.

On the evening of the same day a message was received from the BAS in South Georgia reporting the presence of ARA *Buen Suceso* at Leith. The Argentine flag had been hoisted, shots were heard and military men had been seen ashore. The message was passed to the Governor and I spoke to the Base Commander at Grytviken late that night for confirmation. At 06.30 the following morning (20 March) the Governor came on board to discuss the situation with me, to speak personally to the Base Commander and to issue instructions. When this was completed signals were sent to the FCO and Naval Authorities informing them of the situation. For the time being, at least there was very little more that the Governor or I could do. And the ship was among friends in Stanley; we were not going to allow the Argentines to spoil that.

The ship's company were in particularly good spirits and put on a winning performance in the Stanley Shield, a local FA Cup. This success was followed by a splendid buffet supper given by the Manager of Cable and Wireless, Mr Iain Stewart and his wife Hulda, where our officers joined the Hunts, the Buxtons and a number of local friends. Despite the deepening crisis there was a mood of jovial determination at the party. I believe everyone sensed the conflict to come and in a typically British way responded with resilient cheerfulness. The mood was shattered in the middle of the party when an eminently moist duty officer put a damper on the evening. He had come ashore by boat in very heavy weather with the signal we had anticipated:

C-in-C Fleet is sending instructions to Capt. HMS *Endurance* to leave for South Georgia at 0930 21st. March.

Our first Council of War, for surely that was what it was, was held right there in Hulda Stewart's kitchen. Plans were made to re-embark the flight immediately. The ship's Royal Marine detachment was to be beefed up to platoon strength with nine marines from the Falkland garrison. The surveyors, we decided, should remain in Stanley and continue their work using the survey launch.

Lord Buxton was then brought out of the party because he and Maria had been expecting to go to Montevideo in *Endurance*. I arranged a boat for them at first light next morning to remove their baggage and an onward flight to Argentina.

Rex Hunt came on board the following morning and spoke to Steve Martin, the Base Commander, on the radio. He asked for the following message to be delivered to the leader of the Argentine shore party in Leith:

1. You have landed illegally at Leith without obtaining proper clearance.

2. You and your party must go back on board the *Buen Suceso* immediately and report to the base commander, Grytviken, for further instructions.
3. You must remove the Argentine flag from Leith.
4. You must not interfere with the BAS depot at Leith.
5. You must not alter or deface any of the notices at Leith.
6. No military are allowed to land in South Georgia.
7. No firearms are to be taken ashore.

Rex then reported the situation to the FCO reinforcing his opinion that the Argentine Navy were using Davidoff as a front to establish an Argentine presence on South Georgia and suggested, that since this was the second violation by Davidoff, the party should be ordered to leave South Georgia even if it did report formally to Grytviken.

On this occasion the FCO demonstrated the speed with which Whitehall could move in a crisis. They agreed Rex's instructions to the Base Commander and instructed the Ambassador in Buenos Aires to tell the Argentine Ministry of Foreign Affairs that the incident was regarded as serious and that if the *Buen Suceso* did not leave South Georgia forthwith the British Government would have to take whatever action it saw necessary. The Argentine Chargé d'Affaires in London was also summoned and given the same message.

The FCO had required the *Endurance*'s change of destination be kept secret from the Falklanders but that was a forlorn hope. Too many of the islanders were aware of, or involved in, the arrangements being made for her originally planned departure for Montevideo. What was more the ham radios were already buzzing with news of the Argentine landing at Leith.

Then came the announcement that the *John Biscoe* was returning to Stanley with the new Royal Marine detachment from Montevideo.

On a cold and bleak Sunday morning, 21 March, Rex Hunt, with Aubrey and Maria Buxton, came aboard to say farewell and Rex spoke to Steve Martin at Grytviken.

Sir Rex Hunt takes up the story:

135

Back in Stanley, shortly after lunch, the new police officer, Ronnie Lamb reported an incident at the LADE, which is actually the Argentine Air Force office. Apparently somebody had entered the office the night before, using a key, draped a Union Jack over the Argentine flag next to the Vice Commodoro's (Wing Commander's) desk, carefully removed the trays from the desk, stacked them neatly in the corner and ascribed on the desk top in toothpaste, 'Tit for tat you buggers'.

When asked why it had taken him (the Argentine Officer) so long to report the incident, he explained that he had been trying to work out from his English/Spanish dictionary what the words meant.

Two nights later somebody sprayed the LADE office window with the letters 'UK OK' in aerosol paint. These two incidents were magnified out of all proportion by the Argentine press: 'Barbarous Piratical Reaction – LADE Offices Attacked' was one of the more sober headlines. Our Embassy in Buenos Aires quoted: 'The Ministry of Foreign Affairs is alleging that this was a parallel insult to Davidoff's party hoisting the Argentine flag at Leith'. More realistically, a second official pointed out to Anthony Williams that the Captain of an Argentine Naval Support vessel should not have expected to request permission to enter what Argentine law did not recognize as a foreign territory and that these problems should have been faced before the salvage contract was authorized. This is one point on which we could agree.

We sailed with John Tippey and his film crew still embarked.

On the following day at 04.00 I was shaken in my bunk with news that the *Bahia Paraiso* had disembarked troops and stores and had sailed. We began to plan an operation order for the retaking of Leith and tested the ship's helicopters and weapons. At 15.30 I received a signal advising me 'to resume programme'. This was confusing to say the least. Did 'resume' mean we were no longer the teeth of the bailiff's dog on a eviction mission, and were instead to proceed to Montevideo? An hour later this was clarified. We were to continue to South Georgia.

It was Rex Hunt who finally sorted out the confusion about whether or not we were to continue our passage to South Georgia. After recording his discussions with the South Georgia

Base Commander, particularly with regard to the difficulties of maintaining up-to-date activity reports with too few men and too few key observation posts separated by seven hours on the hoof, he adds:

> Davidoff has not only failed to comply with the laws of the Falkland Island Dependencies, he has also allowed his men to act in breach of his contract with Salvessens. I strongly recommend that *Endurance* be instructed to proceed to Leith and remove all Davidoff's men, and that Davidoff be told that he has forfeited his right to purchase scrap. I consider that his behaviour over the last three months makes it impossible for the Falkland Islands Government to give their approval for him to carry on with his salvage activities in South Georgia.

This was Rex at his best. I have no doubt that this signal changed the mood in Whitehall and allowed us to continue our passage to South Georgia.

At that stage our role seemed to be unequivocal. We were to land and invite Davidoff and the Argentines to leave. We would try to do this by peaceful persuasion and would also try to avoid provoking an incident that could lead to escalation. We were, however, to be fully prepared to respond to opposition.

By the evening both helicopters were serviceable. One was armed with the sight for the AS12 missiles and the other with GPMGs (General Purpose Machine Guns) as a helicopter gun ship.

On 23 March we encountered gale force winds from the north-west. But the warlike wind from Whitehall was waning. A signal from MOD UK to C-in-C Fleet scuttled the anticipated pleasure of throwing the Argentines off the island. It read:

> In view of continued diplomatic activity at ministerial level aimed at allowing Argentine authorities an opportunity to remove party and equipment by Argentine vessel, HMS *Endurance* should proceed to Grytviken and await further instructions. Pending these instructions, HMS *Endurance* should not, repeat not, enter nor conduct any Naval operations in the vicinity of Leith

harbour. In event that it should be decided that HMS *Endurance* should remove Argentines and their equipment, contingency, repeat contingency, guidance follows by separate signals.

We were disappointed. The taking of Leith had been rehearsed carefully and we were rather looking forward to it. We knew the ground well. Each one of the marines had a job to do and the sailors were fully briefed for their backup roles. We were ready and quietly confident of success. To be told to stop everything the evening before we went to work did little for morale, and I was starting to suffer acute toothache. We waited in some frustration for something rather more purposeful. I signalled to the Governor:

I suggest that Royal Marines could now be used as an observation party and that I take over communications from Grytviken, sending new SITREPS as required. If you agree with these proposals, I will seek agreement from C-in-C (Fleet).

Meanwhile the MOD UK were clarifying the way the eviction should be handled if it was approved:

The guidance below should be used if approval is given to remove Argentines and their equipment. On arrival on the scene the Commanding Officer should inform senior Argentine that he is come to convey them back to Port Stanley for onward passage to Argentina.

After giving party adequate time to get ready, CO should invite them formally to embark on board *Endurance*. It should be made clear to Argentines there is no alternative but to comply with his instructions and that neither personnel nor equipment can remain on the island. Every attempt should be made to conduct operation in a friendly atmosphere and as low key as possible. Minimal physical force is to be used in order to compel Argentines to comply.

In this context the CO should be reminded that the Argentine Government may seek to overdramatize the way in which this incident is handled and of the need to ensure that nothing is done that might be seized on as evidence of over-zealousness. Personal arms may be carried only if deemed necessary by CO and then used only for the purpose of self-defence. Firearms are not, repeat not, to be used to compel Argentines to comply. If armed resistance is encountered, landing party is to withdraw to the ship. Further guidance should be sought from London.

Every attempt should be made to recover boats and equipment to either Port Stanley or Grytviken; if not practicable, equipment should be left in as secure a position as possible. If taken to Grytviken, equipment should be placed in custody of Base Commander. Whilst on board *Endurance* and in passage to Port Stanley, every effort is to be made to treat the party with due courtesy. If the party refuses to co-operate, the CO has authority, as a last resort, to place them in confinement.

On arrival in Port Stanley the party should be met and handed over to the civil power who will make arrangements for their repatriation to Argentina, together with any equipment which might still be on board.

It is possible that *Buen Suceso* may still be in the vicinity. Should she turn up before the party have been embarked, the CO is authorized to hand them over, together with their equipment, and satisfy himself that they have been taken off before returning to Port Stanley. Should the ship be encountered on the high seas, its CO should be informed that the party are being taken to Port Stanley for repatriation to Argentina. This would both help ensure that the party did not double back to Leith and would also avoid the risk of any accident being caused while members of the party were being transferred. Further advise the presence of French yacht at Leith jetty is to be politely, but firmly, told to stand aside.

Rules for use of small arms based on NUJ (a joint services document) to follow. Suggest numerical rules of engagement drawn from (another publication) are not appropriate at this stage. The above instructions to be read in conjunction with instructions for *Endurance*.

So at 06.00 on 24 March, instead of going into action, I went ashore at Grytviken to meet the Base Commander for a full situation update. I was accompanied by the officer commanding our Royal Marine Detachment, Keith Mills, and my Flight Commander, Lieutenant-Commander Tony Ellerbeck. Steve

Martin returned with us for lunch accompanied by Bob Headland, an articulate and intelligent boffin who was to become librarian at the Scott Polar Institute at Cambridge.

An example of the mood at home came from C-in-C Fleet:

Minister of State at FCO, Luce, was questioned in Commons last night on the South Georgia incident and the subject was given wide coverage in today's papers:

The *Daily Telegraph* front page reported that *Endurance* was closing South Georgia at full speed to deal with Argies. Although the FCO was silent about *Endurance*'s movements, it was reported that the ship was poised to eject a handful of Argentine scrap merchants. The Argentine ship had left about ten Argies behind. It was also reported that the *Endurance* is on her final patrol before being withdrawn as economy measures to save £2 million.

This was received with glee by Argentine press. The *Endurance's* movements were kept secret to avoid alerting the Argentine Navy. FCO ministers in Commons last night said that arrangements were made for the Argentines early departure.

Other reports in the nationals were headed, 'NAVY GUN BOAT SAILS TO REPEL INVADERS,' 'CUT SHIP SAILS TO OUST INTRUDERS,' and 'MINISTER'S PLEDGE ON THE FALKLANDS.' *The Times Parliamentary Report* was headlined: 'CALLAGHAN WARNING ON SOUTH GEORGIA'. He said it would be gross dereliction of duty for the government to persist in withdrawing *Endurance*. Luce of the FCO said the incident was unhelpful.

Denis Healey asked if action taken by the Argentines was supported. Luce said that the Argentine Government claimed it was not.

Sir Bernard Brain said: 'While it is important not to overreact, it is pointless to go on asserting that the islands will remain British while removing the signs of tangible support, such as *Endurance*.

Other MPs asked Luce to ensure that *Endurance* remains on station. He said that this was a matter for MOD. Healey drew laughter with his comment that 'the only option open to HMG was to ask Australia to allow the *Invincible* to visit the Falklands on her way to the Royal Australian Navy.

140

It was now clear that the Argentine landing on South Georgia was not only front page news but that *Endurance* herself was in the national spotlight. But I was more concerned with maintaining the morale of my ship's company. Later that day I signalled.

There are three main constraints for the ship remaining on station – morale, food and fuel.

1) Morale

The company and their families are well aware that the ship is due to return UK 20 May. Important though this is there are no other constraints for returning to the UK as the ship is due to pay off anyway.

2) Food

The ship only has provisions for another three weeks before it will be necessary to replenish at Montevideo. Provisions in any quantity are not available at Stanley and storing had been planned for 24 March in Montevideo. Allowing for passage time it will therefore only be possible to remain in the South Atlantic region for a further 14 days.

3) Fuel

80% remains. This is sufficient for 25 days steaming at 12 knots, or 50 days at anchor. It would be highly desirable to fuel again at Stanley before leaving the station. My survey boat and survey party are still in the Falklands.

Summary

The ship could remain in South Georgia for a further two weeks before reprovisioning. There is no bar to the length of time on station, except morale. In order to return to UK by 20 May, with just two two-day stopovers en route, the ship would have to leave Stanley by 20 April. In short I would prefer to do the job quickly, and am fully prepared transport the Argentines to Stanley or Argentina, and to resume my original programme.

*   *   *

We were still at anchor on the 25th. I went ashore to speak to all the BAS men about the situation and to thank them for their sterling work; they were civilian scientists who had all performed beyond the call of duty and at some risk to themselves. They had set up the observation posts that had been the source of much of our information.

In the afternoon I went over to Stromness harbour to watch ARA *Bahia Paraiso* using three LCVPs to unload plant. The *Paraiso* had come up from Southern Thule in the Antarctic with all this equipment, a fact which provided at least moral evidence of forward planning ahead of the arrival of the military, and all the necessary stores and equipment. Although the *Buen Suceso* had carried the basics, suddenly, out of nowhere appeared the *Bahia Paraiso* with all the right sort of kit and equipment with her military escort. A coincidence? I hardly think so.

Tony Ellerbeck flew me to the top of one of the mountains and we landed at 3,000 feet on a narrow section of flat ground with excellent binocular vision over Leith Bay. We spent much of the afternoon watching. Towards the end of our stint an Alouette helicopter from the *Bahia Paraiso* spotted our blue-painted red-nosed WASP. We were uncamouflaged and there was no ground cover. I have no doubt that the pilot had already spotted us making a pathetic attempt to look like boulder débris.

The Alouette came down almost on top of us. We expected a present in the form of some incendiary device lobbed out of the open door. As it happened we had a greeting that was less explosive but just as warm. A large beaming face looked out of the helicopter and the hand gave me a cheery wave. I immediately recognized Captain Cesar Trombetta, the officer in charge of the Argentine Antarctic squadron. He waved again – using an international gesture roughly translated as 'go away' – as the Alouette turned and left us. This game of watching you watching us was gentlemanly enough, but we both knew that when hostilities were officially declared things would have to be rather different. Naturally I informed London of all I had observed.

Following my earlier signal there were now urgent discussions about the logistics of keeping *Endurance* at South Georgia. C-in-C Fleet informed me:

The decision may be made by HMG at short notice to extend the presence of *Endurance* in South Atlantic. That decision will entail provision of supplies. RFA *Fort Austin* is the most suitable vessel with Sea Kings embarked. Rendezvous could be Monday, March 29th. The intention is direct transit at 16 knots probably to South Georgia where *Endurance* is currently holding at Grytviken. *Endurance* is to signal operational spares requirements to C-in-C (Fleet).

Meanwhile all we could do was to sit and watch. We noted the continuing disembarkation of stores from the *Bahia Paraiso* and it was clear to us that the operation had been long pre-planned.

In his signal of 26 March Rex Hunt agreed that the operation had been planned by the Argentine Navy, if not the Argentine Government. He was also considering the possibility of giving 16-week entry permits to the Argentines if they presented their passports to the Base Commander. This was clearly some kind of diplomatic compromise suggested by HMG intended to defuse the situation, but at least maintain the principle that Davidoff and his men must have proper documentation. I imagined the frantic scuttling around the corridors of Whitehall that had induced this formula of retrospective approval. Before the outbreak of another war it had been called appeasement.

The press summaries we were sent suggested widening political divisions at home. The campaign of some Conservative MPs to save *Endurance* was gathering new momentum: an Early Day Motion had won support from members of all parties. The Minister, Keith Speed, was now saying that the Government may change its view. Ministers were clearly embarrassed, particularly because the former Labour Prime Minister, James Callaghan, was the most powerful voice in support of *Endurance*.

And the newspapers were having a field day. The *Daily Telegraph* said that the UK had sent a 'leave or we throw you out' message to Argentina. But, as part of the diplomatic initiatives intended to avoid escalation, the Argentines were invited to send their own ship to take the men and equipment off South Georgia.

Whitehall was refusing to give the UK press any information

about the position of *Endurance*; this, however, was readily available from sources in Argentina. The *Daily Express* had perhaps the most predictable tabloid response. Readers were invited to send greetings to the Falkland islanders, by way of moral support, on St George's Day. It was the beginning of the jingoism which was soon to create momentum for the deployment of the Task Force.

On 26 March we intercepted a signal from Naval Attaché, Buenos Aires:

> The Minister at the Chilean Embassy informed us today that all submarines at the Argentine Naval base at Mar del Plata had recently put to sea. This event may not necessarily be sinister as a naval exercise is at present taking place with Uruguayan Navy, probably in River Plate area.

This was as worrying as it was infuriating. It was also nonsense – 'unlikely as water in River Plate is too shallow'. And it was scarcely believable that nobody had been dispatched from the Embassy to the Golf Club House at Mar del Plata with a brief to count the number of submarines at the base. Even by the standards of Embassy incompetence I had not anticipated this new low.

In a signal to the Naval Attaché I suggested I would be grateful for periodic Situation Reports on the movements of both Argentine Naval and Air Force units.

I was despondent at not being kept up to date with diplomatic moves and wrote in my diary on 27 March:

> Anthony Williams and Whitehall making 'Tut! Tut!' noises is not impressing the Argentines. Rex Hunt and a few others taking good firm stand. C-in-C (Fleet) is sailing some ships in support. In my view some Buccaneers are required.

Meanwhile the Naval Attaché in Buenos Aires replied to my signal, although not to me directly. He signalled MOD UK with more news from the Argentine press concerning the deployment of ships on the exercise with Uruguay. The *Bahia Paraiso*, with a detachment of marines on board, was supposed to be anchored within sight of the *Endurance* and the Argentine corvettes *Drummond* and *Granville* had been despatched to South Georgia area with the *Punta Mendanos*, the Argentine Navy tanker, in support.

It no longer seemed remarkable that the Naval Attaché was garnering most of his information from already outdated, and in some specifics (such as *Bahia Paraiso* being anchored in sight of *Endurance*) inaccurate information. It reminded me in some ways of how years before the police had kept in touch with the activities of the Kray brothers by reading the Sunday supplements.

Even at this stage our Embassy considered this level of activity may still indicate nothing more sinister than a regular Naval exercise. The delusion was entirely consistent with both the Ambassador's interpretation of Argentine intent and the sustained level of incompetence of key members of his staff. I noted my dissatisfaction in my diary. 'The situation is,' I wrote, 'a bloody shambles.'

Chapter 9

INVASION

The days before the invasion were a busy time for signals and telegrams. One of some significance was sent from Anthony Williams in Buenos Aires via Rex Hunt to pass on to *Endurance*. It read:

> Costa Mendes and Ros being unobtainable, I have spoken accordingly to Ambassador Blanco. He is taking careful note but professes to be unaware of the specific journey of the *Buen Suceso*. Although of course, he knows in general about Davidoff, in the circumstances, he felt unable to give an immediate reaction, but was clear of the gravity of my message. I warned him that swift action would be needed if a reaction on our side was not to be set in train.
>
> Davidoff was never of course given any permission by this Embassy, but on the contrary, was warned personally in February by telegram and through his representative here on 11 March told that next time he must follow correct procedures. As seen from here there could well be an advantage in sending *Endurance* to the scene, but I suggest a great restraint be used at least until it is clear whether this is deliberate challenge authorized at high level, or just a piece of low level bravura combined with Davidoff's well-known fecklessness.

The political game of cat and mouse was continuing. Here we had an Argentine official prevaricating whilst his British counterpart covers his tracks. The 'warning' Anthony Williams refers to was issued by Richard Gozney, a fairly junior but very bright

146

member of the Embassy staff. But inevitably it was so weakly worded it was no more discouraging than a few dandelions in the lawn of opportunity.

A slightly more purposeful telegram was sent by Anthony Williams on 21 March:

> Blanco telephoned at midnight with an official Argentine response. He hoped the significance of the affair would not be exaggerated. The party and ship would be leaving South Georgia today. They were in no way official and had no serving personnel or military arms. I asked if they would call at Grytviken and what about the Argentine flag, defaced notices etc? Blanco was not sure about the first and said had no, repeat no, knowledge of the other matters. The BAS observers must have been mistaken about the shooting, since they were not accurate over the flag either. I said I would report what he said, and made it clear the party had left without regularizing their conduct at Grytviken.

Even within this officialese there is complacency. BAS observers are the last kind of people you would expect to be mistaken about their 'home ground'.

At least Lord Carrington was reading the tea leaves. Pulling few diplomatic punches he said he would be grateful if those nations with missions in Buenos Aires, and those with Argentine missions in their capitals, would stress to Argentina the need to find a peaceful and diplomatic solution to this incident. He pointed out, quite properly, that any escalation would be in no one's interest and would not be understood by international opinion. This was the right approach, albeit too little and too late. The chance of getting serious assistance from the international community at this stage was a very long shot.

On Saturday 27 March Anthony Williams sent yet another telegram to the FCO:

> I hesitate to give a definite assessment as requested in your signal without seeing what is in the promised message from Costa Mendes. However, it seems almost certain that his new instructions contain something less than what is asked as a minimum. There is little comfort to be drawn from recent information from

secret sources and I understand from my Naval Attaché's telegram that the Argentines could have a dominating Naval presence in the area by early next week. I suspect Argentine intentions may be the subject of debate within the Junta – the Navy being the most, and the Army the least, hawkish. I cannot, however, discount the possibility that any action on our part to disturb the Argentine working party at Leith will be taken as a trigger for armed action by the Argentines.

Here Anthony Williams' assessment was spot on.

On the following day we came back from sea to anchor off Grytviken to take part in a quiet service in the little church.

The Base Commander came on board in the afternoon. While he was with us things started to liven up a bit. A green helicopter, presumably from *Bahia Paraiso*, arrived at Leith during the afternoon. Later *Bahia Paraiso* was sighted to seaward by our helicopter recce flight. In the evening the long-awaited reply from the Argentine Foreign Minister was received by Ambassador Williams. The reply was little more than the standard Argentine dogma on the Falklands and Dependencies.

Later on, sitting on my bunk, I dreamt up a way of boarding *Bahia Paraiso* personally in order to try to defuse the situation. First thing the following morning I signalled the MOD with my thoughts:

> *Bahia Paraiso* and *Endurance* are the ships which are physically in confrontation, and I am informed that Captain Trombetta, whom I know and like, is still on board.
>
> It occurs to me that there might be some mileage in attempting to defuse the situation at local level. This may sound somewhat far-fetched, but in the light of little progress in any other direction another line might be worth trying.
>
> Today I shall be at sea and within helicopter range of *Bahia Paraiso*. My suggestion is that I should be allowed to fly on board and talk to Trombetta. If approved, I recommend that I should go on board alone, unarmed, and put the following suggestion to Trombetta:
>
> The DIPCLEAR [Diplomatic Clearance] should be waived and both ships anchor for 24 hours in the vicinity Grytviken, and out

of sight of Leith. Then Trombetta and I could be flown to Leith, in separate helicopters, to tell the leader of Davidoff's men at Leith that the whole party should embark either in *Bahia Paraiso* or *Endurance*, and be taken to Grytviken for the issue of proper immigration documentation. On completion the party should be taken to Leith and legally allowed to remain for a further fifteen weeks and military support by the Argentines should be discontinued.

During course of conversation with Trombetta it should be pointed out that we are well aware that the Argentine will have the greatest difficulty maintaining a frigate force at sea. *Punta Mendanos* is a very shaky old tanker. If the situation escalates further *Bahia Paraiso* could be faced with an SSN (nuclear submarine), surface or even air threat.

Might it also be worth pointing out that the issue has only one thing in common with similar issues over sovereignty – it is designated a Falkland Island dependency. The Argentine has no historical territorial claim to this island and therefore the two issues should be considered in isolation.

If Trombetta refuses to consider this eleventh hour offer, then it will be clear to everyone that this is a sovereignty issue involving the Navy and using Davidoff as a front.

If this option is approved in part or whole it will be necessary to ask the Argentine Navy to instruct *Bahia Paraiso* to lift radio silence, at least on VHF, in order that I may suggest the initial move. I have not been able to raise His Excellency, the Governor of the Falklands this morning for our usual communications schedule, but I am of the opinion that he would approve this proposal in principle.

Meanwhile the UK Sunday papers had highlighted the increasingly tense situation. The *Sunday Telegraph* put it like this:

A confrontation between *Endurance* and several Argentine warships off South Georgia was threatened last night with warnings in Buenos Aires of the grave situation. *Bahia Paraiso*, with troops embarked, was off Leith to protect their party ashore. Reports from Buenos Aires said that their frigates, *Granville* and *Drummond*, both 950 tons, were on their way carrying Exocets. Waiting to meet them is the *Endurance* with her 21 Marines anchored in sight of *Bahia Paraiso*. It seemed last night that one government or the other would be compelled to retreat or lose face in a Naval showdown.

The *Sunday Mirror*'s Woodrow Wyatt was typically forthright:

> There's more to this situation than musical comedy. Falklanders want to remain British. Whatever economies we have to make in defence, there must be no cuts in the vessels that are needed to protect them. The Foreign and Commonwealth Office have long toyed with concessions to Argentina. Such wet notions must be stopped.

Under the banner headline 'LONE BRITISH SHIP FACES TWO PROWLING FRIGATES' the *Sunday Times* leader began:

> Two of Argentina's most modern, missile-carrying frigates, the cream of the Argentine's expanding Navy, were loose in the South Atlantic last night as tension rose over the fate of South Georgia.

C-in-C Fleet hardly needed to remind me that:

> The present situation remains extremely delicate and every effort should be made to avoid any encounter which could be construed by Argentines as escalatory.

Later on Sunday afternoon Anthony Williams reported the official reaction from the Argentine Foreign Minister. Costa Mendes had told him we were making a mountain out of a molehill, as the workmen had the necessary documentation, by virtue of the 1971 agreement. Mendes had also professed ignorance about the personnel on board the *Paraiso*. Williams added that he had told Mendes about the marines on board *Biscoe* and that he would transmit Mendes' message and the fact that he (Mendes) had withdrawn his earlier proposal, stating that it was merely one of several ideas.

Meanwhile, in London Lord Carrington had decided that it

150

was time that General Al Haig, the US Secretary of State for Foreign Affairs, be fully appraised of the situation. His message was timed at 19.30 on 28 March, 1982. In it he made it clear that the British assessment of the situation accepted that the Argentines were no longer interested in negotiations over the vexed question of sovereignty. It informed him of *Endurance's* presence and that of the Argentine Naval vessels and outlined the possibilities for escalation, whilst maintaining the British Government's resolve to seek a peaceful solution. He concluded by requesting that Al Haig intervene with the Argentines and try to persuade them to call off their Military plans.

Eventually I got through to Rex Hunt and made my proposal to him. He thought it was worth a try, but in view of the uncompromising nature of Costa Mendes' reply to Lord Carrington he doubted whether Captain Trombetta would be given authority to negotiate, or do as I had suggested. Lord Carrington had already offered this way out and it had been ignored.

At last the MOD got back to me on the 29th and said:

> Your constructive suggestion for a course of action to attempt to defuse the situation at local level is welcomed. However, the view is that proposed actions are likely to complicate a delicate issue with small chance of success due to the extent and high level of present political involvement. Optional powers cannot therefore be approved at present. Further consideration will be given and outcome signalled.

This increased the irony of what Ambassador Williams had to say the following day when he spoke to his opposite number in the US Embassy who suggested that Admiral Hayward, outgoing C-in-C US Navy, was due in the area and may be of some use. He then went on to suggest that the US intervention might not carry sufficient weight to allow for an Argentine climb-down and the removal of the workmen by a third party.

We had also intercepted a signal from the Naval Attaché to the MOD which was later relayed to us:

South Georgia deployment of Argentine Navy: two destroyers, two corvettes and one submarine despatched South Georgia. *Biscoe* overflown by Argentine Navy aircraft. Personnel restricted to stay within 60 km of Puerto Belgrano. US Naval Attaché confirms destroyers are *Comodoro Py* and *Piedra Buena*. *La Nacion* states all this as being part of routine exercise, but *Le Clarin* states there has been a rush to put missiles on board the *Santissima Trinidad*.

There could be no doubt now that the Argentines were closing in on us quickly. We were also receiving worrying signals about submarine activity off the Falklands. It was time to look after our people as best we could. Cindy and Annie, who had been on board, were flown back to St Andrew's with Peter Stark, one of the BAS staff. It seemed a good idea to have a chap there in case the Argentines came over the hill for a social call.

A Russian tug, the *Styki*, which had somehow got into the middle of all this, called at Grytviken for water. They were to stay for two or three days. It was all very odd. Why come to Grytviken at all when their fishermen were operating off Elephant Island and the Bellinghausen base was at least ten hours steaming from the fishing grounds? I had little doubt that the Russians were picking up the signals too and they wanted to have a closer look at the situation.

The tension was increasing by the hour. In my later report of proceedings I tried to summarize the situation dispassionately:

I was well aware of the Argentine Naval build up and discussions that were taking place in the diplomatic world, but very concerned at the way that many of those involved in the discussions were underestimating the impending danger and also the determination of the Argentines. I asked to try and defuse the situation locally as I knew and liked Captain Trombetta, my opposite number in the Argentine Arctic area, but the situation was beginning to get out of hand and anyway Trombetta was getting bolder by the day, making a much better job of his relative velocity at sea and trying to head me off when we were patrolling in close proximity. He did not succeed, but we both knew he was soon to have support from frigates and destroyers.

152

As the Argentine Naval buildup continued, the BAS scientists became more nervous. We did our very best to placate them, for even though the ship did not exactly bristle with guns, at least we were there to manage the situation and to evacuate them if it worsened.

My main concern was to know what Argentine sub-surface forces were likely to be deployed. I asked the Embassy at Buenos Aires for clarification. After some considerable time I was rewarded with a quote from the *Clarin* and *Prensa* which 'confirmed' that the Argentines were carrying out Naval exercises. This again did little to instil confidence in our Intelligence resources. I began to feel sure that the FCO was never going to take a strong line over the Falklands or South Georgia. And this could all too easily mean that *Endurance* was to be the sacrificial lamb.

As the days had ticked by and the diplomatic exchanges continued, it had become absolutely clear that the Argentines were paying no more than lip service to overtures made by Britain and the United Nations. By now I was sure that their Naval preparations were almost complete and that an invasion of both the Falkland Islands and South Georgia was imminent. I noted in my diary:

> It does seem the best source of intelligence in Argentina is Chilean. The British Naval Attaché in Buenos Aires guessing – as usual – from what he reads in the papers and the Ambassador seems to have thrown in the sponge. We were also having less than pleasant encounters with the *Bahia Paraiso* on our patrols.

In his book *Operation Paraquat* Roger Perkins begins his description of the dramatic events of 30 March like this:

> *Endurance* made another search to seaward for the *Bahia Paraiso* and found her patrolling about 15 miles to the north-east of Cumberland Bay. Nick Barker did not close, but cruised back and forth trying to keep the Argentines under observation in moderate visibility.

Captain Trombetta had been pottering about in the same location for about five days. He was under orders to mark time pending further developments. The obvious implication was that he expected more Argentine ships to arrive in the near future. Nick Barker accordingly kept his two Wasps busy with constant reconnaissance flights up and down the coast, but nothing was sighted that morning. These flights pushed the total flying time of the two Wasps to a new record for any one month – 107 hours.

Early in the afternoon, a signal was received from Northwood, ordering Captain Barker to return to Port Stanley with all despatch.

In the same way that Royal Marines on East Falkland gave some credibility to Great Britain's stance for sovereignty there, a military presence was required on South Georgia. The military personnel could also provide protection, if required, for the unarmed BAS civilians. One platoon defending an island a hundred miles in length could be nothing more than a token force but there was no alternative.

During the evening Lieutenant Mills and his men were ferried ashore with a full allocation of platoon weapons and ammunition. This was the first occasion that armed troops had ever garrisoned the island. Steve Martin, the Base Commander, was not happy with this latest development. He would have preferred not to have any troops on the island, particularly when they were billeted on him at only 30 minutes' notice. He was the magistrate, and therefore answerable to the Falklands Islands Government for everything which happened on the island. He had received no advice from Rex Hunt, nor indeed from anyone other than Captain Nick Barker.

The base was being turned into an armed camp, with all of the implicit perils. Martin himself had no instructions as to how he and his personnel should conduct themselves in the event of serious trouble.

At a Conference on board *Endurance* shortly before she sailed, Steve Martin voiced his anxieties to Captain Barker and Commander Francis Ponsonby. Captain Barker told Steve Martin that the order to leave Keith Mills and his men at King Edward Point had come from London. Steve Martin was not entirely reassured. He was a university graduate and boatman, not a soldier or diplomat. Everything was happening very quickly and he felt himself being carried along by circumstances which were totally unfamiliar to him. Who was now in charge of the island? Was he still the Base Commander or had Keith Mills taken over? As magistrate and therefore legal representative of Governor Hunt he had considerable powers, but these appear to have been in part overridden by orders coming directly from London via Captain Barker.

After some discussion his dilemma was resolved with a commonsense agreement between Martin, Nick Barker and Mills, that there would be no change to the usual administration of the base as long as the present situation continued. However, in the event of an emergency, and if fighting broke out, all BAS personnel would conduct themselves as non-combatants, keeping well out of the way and Keith Mills would subsequently command.

Martin was not alone at feeling worried; although elated at the prospect of independent command under novel circumstances Keith Mills had the anxiety of not knowing exactly what was required of him. In the phraseology of his profession, what were the rules of engagement? Nick Barker responded by spelling out the terms under which the Marines could resort to force. Mills instantly recognized the parameters as being those defined in the yellow card rules.

These yellow card rules are reasonably straightforward, but the problem was that I was as usual being back-seat driven from Whitehall and so the rules of engagement were changing by the day. I had to interpret them and didn't want to keep breaking radio silence to inform Keith of each new interpretation. The only realistic option was to filter the information as best I could and keep Keith reasonably well informed as to what he could and could not do.

Our order to proceed immediately to Stanley had now been confirmed. I had signalled C-in-C with the suggestion that it could just be better to stay in South Georgia, where we could actually face and deal with the enemy. From the signals we had intercepted it seemed there was a strong possibility of being caught between the two tactical areas and therefore relatively useless. But Stanley it was. And we had to devise a plan to slip out without being spotted.

Once again I cannot do better than allow Roger Perkins to tell this part of the story exactly as it appeared in his book *Operation Paraquat*. Roger taped my account soon after I returned to England when the detail was still very fresh in my mind.

The entrance to East and West Cumberland Bays is approximately 4.5 miles in width, any ship leaving by the normal track would be spotted instantly by the *Bahia Paraiso*'s radar operators. The only answer would be to hug the shore line and creep away, hoping that the radar scanner would be unable to distinguish the ship against the steeply rising cliff. The surface of the sea was littered with rocks and small icebergs, and as Nick Barker told his officers, 'We've got to pretend to be one of them'.

Announcing his intentions to the ship's company he emphasized the need for secrecy. Navigation lights would be extinguished; all deadlights (those are the porthole covers) secured; the ship must be darkened as she had never been darkened before; there would be strict radio silence; the radar would be used only in brief squirts to confirm the ship's position, otherwise pulses transmitted by *Endurance* would be identified in the *Bahia Paraiso* and by any other Argentine vessel which might be in the area. The sole navigational aid, apart from the naked eye, would be the echo sounder, but this would have limited value in such a poorly charted area. Bill Hurst was given the task of conning the ship away from King Edward Point and out to sea.

At 19.00 on 31 March *Endurance* weighed anchor and moved very slowly across Cumberland Bay East until she was under the high ground of the east headland. The wind was blowing from the west at about 7–8, kicking up the surface of the sea into waves three to four feet high. Although the night sky was overcast, the horizontal visibility was six miles. This was much greater than Nick Barker would have wished. It was important not to let the ship's silhouette show against the horizon.

Bill Hurst maintained steerage way as he nursed *Endurance* along the black jagged shore. About 200 yards to starboard a white line of bursting waves signalled the waiting rocks. At this slow speed, with the beam wind pushing hard against her high superstructure, the *Red Plum* was all too ready to drift to leeward.

Gradually the extremity of Barff Point came in sight. Here

there is a narrow gap less than 400 yards wide, between the headland and the Right Whale Rocks. It is unlikely that this current-swept stretch of water, known as the Merton Passage, had ever previously been attempted by any vessel larger than a motor boat. The charts show a minimum of eight fathoms, but the seabed had never been charted in detail and only extreme necessity could tempt a ship's Captain to hazard his vessel in such a place.

Bill Hurst quietly ordered the helm to starboard and eased the ship into the neck of the passage. *Endurance* had found herself in many curious places in 26 years since she was launched, but the transit of the Merton Passage on this night was by far the most perilous. The men on her silent bridge watched as the cliffs and rocky shore lines to starboard and to port passed with almost painful slowness. The echo sounder told them that the seabed was shoaling steadily closer to the surface. Soon there was a clearance of less than 20 feet between the rocky bottom and *Endurance*'s keel and still shoaling. Even one large outcrop would have been enough to bring total disaster. But all went well and she passed through safely.

With the passage behind them, the people aboard the *Plum* were now faced with the task of getting completely clear of South Georgia without their departure being reported. It was known that there were several other ships in the area, including two Russian vessels.

To avoid observation, Nick Barker chose the southerly route, heading for Cape Disappointment. Icebergs had reached the adjacent waters as the onset of the Antarctic winter carried them northward. He would move slowly down the coast, keeping close inshore and hope that any Argentine radar operators would classify his ship as just one more iceberg.

For the first hour it seemed as though the worst was behind them, then, approaching Royal Bay, the lookout saw a brightly lit ship off the port bow. It was impossible to know her nationality or reason for her presence. Captain Barker debated whether she was an Eastern Bloc ship or whether she was another Argentine vessel coming in to join the *Bahia Paraiso*. He ordered the course to be altered even closer to the coast, accepting the hazards of offshore reefs, Bill Hurst conned the *Plum* slowly past the unknown ship until she disappeared into the darkness astern. Either she had failed to spot *Endurance*'s blip on her radar scope or had simply not been interested. The evidence later suggested that she was a Communist fish factory ship.

By dawn on 1 April Nick Barker had cleared the southernmost tip of the island and was pressing hard for the Falklands, into a Force 10 gale. In *Endurance*'s cavernous engine room the 5 big pistons thundered up and down making conversation impossible as the engineers coaxed maximum power from the elderly machinery. For Bill Hurst it was the end of what he subsequently labelled 'a bloody gruesome night'.

The ship rolled like an empty barrel as she buffeted her way across the heavy south-westerly swell. Nick Barker's usually mild temper was strained to the limit by his current frustrations. Everything which he had forecast was coming to pass. The Argentine fleet was at sea and within striking distance of the Falklands and South Georgia. Reports spoke of major units to the north of the islands with a second force approaching from the south.

Possibly two frigates armed with Exocet missiles were deployed somewhere between the Falklands and South Georgia on the *Endurance*'s present track – and a submarine was rumoured to be en route for the same area. To counter this display of power Rex Hunt and Nick Barker had seventy-three marines in East Falkland, twenty-two marines on South Georgia and the dear old *Plum* wallowing along half way between the two. The nearest support was at Gibraltar, 5,500 miles and two weeks' steaming away. If ever there was a moment which exposed the poverty of the British Government's policy in the South Atlantic this was it.

I still think of it as my worst nightmare. I wished those who had let us down so badly could have shared the battering of that Force Ten gale and the private fears we must surely all have experienced. And almost worse than all of this was the feeling of impotence. Our marines we had left behind on South Georgia knew what they had to do. The force on the Falklands were preparing their own response to the now almost certain invasion. But we, who could have supported either, were in the middle of nowhere bobbing around like an old tin bath that could soon be used for target practice by a gang of likely lads from the Argentine.

It was 1 April, the April Fool was the British Government and the jokers were in the opulent rooms of Whitehall and our Embassy in Buenos Aires. I wrote in my diary:

Anything could happen today. Anything. The weather is not good, from the west, 7–8 with a westerly swell. We're making good 9.5 knots with 160 revs rung on, taking a devious route to Stanley.

Sent a signal to DNOT (Director of Naval Operations and Trade) asking for information, diplomatic telegrams and so on, but no reply. No news from Fleet or from the British Naval Attaché in Beunos Aires – in the latter case not surprising.

The Fleet has ordered me to set watch with the Royal Marines in the Falklands. I recommended listening only. It is suicide to transmit, especially since I have eluded the Argentines since leaving South Georgia.

The Argentines have announced internally they will invade the Falklands at 06.00 tomorrow. Some Naval exercise this turned out to be. It may still be some form of bluff, but I doubt it. They're not to be underestimated these bastards, particularly when their hand is on the trigger.

The Press say an SSN and *Exeter* are on the way, but this may be a controlled leak. *Fort Austin* has been diverted, so has a tanker. I long to get stuck into this situation, but may be hidebound by rules of engagement, or the positioning of Argentine forces. It's all been bloody frustrating.

Signals during the night were thick and fast starting with a clear indication of D-Day and H-Hour – 06.00 on the 2nd. Although the invasion had been planned for the 2nd for some time, no one knew it would be timed for first light.

The initial signals from Sir Anthony Parsons, British Ambassador at the United Nations, were pathetic as in fact most of the diplomatic exchanges have been. Where did we find such weak-willed diplomats? My predicament is a direct result. Argentine threat assessment thinks we are still at Gritvyken, so at least we've hoodwinked them. That part at least is satisfying.

Meanwhile Lord Carrington had sent a message to the Governor of the Falklands informing him of the request for American intervention. Then he dumped any action – and its potential consequences – into Rex's lap.

At this stage Ambassador Parsons was still making placatory noises and virtually refusing to acknowledge that the threat was real. Days later, when he was finally convinced that the situation was serious, he began to become an important player in the diplomatic game. I wrote in my report:

> The odds of one ice patrol ship armed with AS12 missiles, and by now without most of her small arms, against the might of the Argentine fleet was daunting, but my aim was to go for the Argentine fleet oiler, *Punta Mendanos*, which was reported to be in the vicinity of Beauchene Island. I felt that if I could knock out the oiler, the consequent threat posed by the very thirsty old ex-American destroyers would be reduced considerably.

I talked to my officers. I felt instinctively it was better to get back to South Georgia before it was too late to support the Royal Marine detachment. We also hoped to evacuate the scientists and to attack the *Bahia Paraiso*, and hopefully one or both of the corvettes.

On 1 April the ship was ordered back to South Georgia and at best speed. I made for the south-east corner of the island. This was because we had a report that two corvettes, two destroyers, a submarine and a tanker were heading for South Georgia; the assumption was they would make their approach from the north. By using the cover of the icebergs to the south and hugging the coastline I knew well it should be possible to escape detection before arriving back in the vicinity of Grytviken.

2 April, my diary:

> D-Day finds *Endurance* nearly halfway between South Georgia and the Falklands. Despite my request to return to South Georgia knowing that Grytviken would be invaded, I was at first told to continue towards Stanley. Happily that decision was later reversed but I fear we have lost precious time. Signals poured through all night. Stanley went off the air at 05.45 saying that Government House had surrendered. It was defended at the time by Royal Marines and *Endurance*'s sailors. At 08.15 it was

confirmed by one of the BAS radio operators that Stanley had been captured. Happily there appear to be only three casualties – all Argentine. One Argentine officer is dead. Two thousand troops were landed by the Argentines. Of course it is being hailed as a great Naval victory. If so then this mighty victory was against one enemy ship which was virtually unarmed and hundreds of miles away at the time. The Argentine line is that they have recaptured the Malvinas, South Georgia etc. But we know they have not yet tried to capture South Georgia. The opposition is *Bahia Paraiso* and a corvette. I believe I can deal with them.

We received a transcript of a message from Port Stanley:

Old and new fighters buzzing all around and a lot of transport aircraft movements. There are heavy, probably amphibious, vehicles moving around the streets, driving on the left, apparently taking the fences and hedges with them as they manoeuvre round corners. A few houses have been riddled with bullets and one or two buildings have lost their water supply as a result of mortar fire. It appears that the Kelpers [nickname for the Islanders] are attempting to move their children away from Stanley and get them to the West Island. Argentines are starving the population of any world news. As soon as any Kelper put the World Service News on the box it was turned off by the Argentines. This starvation has not helped the situation and the Islanders feel particularly helpless. They think there are grey ships on the way and three nuclear subs which will blast the Argentines away from the Falklands.

The message came from one of the radio hams. Most of our interceptions of Argentine messages came from Naval sources including an amphibious group. They had been passed back to Cheltenham.

Since we were keeping silence, I had not been talking directly to Rex Hunt, but asked that messages from the Invasion Force be relayed. I was later horrified to learn that the first Rex had actually heard of the Invasion Force was at 15.30 local time on Thursday, 1 April. He had been aware that the Argentine Fleet was putting to sea, but had been misled by the Buenos Aires

Embassy who still appeared to believe that the Argentines were at sea for anti-submarine exercises with the Uruguayans. He had not even been told that the Argentines had subsequently sailed one or more amphibious ships, or that a full battalion of Marines had been seen embarking with armoured personnel carriers.

Like most of his ex-colonial service contemporaries, Rex Hunt was a pragmatist. He believed that some of the Argentines would proceed to South Georgia and that was why for the time being we were necessarily out of touch. We had intercepted the signals about the amphibious force but were unable to pass the information directly to him. We could listen but hardly dared to speak. We had to assume that his own channels of communication would keep him informed. All we could offer were our prayers.

The awareness of our diplomats – or rather the lack of it – in Argentina is summed up by a story told in my television film 'War Stories'. Sir Frederick Bennett, who was for many years the Conservative MP for Torbay, is an acknowledged expert on South American countries and a distinguished barrister from Lincoln's Inn. Shortly before the invasion of the Falklands he had been invited to Chile and subsequently to Argentina. He flew out to Chile via Buenos Aires approximately two days before the invasion and he describes how the passengers were prevented from looking out of the windows as his aircraft put down on a military airfield close to the Andes.

> I didn't pull my window blind fully down because I wanted to see what was outside. I looked out – and I know war when I see it. I could see a lot of army vehicles being manoeuvred about near the edge of the tarmac and I wondered where they were heading, or was this just an exercise?

The aircraft flew on to Santiago, Chile, where he was a guest of Mr Heath, our Ambassador. Naturally he asked him what was going on. The Ambassador said to him: 'Sir Frederick, I wish you to complete your engagements here in Chile and then I would suggest you fly home again. You ought not to go to Argentina tomorrow to make a speech at the lunch in Buenos Aires. We shall be at war by then.'

'What war is that?' he asked.

'The Argentines are on their way to invade the Falklands.'

Sir Frederick picked up the telephone and rang Anthony Williams to explain why it would be imprudent to make his visit.

'I've been advised not to come,' he said, 'because I understand we're going to be at war.'

Allegedly Williams replied, 'What war?' He even went on to suggest that failure to fulfil the commitment could give cause for offence.

Sir Freddy was somewhat bemused with the mixed signals he was receiving. But if the British Ambassador in Argentina believed everything was OK then there was really no reason for cancelling his visit. However, before leaving for the airport at 06.30 the following morning he was surprised to receive another call.

'I'm sorry Sir Frederick,' said Anthony Williams, 'but I don't think you should come over today. It appears, after all, that we are at war with Argentina. They have just begun invading the Falklands.'

Sir Rex Hunt later wrote:

'Not mentioned in the telegrams is the crucial information that in the early evening, Mr Nott, then Secretary of State for Defence, had been briefed by the MOD officials on the latest intelligence report, presumably originating from *Endurance*. This indicated that the early morning of the second of April had been set by the Argentines as a time and day for action. Taken with earlier intelligence reports analysts had presumed that the action intended was an invasion of the Falkland Islands. The FCO had also seen these reports. But we were in ignorance of what was to befall us. Mavis and I had hosted a party that very evening . . . .

April 1 began the same as any other. My early morning schedule with Steve Martin was uneventful. He could not tell me over the radio that *Endurance* had sailed and there was nothing from Nick because he was maintaining radio silence. Telegrams arrived from London during the morning via New York, but nothing about the invasion on the 2nd. Bill Luxton flew in from

Cap Chartres and called to see me. I explained the gravity of the situation, but could not forecast what might happen.

Rex returned to his office until about 15.30 when the fateful telegram arrived. Couched in typically FCO language it read:

> We have apparently reliable evidence that an Argentine task force will gather off Cape Pembroke early tomorrow morning, April 2nd. You will wish to make your dispositions accordingly.

Brian Wills, cast in the role of bearer of bad tidings, put the telegram on his desk and added, 'They might have said, "Goodbye and the best of British".'

Rex made a quick calculation. He had 15–16 hours at the most to make whatever dispositions he could. He was fortunate in having sixty-nine Royal Marines available – the forty-three of the new detachment plus the twenty-six of the old. He also had the twelve hydrographers from *Endurance* who, though primarily trained to hold a mapping pen, could doubtless also be relied on to fire a weapon. In addition there was the Falkland Island Defence Force.

Meanwhile, in *Endurance* we were still fighting against the heavy south-westerly swell whilst painting our helicopters khaki to camouflage them against the Falkland hills.

The attack on the Falklands began at 04.30 local time when the Argentine assault force went ashore in the vicinity of Mullet Creek. The main attack was to be an hour and a half later at York Bay where personnel carriers were landed to move along the airport road towards Stanley. The leading vehicle was struck by a Carl Gustav missile fired by the defending Royal Marines and the crews of the remaining vehicles disembarked.

Lieutenant Chris Todhunter, our hydrographer, was detailed to keep guard on some Argentine contractors in the town hall. The rest of the survey team operated an information service in Government House until they joined in the active defence of the building. After four hours of fighting the Governor declared a surrender and the British flag was lowered. The survey party was flown home from Uruguay with the Governor, his wife, the

164

Royal Marines and Naval party 8901. We lost communications on the London–Stanley link, but the BAS base at Signy confirmed via Grytviken that no civilians had been injured, though some Argentines were in hospital.

The new Argentine Military Governor began issuing communiqués to the Islanders. I was asked to transmit a message to them from the Director of BAS at Cambridge to the base at Grytviken, but decided against as this meant breaking HF silence. The priority simply had to be the survival of my ship. However, I asked the MOD to pass the Director's message to the other bases by telex and then it would be relayed to South Georgia.

On 2 April at 05.00 I lost all contact with Port Stanley and expected to lose contact with South Georgia soon afterwards. Throughout the day world news bulletins referred to the Argentine proclamations of a great Naval victory. Although this was a considerable exaggeration, it was nevertheless humiliating.

We now had to formulate our ideas for dealing with the enemy action at Grytviken. With the ship pounding back to South Georgia, the situation ashore was beginning to hot up. Hearing about the invasion, the Royal Marines at Grytviken set about preparing their defences. They placed two troops on the Jason Ridge to observe activities. The main base also learned that the *Bahia Paraiso* was at anchor at Leith and a corvette was heading into Stromness Bay.

We made contact with the garrison using the prepared code and informed them that *Endurance* would be in the vicinity by 15.00 the next day, 3 April. However, at 10.30 we picked up the Argentine side of a VHF call from *Bahia Paraiso* to the South Georgia garrison:

Following our successful operation in the Malvinas Islands, the ex-Governor has surrendered the Islands and dependencies to Argentina. We suggest you adopt a similar course of action to prevent any further loss of life.

In an attempt to gain time, Keith Mills asked for clarification. He was not reading back the message on HF so that *Endurance* could hear. He further asked for time to consider the request. He was given five minutes.

The next message from *Bahia Paraiso* was a demand that all base personnel assemble on the beach. I broke in with instructions to the Base Commander to wait until I had asked London for their intentions.

I spoke to the MOD Duty Commander and the Assistant Chief of Naval Staff Operations. There was no 'answer' from them other than to confirm that I was not to help unless provoked. Only then could I engage with AS12 missiles. I felt rather like a prize fighter under instruction to take the blows for a couple of rounds so that somebody could get better odds with the bookie. Of course they were anxious to keep the whole Argentine Navy off our backs by avoiding unnecessary provocation. From where we were standing an invasion of the Falklands and South Georgia seemed sufficient cause to invite us to do what damage we could. But this was largely academic. We had been warned off having a pop at Argentine ships and, because of the order to return to Stanley, were still frustratingly out of useful range of South Georgia.

Then came another surprise. I was concerned to hear there would be a delay in sending Naval forces from Gibraltar, or perhaps further north, to the area. We really were being left to stew without even the satisfaction of aiming one good kick at the enemy's shins. Meanwhile I was expected to maintain a dignified calm.

My safety valve was my diary. I wrote: 'This is an operation – not a fucking exercise! British lives and possessions are at stake. The Argentines will ignore our diplomats until they speak with strength and that means military might on the station.'

3 April was the day when the feeling of impotence hit hardest. I hated what I had to do only slightly less than I despised those who had brought about this situation. In the most matter of fact way I had to pass on instructions to Keith Mills about defending the base. Like a hangman I could not permit any emotion to be heard in my voice. I repeated his rules of engagement and informed him he would not be required to continue the fighting if lives would be lost unnecessarily. I told him that his key rôle

was to make it be seen that the Argentines took South Georgia by force. Other signals followed as I clarified the situation with the Base Commander. Then I was forced to silence again. We were most fearful for Keith and our marines. The situation they faced was untenable. Their lives depended on an honourable adversary and the common sense to know when to admit defeat.

When you join the armed services you accept the risks. But you do not expect to fight, and perhaps die, on some Godforsaken windswept mountainside just about as far from home as you can get. At this moment South Georgia seemed unimportant, an irrelevance. What could Argentina do with it anyway?

Endurance was pretty well stretched by now. With the dozen of the survey party left behind in the Falklands, and full Marine platoon ashore in South Georgia we really had just ourselves, our flight, and our couple of 20 mm pea shooters. There was also an ominous silence from Grytviken. All the BAS stations were on net, but Grytviken said nothing. We knew that the battle had begun.

We heard the details of what happened much later. First the Argentine corvette *Guerrico* rounded the point and headed into the cove off the BAS base, while a helicopter, which could have come from either ship, reconnoitred overhead. The *Bahia Paraiso* was then informed that there was a British military presence and that any attempt to land would be repulsed. Having completed his task, the Base Commander, Steve Martin, withdrew to the civilian sanctuary of the Norwegian whaling church.

Lieutenant Keith Mills moved down towards the jetty at King Edward Point. His intention was to talk to the Argentine landing party which he assumed would arrive. But as the corvette turned and headed back out into East Cumberland Bay Keith was surprised by an Argentine helicopter disgorging marines close to him. As the Argentines took up positions of cover, one of the marines raised his rifle. Keith withdrew as fast as possible to a defensive position.

Then a Puma from the *Bahia Paraiso* attempted to land on the foreshore. It was supported by a volley of covering fire aimed at Keith's position from an Argentine machine gun mounted at the opposite side of the bay. Keith gave the order to open fire. Around 500 rounds were pumped into the Puma which remained in the air only through the efforts of an excellent pilot. It covered the 400 metres or so to the other side of the cove, trailing smoke, and made a very heavy landing. No one was seen to climb out. Two months later the Puma still lay where it had landed. So far as Keith could determine, the occupants were all dead.

It was an Alouette that came next, intent on making further marine insertions on the opposite side of the cove. This was also fired on by our marines, causing it to drop out of the air immediately. It was severely damaged.

It was then that the corvette returned to the scene, blazing away with her 40 mm gun from the after-end. An immediate landing was anticipated, but, to the marines' surprise, she steamed on her slow relentless course to within about 300 yards from the base. Our marines let rip with a Carl Gustav (anti-tank) round which fell into the water about 10 yards short of the ship. At first there was nothing, but then came the explosion. The round had hit the starboard quarter below the water line.

The Royal Marines maintained the pressure. Their next success was with 66 mm heavy machine-gun fire which rattled the superstructure. The corvette turned out towards the safety of the bay. Our marines were determined to mark her departure with a further acknowledgement of their presence. They found their target again when anti-tank rockets bored into her Exocet launcher. The Argentines later disclosed that 1,275 hits were scored on the *Guerrico*. The ship's detachment had knocked down two helicopters, killed an entire landing party and crew, and pretty much put a corvette out of action – not bad for one platoon. From a safe range of about 3,000 yards the corvette turned again and began shelling our positions.

By this time the Argentine marines ashore had moved round the cove through the whaling station and cut off our marines' withdrawal route. We had also suffered our first casualty. Corporal Peters had been shot twice in the left arm.

Keith properly decided this was enough. The point had been made and his position was now hopeless. A coat was turned into a makeshift flag and held aloft. The shooting stopped immediately. The two Commanding Officers met to negotiate the surrender. The twenty-two British Royal Marines were to become prisoners of war with the promise of good treatment. The civilian scientists were released from their refuge and all were put on board the *Bahia Paraiso*. Eleven days later they were disembarked at Puerto Belgrano and housed at a swimming pool on the base.

The Royal Marines were returned to England on 22 April via Montevideo. For his brave defence of South Georgia against a force of 100 Argentine marines, three helicopters and two ships, Keith Mills was awarded the DSC. His second-in-command, Sergeant Peter Leach, was awarded the DSM.

It was to our huge regret that all this happened while we were heading east round the southern tip of South Georgia. I had every intention of bringing helicopter support to our marines by mid-afternoon. We were too late.

When the ship was at extreme range for a recce flight WASP 434, now fully camouflaged, was launched and landed in the cover of the mountains. Lieutenant-Commander Tony Ellerbeck and his observer, Lieutenant David Wells, climbed to a high point, leaving the WASP obscured by the high hills. They watched one oddly calm sequel to the battle, *Guerrico* moving away at Zimmer speed. *Bahia Paraiso* was hidden from view supporting her personnel landing craft, but her position could be guessed at by the flight pattern of a helicopter heading for the shore. There was no sign of any of our men. We had to assume they were now being held in one of the ships. Any thought of an AS12 rocket attack was therefore stillborn.

It was my belief that the Argentine force consisted of the *Guerrico* and her sister ship *Granville*, supported by two ex-US destroyers and possibly a submarine. The outcome of a battle against such naval power, while hopefully causing some damage to the Argentine ships, would inevitably have led to the destruction of *Endurance* and the death of most of her men in freezing water. I later learned that the Argentines knew *Endurance* had arrived back in the area.

*   *   *

Command at sea can be a lonely business at any time. Command of the only British ship in the southern hemisphere when there are trigger-happy Argentines in the area is the closest thing I have experienced to complete isolation. To make things worse my very good friend and second-in-command, Mike Green, had been taken ashore with appendicitis and by that time had returned to England. I was perhaps irrationally upset about that. It was hardly Mike's fault and this was not something I could blame either on incompetent diplomats, bloody-minded mandarins or lying Argentines. In my darkest hours it just seemed another example of Barker's luck. But, in an odd sort of way, now that we were fighting for our lives, apportioning blame for the situation seemed irrelevant. If we survived that could be dealt with later. If we survived . . .

I knew intuitively that the time had come to channel all that anger positively. We were, after all, quite literally in the same boat. I took stock of what I did have. The *Endurance* was not a warship in the conventional sense, but she was armed to an extent that the enemy could not have expected. She also had one of the most sophisticated listening systems fitted to anything afloat and could go places that the conventional warship could not, or dare not, go.

I also had considerable human assets. First amongst these was Commander Francis Ponsonby, the nuclear submariner, who had come on board with the film team. Francis had every right to ask how he had fallen into such misfortune. To his great credit he never did. He had already proved to be a more than capable Chief of Staff and exactly the right sort of sounding board for ideas and help to rationalize our options. We both recognized that the equation of war is simple enough. We were determined to go and sink Argentines if we could: the cost was all too likely to be the end of *Endurance* and all who sailed in her. But this was the job. It was time for UK Ltd to get a return on the considerable investment they had made in our training.

Uppermost in my mind was avoiding an early bath in South Atlantic waters. That meant evading the enemy until we encountered him on something like our own terms. Our belt and braces strategy was to hug the inshore areas of South Georgia. If we came to grief on the rocks, or were caught by an Exocet missile, there was at least a change of beaching the ship, or pushing her up on a rock so we might have a short swim for the shore. The chances of many surviving hypothermia with nobody to rescue us were not good, but at least there was a chance.

My experience of commanding *Arrow*, the first Exocet-fitted frigate, was invaluable. I knew exactly what sort of tactical advantage the *Guerrico* or the *Granville* had to get to fire a successful shot at the *Plum*. This meant we were to spend a lot of time in the fjord – hiding behind a rock by day and emerging like Dracula after dark. Again the idea was to look like an iceberg. That was not easy for a red-painted ship during the day.

One worry was that we had little idea of the extent of the submarine threat. I knew only that their submarines had sailed and that underwater *Endurance* sounded like Big Ben. We had no capability for dimming the noise of the generators or the main diesel engines. In submarine terms this made us an almost ridiculously obvious target.

We turned the Main Signal Office (the MSO) into an operations room. This is where we conducted our strategy meetings. I had another excellent ally in Bill Hurst, a mariner of my own vintage who for some extraordinary reason had not been promoted to full Commander. He certainly proved his worth in *Endurance*, not only as a particularly efficient Navigating Officer but as a highly resourceful and valued confidant.

Tony Ellerbeck was a different sort. There is invariably someone like him in every ship. He could be erratic, but he was also hugely resilient and had an enormous store of initiative and courage. On the day South Georgia was invaded I dispatched him, armed with a machine gun to do a covert recce. This was a high-risk operation; if he had carried the AS12 missiles he would not have had the range to reach Cumberland Bay before nightfall. It was like going into the lion's den with a peashooter. For this, and later for flying operations during the recapture of South Georgia for the most part in the sort of weather in which you wouldn't even let a domestic cat out of the house, he thoroughly deserved his DSC.

There were many problems as we approached the battle area.

Tony's recce lasted from 15.00 to 17.00 when the Wasp returned and reported that the *Guerrico* was underway from Grytviken but damaged, and that *Paraiso* looked relatively normal. We could only guess at the damage wrought upon the *Guerrico* by our marines. The report indicated that she was limping about in the harbour with at least some smoke coming from the super-structure. This was mightily cheering news. At least it was one blow against the Argies.

Nobody was sighted at the base and we presumed they had all been taken prisoner. Again, though it was pure supposition, we thought it was likely they were embarked in the *Bahia Paraiso*.

Our discussions now turned to a missile attack on the *Guerrico*, but this was not to be. I was instructed firmly from Whitehall that preservation was the name of the game. We were to hole up as much as we could during the day and observe what we could of the Argentine ship movements. It was back to the waiting game while the Task Force steamed down from Ascension. We knew that was likely to take several days. But at least we could begin to plan the next phase. Every Barker brain-wave was discussed with the Command Team, refined and honed. I think this had much to do with our survival.

On 4 April I sent the helicopters on another covert recce to St Andrew's Bay and beyond. There was no sign of the *Guerrico* or the *Paraiso*. Our assumption now was that they were at Leith. Was the *Guerrico* still licking her wounds? We thought, wish-fully, that it was likely. Later the Wasp overflew Cumberland Bay and confirmed that neither of the ships were in the Bay area.

Our choice of hidey hole was less easy. There were plenty of options but none with which we were completely comfortable. But it was a decision that had to be made quickly. I opted for Larsen Harbour and hoped that this uncharted creek did not present any unforeseen dangers.

My old friend Captain Freddy Fox, then Chief Staff Officer Operations at Northwood, telephoned to ask about the possi-bility of evacuating the remaining personnel, including the one field team who had not been captured – Trevor Edwards, Damian Sanderson, Campbell Gemmil and Ian Barker – who were still up country in the survey hut at Lyell Glacier. We were of course also deeply concerned about Cindy and Annie, particularly as we now knew that Argentine troops were soon to be put ashore to garrison Leith and Grytviken. By that stage Peter Stark had been joined by two other BAS personnel, Tony North and Miles Plant, to look after the girls.

It could only be a matter of time before the BAS was captured. This meant that other parties, such as the group on Bird Island, would be isolated. They may escape immediate capture, but if the area was occupied by Argentina for any length of time their position could become precarious.

In war conditions one is sometimes asked to do faintly ridiculous things. I was ordered to make voice signals, on either UHF or VHF, to an imaginary submarine. The logic of this was reasonable enough, other than the insistence that I should communicate in plain language. I do not imagine that the Argentines believed for a moment that we would be imprudent enough to hold 'on air' discussions in this way.

On board *Endurance* we were more concerned about another kind of disinformation. How could we judge the prospects of the UK media picking up some of the more outrageous Argentine propaganda? Thus far the *Endurance* story had been handled responsibly, most typically along the lines of a 'lone vigil'. But how would they respond to Argentine radio claims that all that was left of *Endurance* was a smouldering wreck in a South Georgia harbour? As it happened Whitehall dealt with this efficiently. The fantasy never appeared in the UK press, although it was picked up in the Falklands and many of the Islanders were concerned about our fate. Happily not much of our premature obituaries was communicated to our families.

My main worry was the unique and special family that the ship's company had become. They came on the bridge and aired their views as usual and, whenever possible, I would find my way below to see how they were getting on. I was invariably greeted with a smile and a joke, but knew that deep down they were all as worried as I was. I shared what information I could as soon as I could. Nothing is worse than uncertainty and second guessing.

The men in the Senior Ratings' Mess were an absolute tower

of strength in the example they set, and they gave me support which went way beyond the call of duty. At the first hint of dissent among junior ratings, they would jump in and say, 'Well this is what the skipper wants and this is how we're going to do it.' It was a measure of support that I was not sure I deserved, but it made me more determined than ever not to let them down. On reflection I have little doubt that this was the force of group psychology working on me. I was not to be given the luxury of seriously considering my own fallibility. If they believed in Nick Barker then what right had he to doubt himself? I just hoped that if the worst came to the worst, I could borrow a trick from someone with genuine messianic credentials. But then don't ice patrolmen always walk on water?

Some members of the film team were openly apprehensive and were determined to get ashore just as soon as possible. In their situation I may well have reacted in the same way. I could only promise to put them on board the first homeward-bound grey ship we met. But senior members of the team were more resilient. John Tippey and his sidekick, Bob Mahoney, were keen to stay with us and see out the situation. So were some of the others.

Our orders were to remain in the area. That did little to prevent feelings of fear and isolation building inside each of us. And we were hungry too. We had missed our victualling stopover at Montevideo so it was strict rations now. We tried to vary it as much as possible but even the miracle workers of the galley could do little to disguise another round of powdered spud. As the freezers emptied the Magellan crabs were rediscovered. This Chilean contribution to the War Effort was hugely appreciated.

Chapter 10

RETAKING SOUTH GEORGIA

On 4 April I was ordered to proceed immediately to Ascension. I noted in my diary that this was the third time I had been ordered to proceed somewhere forthwith. Each time without apparent good reason, each time suddenly, and each time without discussion. Perhaps, I thought, this is due to a new Staff exerting their influence, but I suspected it was knee-jerk thinking. If decisions can be so muddled over one ship I feared seriously for the fleet coming south.

So on 5 April, after seventeen days in and out of the South Georgia area, we did our best to reassure Cindy and Annie, and the scientists left in the hinterland, that we would soon return. Given our recent progress, I was less than convinced about that. We also dropped private messages for them in empty beer cans asking them also to communicate with us as if we were still in the area, and to make the kind of noises that amounted to false trails.

We already knew that our passage north was not in fact to Ascension, but to a rendezvous with one of the RFAs, the *Fort Austin*.

For the next three days we made steady progress north. During the middle of this period, on the 7th, we were instructed to join a group which consisted of *Antrim*, a guided weapon destroyer, *Plymouth*, a frigate and the tanker *Tidespring*, which had a whole company of Royal Marines embarked. This was part of a forward group deployed to recapture South Georgia. We were delighted to be involved in this group, particularly as we had failed to prevent the capture of the island. It was also an opportunity to transfer my film team at our replenishment rendezvous with the *Fort Austin*, which was well ahead of the warships.

We also had news of our ship's Royal Marine Detachment. This was thanks to the BBC World Service, by far our most useful source of Intelligence during the early days of the Conflict. They were in fact already in Uruguay where they were joined by the other marines who had been captured in the Falklands. They were soon to return to the UK.

Since the news that we were to join the group the ship's company had become decidedly more determined to give the Argentines a bloody nose. But our one and only Chinese dhobi man, Mr Yu, wanted to go home. In fact the poor chap had come to my cabin, full of tears.

'My missy she say me not on ship for war. Me go on ship for laundly. Please to go home with men who make film.'

I had to tell him I did not think this was possible. I only had clearance for the film team at this stage, and the NAAFI staff, who were also civilians, had said that they wanted to stay. He was not happy with this response and I certainly did not want any civilian on board against his will. I promised to do what I could. Eventually he got a deluxe passage in the *QE2*.

By 12 April we had reached warmer waters. This, in itself was a relief to everyone. Morale was further boosted when we met the *Fort Austin*. I had a friendly meeting with her captain, Commodore Sam Dunlop, who was the Senior Officer of the Royal Fleet Auxiliary. It was as if a terrible dark shadow was lifting. I no longer felt I was fighting this war on my own. It was also oddly encouraging to hear his complaints about not being kept in the picture. When ordered to divert, the *Fort Austin* had in fact been on her way home after six months in the Middle East!

We asked for eggs, bangers, spuds and various other things, particularly meat. They couldn't provide the first two items on our list, but we did well enough. I also remember a Wessex coming over to drop joints of meat on our flight deck. Just before she hovered over the flight deck to drop them, she developed mechanical trouble and had to jettison the load of meat straight into the sea. After the privations of recent weeks it occurred to several of us to jump overboard to 'rescue' what we could before it sank.

We also exchanged our film team for SBS and SAS troops, who were all set for reconnaissance incursions in preparation for the recapture of South Georgia. The sailors were somewhat in awe of these men as they sat on the upper deck in the sunshine, sharpening up their knives and garrotting wires and generally checking very anti-social bits of kit. We really did have the trained killers on board this time.

But it's a case of horses for courses. The *Endurance* soon sorted them out when the weather got rough. Indeed, the most violent thing we saw was the shade of green that some of them turned. Given a rough sea any stomach can turn to jelly, but it did help to reduce the awe factor. And I'm sure it added an extra incentive for them to get ashore.

Early on the morning of 14 April we met our group. It was quite an emotional encounter. As we steamed up towards *Antrim* they 'cleared lower deck' for us. All their sailors manned the sides, hands on guard-rails, as we approached, and, as we passed them, they cheered us to a man. It was quite unexpected. *Plymouth* followed with a cheer that was less orchestrated but equally welcoming.

For the next five days we plugged our way south, transferring men regularly by helicopter or boat for meetings. One new rôle earmarked for *Endurance* was that of landing craft. We were to run up the beach just off Grytviken with our ice-breaking bow to deliver M Company, 42 Commando. *Plymouth* and *Antrim* were to provide the covering bombardment with their 4.5 inch guns. We were also preparing to do a reconnaissance, and, if necessary, to take out Argentine positions ahead of the bombardment and landing.

I was beginning to feel really useful. Part of this was to do with my 'expert' knowledge of conditions we were sure to encounter, and of course the island itself. But it was also to do with operating as part of a team. By definition almost, the Captain of *Endurance* has a more solitary job than most. In recent weeks it had felt like solitary confinement.

Captain Brian Young of the *Antrim*, designated as the Group Commander, was a senior Fleet Air Arm Captain. He had been dispatched south to take over command of the area. This inevitably caused some resentment on our part. We felt we were the seasoned campaigners who were best placed to understand the situation and conditions. It was true that we did not have an anti-submarine capability, or anti-aircraft guns, or even all the communications required, but I still believe the best response would have been for Admiral Sandy Woodward to send two or three frigates commanded by commanders, or a captain junior to myself. This would have meant we could have led the recapture.

The ad hoc arrangement that was hurriedly cobbled together was one that was difficult for Brian Young to co-ordinate. Of course we needed a company of marines led by someone of the experience of Major Guy Sheridan, and we also needed special forces to insert at an earlier stage. But they could have been better co-ordinated. The point is either Brian Young was in charge or he wasn't. There were certainly times during the operation when it was hard to tell. Most of the directives came from a variety of sources in the UK.

Whenever signals were made to the Ministry about the state of the operation it was always '*Antrim* this and *Antrim* that'. At times we felt *Antrim* was the only ship involved. This caused massive resentment among the other elements of the force, particularly as the signal traffic conveyed a great deal of uncertainty. We had learned the hard way that flying operations in the South Atlantic, even in relatively good conditions, are extremely dangerous and difficult. My pilots and I tried to explain that landing on South Georgia was like landing on the Alps in the middle of the sea and we should be prepared for this. But nevertheless the SAS insisted on two to three days' reconnaissance in order to establish exactly where the Argentine troops were dug in, where they were based, and how they were operating. After all the previous delays I found this approach frustrating. But it was understood. There is nothing gung ho about the SAS. When they go in, they go in to win.

On 21 April, as we arrived back again in the South Georgia

area, the weather turned from nasty to perfectly bloody. We experienced blizzard conditions most of the time with wind speeds upwards of 30–40 knots. This did little to facilitate our reconnaissance programme, but we did manage to get a helicopter to Cindy and Annie at St Andrew's Bay. Chief Petty Officer Scott, our Stores Chief, replaced Peter Stark as 'chief minder'. We needed Peter for his detailed local knowledge. He also proved invaluable in advising me on the positions of the Argentines. That information was to be vital in deciding where best to insert our special forces.

Our ultimate target was the main base which was now firmly established at Grytviken. One little snag was that between the spit of land from where we were operating and the Grytviken base there was a large glacier and very mountainous terrain. We either had to land our special forces on the other side of the glacier, which would certainly have given the game away, or land them on one side of the bay and boat them across in Geminis to the other side. This too was a risky strategy. It would be all too easy for small particles of ice to puncture the boats. Although we had some problems persuading the SBS, this was clearly the best option.

While at anchor in Hound Bay trying to operate our helicopters in reasonably calm conditions, we got our starboard anchor very firmly stuck under a rock. After various attempts to release it failed we had to slip it, together with three shackles of cable. Despite even greater efforts to retrieve it later, we failed again. In mitigation I could point out that there were distractions. We were in an uncharted bay in blizzard conditions almost within bow shot of an enemy submarine. Souvenir hunters would be well rewarded by a plodge around those chilly waters.

The Special Forces were divided into several different troops, all of whom had different tasks. Some were to cross the glacier at Fortuna, some to make an overland approach. *Endurance*'s men were the mountain troops under the command of Captain John Hamilton, a very fine man, who had earned a reputation as a particularly courageous officer. Sadly he was later killed.

Although 'our' SAS were very popular, there was certainly the view that they were in the wrong ship. If these had been the amphibious group it would have made more sense. And we did have a special problem in getting our local knowledge across to Cedric Delves, the SAS Commander. He came across by helicopter to talk to us. I could tell right away we were not convincing him that the Fortuna Glacier was a rotten option. He even called his HQ in Hereford for 'impartial' advice: I have since learned he was talking to two Everest climbers. But it depends who you talk to and what you want to hear. He was convinced that the glacier should not be an impossible option. The truth is that it matters little if you are experienced or a novice. The weather that constantly changes the mood of the glacier is utterly indifferent.

We pointed out that only Shackleton in 1916, and one other expedition in 1964, had made it across South Georgia and in both cases they had been fortunate with the weather. Crossing a glacier is always a risky business. This could be mitigated somewhat by pacing it steadily – he'd allocated four days – but with a further bad weather forecast the distance from the objective only added to the risk.

Royal Marines Major Guy Sheridan, in overall command of land operations, was an experienced Himalayan climber. He was equally unhappy about the choice of Fortuna and discreetly tried to counsel Delves rather than risk appearing to undermine him. He should, I believe, have taken a firmer line and told Delves to forget Fortuna altogether. But Sheridan's directive was straightforward – to determine Argentine strength and dispositions in Husvik, Stromness and Leith. How Delves achieved that aim was down to him, even if he declined to accept the opinions of those best placed to offer sound advice.

In addition to the marines, SAS and SBS, we had two 'forward spotting officers'. They were Bombardment Support Liaison Officers in the form of Colonel Keith Eaves (in the *Antrim*) and 'Brum' Richards (in the *Plymouth*). Their job was to be parked ashore in appropriate positions so that, when the ship's bombardment came, they could direct the fire onto the target. Of course they could not do their job until the SBS and the SAS had determined exactly what the targets actually were.

The helicopters to be used for the insertions were 2 Wessex 5s

180

(troop carriers from the *Tidespring*, whose pilots, used to insertions, were known as 'Junglies') Another Wessex, an anti-submarine helicopter, (normally based on *Antrim* without as much room for troop-carrying) was piloted by Lieutenant-Commander Ian Stanley.

During the night of 20/21 April two ships, the *Antrim* and the tanker, were given the go-ahead from the back-seat drivers at Northwood to move in to within 15 miles of South Georgia. As there was a gale blowing from the north-east and visibility was down to about two miles with a cloud base of about 400 feet they asked for a delay.

At 09.30 the *Antrim*'s helicopter was despatched to look at the weather inshore which would determine if the operation was possible. This was the first time Ian Stanley and his crew had seen South Georgia. Maps give little indication of the way that majestic mountains leap straight from the sea. 'Why didn't you tell us?' they asked later. We had told them with no little enthusiasm. It is just that the place is so spectacular nobody can ever be fully prepared for it.

When Ian Stanley got to the Fortuna he decided that there were no enemy troops there. He reported back to *Antrim* that the terrain was very much as described by the *Endurance* Officers. Delves and Hamilton (the SAS leader on the ground) asked for a flight in to have a look ahead of their troops. When they went in, they asked the helicopter be put down on the glacier. Apart from kicking up so much snow they had a virtual white-out, and a great deal of buffeting, they had no horizon to judge the inclination of the helicopter. The ice, snow and cloud all blended into one and they put the wheels down into a crevasse. From there they led in the two Junglies. The visibility was poor, but the helicopters went down exactly where they were wanted. The troops jumped out, got their gear and set off roped in groups of four. When the pilots returned to their ships they said they hoped they'd never have to go back to that 'hellhole'.

That night the weather conditions were extreme. The wind had got up to Force 11 or 12, increasing the chill factor enormously. The ships were bounding all over the place. The helicopters were in a perilous state. In the case of *Tidespring*, one was in the hangar and the other lashed on the deck.

On the glacier the SAS made themselves as comfortable as possible in the small crevasses. Some late indecision had meant a delay in putting them ashore and they had made little progress before nightfall. The night took its toll on SAS morale. By morning John Hamilton was forced to accept that any advance or operation in a military context was going to be difficult. A bitterly cold and wet start and very little progress forced him to bow to the inevitable. Another night in these conditions would mean his men would face enemies more feared than the Argentines – hypothermia and frostbite. So, bitterly disappointed, he told Cedric Delves that he was going to pull out. Three dismayed Wessex helicopter pilots prepared to bring the SAS back again.

We tried hard to find flat seas to provide a stable platform for the helicopters. Given the conditions 'flat' could only mean 'feasible' in terms of take off and landing. But for the urgency of the situation no helicopter would have flown that day. But the rescue attempt had to go ahead. The pilot of the first Wessex, Mike Tidd, told Captain Young that, while he was hovering, he saw a snow squall sweeping towards him half a mile away on the crest of the glacier. But apart from that it was clear. As any kind of visibility could not be guaranteed for long he asked permission to lift off ahead of the other helicopters. The snow squall overtook him, he suffered a white-out and he lost the horizon. This was something almost familiar to *Endurance*'s pilots but it was a 'pleasure' he had not experienced before. During the white-out he began losing altitude very fast and hit the ground at about thirty knots. All this was observed through the snow by Ian Stanley, who said Mike was doing well up to the moment he lost visual references. The loss of altitude proved critical; one of the rotor tips hit the surface of the glacier and the helicopter slewed round on its side and came to rest on the far side of a dip. But miraculously there were no discernible casualties apart from a cut above the eye of one of the staff sergeants. They climbed out of the stricken Wessex, were divided into two groups and loaded into the remaining helicopters. Once again Ian Stanley led the way out. His ASW helicopter had the right sort of instruments, including an altimeter, to help take him over the ice ridges. He was, in effect, the 'shepherd'. The other pilot was flying visually as close to the ASW as he dared.

It went pretty well until they were buffeted by another snow squall. The white-out had the same effect as before and the Wessex 5 started losing height. The inevitable followed. The Wessex 5 hit the ground too heavily. A wheel was caught in a small crevasse and she went over on her starboard side. Again there was a pile of entangled legs trying to become disentangled. Ian Stanley landed again and, after picking up another bruised crew, took his haul of survivors back to the ship. This was achieved successfully and Ian reported that the two Wessex 5s were damaged beyond repair. In military terms the whole operation had become a monumental cock-up.

By mid-afternoon the weather conditions improved slightly. At 16.30 the one remaining Wessex was again flying in over the top of Cape Constance and approaching the Fortuna ice cliff. But conditions proved to be worse inshore: the wind was stronger and there was a lot of cloud. So instead of going up the glacier at low level Ian climbed to 3,000 feet to the apex of the cloud bank which gave him about 600 feet clearance over the glacier itself, but nothing to spare over the peaks. It was then that he saw the orange dayglo life rafts below. These had been inflated partly as a visual marker, but also, when inverted, they provided a refuge for the men to huddle together. Ian Stanley managed to land his helicopter without incident close to where the troops were sheltering. He decided that there was no option but to sardine all sixteen of them into an aircraft which would normally have room for about six. The normal laden weight of a Wessex 3 is about 13,500 pounds. When Ian departed from the glacier, still in appalling conditions, he did so with a weight in excess of 15,000 pounds. To our terrific relief he got away with it.

The own goals which led to the loss of two troop-carrying helicopters were more than an embarrassment. They threatened the future of the operation. And all this had been achieved without firing a shot in anger. It was a sickener, but who says 'I told you so' to the SAS?

But the fundamental problem remained. How were we now to put the SBS ashore? Our Wasps were uncomfortable and barely equipped to carry three in the back. They were simply not the right tools for the job. And Tony Ellerbeck was still suffering regular doses of the katabatics – enough to put the wind up even the most experienced pilot.

So far our helicopters had achieved the landing of twelve SBS in appalling weather conditions – no mean feat. With their 'Morris Minors' Tony Ellerbeck and Tim Finding had achieved what the Rolls Royces had failed to do on Fortuna. This was largely a reconnaissance mission, although they were also preparing to attack the Argentine base half a dozen miles away across the bay.

We had seen Tony Ellerbeck's problems and were extremely anxious. Late that night we too decided to call off the operation, and, as darkness fell, we recalled the troops. So we had a different troop of SAS and some SBS on board, all itching to get ashore and get on with their job.

There were more meetings. Cedric Delves and Guy Sheridan accepted that Fortuna was a dead loss, and the next plan was to use the SAS amphibious troop, putting them in pretty close to the base, hopefully without being spotted by the Argentines. To the best of my knowledge, at this stage the Argentines didn't know we were at sea outside the bay, although there had been several overflights by Argentine Boeing 737s and also by Russian radar satellites. We knew the times of the Russian satellites and so we would 'close up the ships', which we hoped had the effect of making the four ships appear as a single contact, probably an iceberg.

I'm sure the damage done by Keith Mills' anti-tank mortar to the *Guerrico* was passing through Brian Young's mind as he crept forward in *Antrim* on 22 April. The intention was to drop the SAS amphibious troops and their Geminis overboard about 3,000 yards short of Grass Island, which was itself some three miles east of one of the Argentine bases. As the later Geminis were being dropped, the first ones were already having trouble with their outboard motors. One boat had to be taken in tow.

Again the weather conditions began to deteriorate. The

boating skills of the SAS also left something to be desired. At one point two boats were being towed by a single source when the engine died. So three were tied together while the troops paddled like hell for Grass Island. Then they decided to cut the lines and let each boat fend for itself.

By 07.30 on the 23rd *Antrim* had a pretty clear picture of the night's events. Only three of the Geminis had made it to Grass Island and these had now been deflated and hidden in the tussock grass. As far as we knew they were undetected. Of the other two inflatables nothing was known. Wonderful troops though they are, the way the first two operations had gone was hardly filling us with confidence. Happily the other two boats were soon found safe and sound.

Plymouth and *Endurance* were operating together, as were *Antrim* and *Tidespring*. Unfortunately relations between the two groups were deteriorating. I believe there was a certain amount of parochialism and jealousy creeping in as we, the 'experts on the spot' were being led by *Antrim*. There were certainly times when I felt like the experienced hand being coached by the rookie. I was sure that more notice should have been taken of my aviators and seaman officers.

Although I liked and admired her Captain, he was making decision after decision with which we disagreed. We still felt that our local knowledge was being undervalued and that if they had only listened to us the mistakes of Fortuna Glacier and Grass Island could have been avoided. And yet *Antrim* and her helicopter pilot were being hailed as heroes from a situation that arose out of a débâcle. Such is the nature of war.

Later that day *Endurance* reported an Argentine C130 Hercules aeroplane which had been sighted by two BAS personnel up in the north-west of South Georgia flying down the coast. This meant that it must have overflown some of our ships and our cover was blown. At 14.30 our 'listeners' intercepted an HF transmission which we believed came from an Argentine submarine. The strength of the signal seemed to indicate that the submarine was within a hundred miles of us. This made it closer still to *Antrim*.

The Intelligence cells in London and Northwood were now

getting their act together. Captain Young was informed by the Chief of Staff, Admiral Sir David Halifax, of the presence of a submarine, the *Santa Fe*, in our area. At the same time *Tidespring* was out to sea doing a pump-over of fuel from another tanker, the *Brambleleaf*, which had just arrived in the area. It was decided that the *Plymouth* should make best speed south-east to be in a better position to defend the two tankers, and thence to escort them to a position 200 miles from the island.

After consultations with his military advisers, Brian Young had decided to try and put M Company of Royal Marines ashore in Stromness Bay at first light. We were to remain in the vicinity of Hound Bay to support the SBS who were already ashore.

The air cover provided by the Hercules for the submarine determined that orders should be given to Captain John Coward, of the *Brilliant*, to head south as fast as possible, leaving his little force of Type 42 destroyers, *Coventry*, *Glasgow* and *Sheffield*, along with my old ship, the *Arrow*, (and another tanker with a full load of fuel) to follow as best they may. Brian Young knew that the *Brilliant* was one of the best equipped ASW ships. The *Brilliant* had accommodation for two Lynx helicopters: most frigates and destroyers could only carry one. But even at best speed, and given reasonably good weather conditions, she would not reach our group until next day, 24 April.

At that stage we did not know that our own submarine, the *Conqueror*, was also in the vicinity. She had been ordered to leave South Georgia and proceed north-west, at reasonably high speed, to act as a forward screen for the *Brilliant* Group.

We were only too aware that our booming diesel engine would act as a magnet for the *Santa Fe*. This meant, yet again, we had to pretend to be an iceberg by night and hide in the fjords by day. To the best of my knowledge we remained undetected by the *Santa Fe* in these early stages, but we later thought we had been spotted by an Argentine Boeing 737.

I had a frustrating morning. The officers commanding the remaining SBS troops, the SAS and the Royal Marines all kept appearing on the bridge, singly, in pairs, and as a full deputation, demanding that they should be landed as soon as possible. I fundamentally agreed with them. In fact I wanted rid of them.

Normally the rivalry between the units would have been pretty good fun, but in their resolve to get to grips with the enemy they were constantly hyped up. You can only take so much of the macho hero stuff and I had certainly had enough. I was also beginning to fear they may dissipate some of that pent-up aggression on each other, or perhaps some poor sailor if he dared to speak a word out of turn or looked at them in a way they didn't like.

Meanwhile I had been trying to get hold of Sir David Halifax on the satellite telephone only to be informed that he was out at lunch. That was at 12.30. I asked if he would kindly ring me back as soon as possible. Without trying to sound over anxious I did make it clear that the matter was pretty urgent. He finally called at around 16.00.

'Are you having a bit of a problem, Nick?' he enquired. His measured tone reminded me oddly of my family physician. It's strange how this automatically demands an equally detached response.

'Yes Sir, we're in a bit of a pickle.'

'Perhaps you'd like to tell me about it?'

'In the background, you may hear the ship closing up at Action Stations. Actually Sir, at this very moment we're trying to bring our peashooters to bear on an overflying 737. Unhappily I believe he is out of range. But perhaps you may care to hear our translation of the 737's intercepted messages in Spanish to the *Santa Fe*. They're giving our position and saying that we're landing Special Forces.'

'Oh I don't think the submarine is that close, old chap,' he comforted. 'There's really very little to worry about.'

It was like 'take two aspirins and go to bed'. There was nothing more I could say. But I'd been listening to them speaking on VHF, which is line-of-sight only. Both signals were extremely clear. And how, from his Northwood bunker, did he know where the *Santa Fe* was?

'Very well sir,' I said lamely.

But I wasn't comforted. I felt it was best to get our special forces ashore before we were sunk. With a multi-threat situation in the offing I believe Brian Young felt that he had left *Endurance* rather exposed, so he decided that *Antrim* and *Plymouth* should head back in our direction. His other preoccupation was in formulating a plan to try and deal with the submarine. The threat of an attack by submarine is every sailor's greatest fear.

This was a situation that should not have arisen. Our main force should not have been taken 200 miles to the east. Worse still, if the right ships had been deployed to screen *Endurance* we would have been in a position to hunt and sink the *Santa Fe* just as soon as we knew the threat was real. We had a massive asset in the submarine HMS *Conqueror* with her first-class ASW facility. If this resource had been combined with say two or three modern frigates, rather than the geriatric *Antrim*, we could have made short work of the submarine.

In the meantime we had intercepted several encoded messages from the submarine which we sent back to UK to be broken. I was woken during the course of the night when one deciphered message came back to us. It confirmed that *Santa Fe* was in our area and almost certainly heading straight for Grytviken where she was to land some special forces. These presumably were reinforcements for Lieutenant-Commander Astiz, the Garrison Commander. The last part of the deciphered message was the worst possible news for us. The *Santa Fe* had orders to sink *Endurance*! This did little to enhance my beauty sleep. The possibilities were whirling through my mind. We had to take the attack to the enemy. We had to find the *Santa Fe* as soon as possible.

Antrim's Wessex helicopter, the 'Humphrey', had been sent on ahead, flying over the wave tops at about 200 feet. Her mission was to search out the entrance to Cumberland Bay. Both of our helicopters were ranged on deck with AS12 guided missiles at the ready should the submarine be located. We couldn't use our Wasps in the search; carrying the AS12s seriously limited their range.

Chris Parry, the Wessex observer, spotted a submarine ahead. It was, however, impossible at the time to determine if this was the *Santa Fe* or the *Conqueror*. But pretty soon the confirmation was made. This was an ex-American Guppy Class, the *Santa Fe*. And she was on the surface.

Chris Parry was in full control of the attack, which left Ian Stanley to do the driving. They had Mark 11 depth charges which in weapons technology terms are just a modest advance on the musket. Basically they are big bangs in a tin. They are most effective in fairly shallow water; the chances of doing serious damage to a surface target are not good. The Wessex dropped a couple of these and two big splashes straddled the submarine. These may have shaken things around a bit but the damage was not enough to halt *Santa Fe* in her tracks. She turned and headed back towards Grytviken. But if the attack had achieved nothing more it must have caused some ringing ears.

Following this first attack, a Lynx, armed with a single homing torpedo, was dispatched from *Brilliant*. This is a much more sophisticated weapon, particularly efficient when used against deep draft surface targets, or submerged submarines. The Lynx also had a machine gun.

We were pretty close to the action and I thought it was about time to join in. I launched one of our Wasps – the 434. Tony Ellerbeck had been on 'deck alert' since the night before pending a sight report. He was itching to have a go but there was a snag – the success of attacks on *Santa Fe* depended on co-ordination. However, *Endurance*'s Wasps were fitted with radio kit which was entirely different from the rest of the Royal Navy and the two systems weren't compatible! The only way round this was for the ship to be a communication interface which was less than ideal in a situation where responses may have to be made very quickly.

Tony had just reached the tip of the peninsula at the edge of the bay when we called him to say we'd overheard a Mayday call from the *Santa Fe*, giving her position. The observer, David Wells, picked up a target at two miles and they went through their pre-release checks. But when he tried to fire the port missile nothing happened. He repeated the checks and the starboard AS12 went away. David steered it through the turbulence and obtained a hit on the starboard side of the fin.

A machine gunner who had been firing earlier at the Lynx was knocked back through a door and fell down the hatch into the control room. His sudden arrival, complete with a mangled

189

blood-stained leg, caused much anguish. But the AS12 had not exploded on impact because the fin is made of glass-reinforced plastic which provides little resistance.

Tony Ellerbeck lined up for another attack and David Wells launched the port AS12 from a height of 100 feet and a range of three miles. He was aiming it at the junction of the fin with the hull. But the missile dived into the sea 30 yards short of the submarine's port quarter. The 434 then turned away and flew back to *Endurance* for a reload.

The submarine's captain had just two options. He could head back for the quayside at Grytviken and unload the ship's company quickly, or he could dive and hope to escape with no more damage than had already been inflicted. We learned later that the *Santa Fe* already had a damaged hatch which meant her water-tight integrity was not complete. Also a torpedo from the Lynx would be more likely to score a hit on a submerged submarine. Her Captain decided to stay in the control room and try to pilot the submarine back alongside the jetty.

Meanwhile Tony Ellerbeck had reloaded his Wasp with another pair of AS12s in double quick time. Returning to the attack he came round the tip of the peninsula at about 100 feet, heading straight for the submarine. As he approached her port quarter David Wells fired the missile. This one was a 'rogue' which dived all over the place on the end of its wire and finally disappeared from view. Tony closed again, David fired again. This one plunged straight through the fin. The cry of 'Bull's eye!' from the Lynx resounded through the radio net. Tony observed the submarine for several minutes before flying back to *Endurance* to rearm again.

At this stage a Wasp from *Plymouth* joined the AS12 attack, and our other Wasp, the 435, piloted by Tim Finding, closed on the *Santa Fe* and found a line of sight with the port missile. This struck the surface of the sea just short of the submarine. Tim continued closing at 60 knots whilst observer Bob Nadin selected the starboard missile. They let it go at a range of two miles. Nadin's control of the missile via the joystick was as good as his control over a football. The missile went straight through the fin but again failed to explode.

Although the *Santa Fe* was now close to the jetty she was a spent force. She even struggled to park alongside. Although none of us appreciated the historical significance of the event at the time, this was the first time since 1945 that helicopters had been deployed against a submarine. It was also the very first time that a submarine had been effectively destroyed exclusively by helicopter action.

By 10.45 all helicopters had returned to their parent ships. None of them had been damaged and all the aircrew were safe. There was understandable jubilation all round. In *Endurance* it was not perhaps so much for what we had achieved but for the fact that we had helped to eliminate our most feared enemy. There was also a sense of enormous relief that we had joined our Royal Marines in firing a few shots in anger. The only slightly subdued congratulations came from the aircrew and marines on board the *Tidespring*. This was understandable. We knew all about the pent-up frustration of waiting to engage the enemy. The sight of the submarine leaking oil into the harbour and her ship's company scurrying up the hill dispelled any slight doubts we had that she could still be a threat.

There were now more meetings on board *Antrim*. Perhaps the success against *Santa Fe* fostered a greater unity of purpose. We decided the time had come to abandon convoluted schemes and strategies. The time had come for a direct attack on Grytviken. Gun spotters were to be put ashore and four-and-a-half-inch guns were to range on to specific targets. The bombardment would be followed by an attempted helicopter landing of troops. Of what we had left, *Brilliant*'s two Lynx were best able to cope. They could carry eight fully armed men each, and at a pinch the Humphrey could take a similar number. Our little Wasps could only manage four at best.

In order to maintain momentum we had to round up resources as soon as possible. The main troop force was still on board *Tidespring* 100 miles away and we judged it best not to wait for them. In all we could muster just seventy-four men – the SAS now recovered from Fortuna, Captain Chris Nunn and some of the men of 42 Commando Royal Marines, plus a

191

mortar troop and parts of various smaller units. This little ad hoc army would lead the recapture of South Georgia.

At about 14.00 *Antrim* and *Plymouth* got into formation and went up and down the coast pouring shells behind the enemy positions. Tony Ellerbeck was now airborne with a borrowed portable HF radio so that he could communicate direct with the other ships and helicopters taking in the advance parties. They flew in as low as they dared – at about 15 feet to try to 'hide' behind the cliff as they went through the narrow gap of Merton Passage. This was the same channel that *Endurance* had used to avoid detection. It was hardly less dangerous for the helicopters in the funnelling wind. This was a commando style assault force without the benefit of commando helicopters. Furthermore, none of the pilots was trained for amphibious warfare and the troops would not be able to make the characteristic rapid exit on landing.

Those being dropped ashore knew it was a death or glory operation. Reconnaissance had been sketchy to say the least. Nobody could be sure of the defensive positions or indeed how well they were defended. I have heard it said that Military Intelligence is a contradiction in terms and that has sometimes proved to be the case. In this instance the men had to rely purely on their own instinct and intelligence and in my view that may well have contributed to their success.

There is a flattish area to one side of Grytviken called Hestesletten. This is where the majority landed, ready to make their relatively short and easy approach over gently sloping terrain towards what we believed to be the main Argentine base. Meanwhile the *Plymouth* was creating a diversion to the north by shelling Brown Mountain. We hoped that the Argentines would believe that the main ground attack would follow from the same direction.

In those two hours *Antrim* had fired seventy rounds and *Plymouth* 150. Nobody stopped to think then, but this must have added up to several months' training allowance. Under the cover of *Plymouth*'s fire, *Antrim* moved into the bay, to one side of the cove. I felt hugely optimistic about the chances of success. My only regret was that *Endurance*'s marines, who had

192

defended their position so valiantly, were not going to have the pleasure of recapturing the island.

As Cedric Delves and his SAS moved over the top of King Edward Point they passed a number of Argentine positions. None of them offered any resistance; they just threw their arms up and surrendered. And it seemed hardly any time at all before a white flag was hoisted on the one and only flag pole at the base itself.

It has to be said that our troops were fortunate. Any serious resistance could have caused heavy casualties. Guy Sheridan in particular was unhappy at the way in which sections of the ad hoc force seemed determined to do their own thing. On the ground at least, the operation, with better communications, was better co-ordinated than anything to date.

One disaster in waiting was overcome ridiculously easily. The base was heavily mined but there were any number of Argentines ready and willing to point out exactly where they all were. Indeed the Grytviken garrison and the ship's company from the *Santa Fe* were almost too eager to be rounded up. By 17.30 it was all over at Grytviken. The whole operation had taken less than four hours. Brian Young sent a confident, if somewhat premature, signal to the Commander-in-Chief. He said:

Be pleased to inform Her Majesty that the White Ensign flies alongside the Union Flag at Grytviken, South Georgia. God save the Queen.

But it was not over. The small garrison at the other old whaling station at Leith, round the other side of Cumberland Bay, was still very much intact. The task of capturing it fell to *Plymouth* and ourselves. We persuaded the submarine captain, Lieutenant-Commander Bicain, to talk to Garrison Commander Astiz. the idea was to tell him that the game was over and that he may as well surrender. There was indeed a convoluted conversation in Spanish, at the end of which Bicain reported: 'Astiz says that he will not surrender. He will fight to the death.'

David Pentreath of the *Plymouth*, although much my own vintage, was slightly senior to me, so once again Barker was to wear the number two shirt. He, however, authorized me, as the local resident, to make a further appeal to Astiz to surrender. At first Astiz agreed because of the presence of the 'civilian' scrap metal dealers. Then, he changed his mind.

At about 21.00 I went over to *Plymouth* with some of my officers. There we decided on a sustained bombardment on Leith. We communicated this to Astiz and again invited his surrender. He responded by informing me that he was a trained underwater attack swimmer who may well be inclined to pop a limpet mine on the bottom of one of the ships during the night.

We still had 'D' squadron of SAS on board, minus the three men still missing from the Grass Island insertion. Our next move was to put them, plus our few SBS men, ashore. Their instructions were to surround the enemy but not to engage them. By this stage Astiz was again talking about surrender. It was decided that we would go in at 08.30 and accept the surrender on the football pitch. However, at about 07.30, I had second thoughts about trying to land in an area which was still effectively controlled by enemy troops. I changed the rendezvous at the last moment and Astiz reluctantly agreed.

The surrender went smoothly enough and Astiz confirmed our assumption that the building was heavily mined. In fact it proved to be so heavily mined that our suspicions were further aroused. One of the booby traps we found was particularly fiendish. There were wires leading out to the middle of the football pitch where they had marked an H for the helicopter landing. That could so easily have been the end of helicopter, crew and the poor mug who had been delegated to accept the surrender. Astiz told me he had found the prospect vaguely amusing. I told him that the white flag obviously meant nothing to him and that I did not share his sense of humour.

But there was also a moment of light relief. Tony Ellerbeck and his gang found a large quantity of condoms in Astiz's room. I asked the Argentine what he expected to find on South Georgia and he replied in excellent English, 'You never know. You have to be prepared for anything!'

I remember feeling deeply grateful that Cindy and Annie had not fallen into his clutches. Indeed I felt sorry for any woman

Yo por este medio rindo sin condiciones La
Base De Leith y las Cercanias en nombre del
Gobierno Argentino a representantes de Her
Britannic Majesty's Royal Navy, esta dia de
la fecha Lunes el 26 de abril 1982

Debido a la superioridad de las fuerzas
enemigas me entrego a fuerzas ~~Argentinas~~
Britanicas

TNCB ALFREDO ASTIZ

David Pentreath
Captain Royal Navy
HMS PLYMOUTH.

Captain
Royal Navy

195

who had encountered such a charmless man. This may seem like condemning him without a trial, but later investigations did reveal a pretty seedy background. He had been responsible for the deaths of a significant number of left-wing activists in Argentina and had been given the command of the South Georgia garrison as a reward for services. Astiz was certainly not a man to be trusted. We flew him out to the *Plymouth* in their Wasp. I had drafted their surrender document which was then translated into Spanish by one of our interpreters and beautifully calligraphed by one of our hydrographers, Chief Petty Officer Ginger Woodhouse. It was a capitulation document worthy of a mighty warrior, far too good for a slug like Astiz.

As we sat round the table for the formal submission Astiz was invited to sign the formal surrender and to write a sentence on the paper. As he was writing, I asked the interpreter what was being written. There was a pause. Then Astiz broke the silence and announced that he was recording his reason for surrender: 'the superiority of invading forces'.

'No chance of that,' said David Pentreath as he struck out the offending word. Later he told me, 'I did not care much for that man's arrogance. I was pleased to transfer him to *Endurance*.'

The mopping-up operation was not a simple task. Leith was a fortress built on mines and explosives. I was keen to get some of my people ashore; they had not set foot on land for more than two months. But there was no way I was going to let one of Astiz's little games add to the UK count of widows and orphans. Nobody went ashore until we were as certain as we could be that the area was clear.

Argentine radio was putting a different interpretation on events. We were, apparently, guilty of 'a treacherous act of war'. They also said that the Argentine forces on South Georgia, though hopelessly outnumbered, were still fighting fiercely against the British 'aggressors'. There were, of course, dozens of British casualties, and our ships were sinking all over the place.

Monday heralded the arrival of *Tidespring* with the remaining assault troops of 'M' Company on board. The poor chaps missed out on the entire operation, and, as it happened, they never made it to the Falklands either! But they did later have the satisfaction of recapturing Southern Thule and doing an excellent job as the South Georgia garrison.

The problem at this stage was prisoners. We had a ship full of stinking scrap dealers, sleeping all over the passages. We also had the obnoxious Astiz and his henchmen who we put down into the hold under SAS guard because we felt that given even half a chance they would have gutted any one of us.

We also had a ship's company of submariners who were a very different sort. Lieutenant-Commander Bicain, Captain of the *Santa Fe*, had been sitting on a beach in Mar del Plata with Tony Ellerbeck and their respective wives only a few weeks previously. Now he was a POW in our wardroom. Intrigued to know who was right about the *Santa Fe*'s position during the intercepted VHF messages, Tony asked him directly.

'So what were you doing last Saturday afternoon, about 16.00 when our boss was talking to Northwood?'

'Looking at you lot through my periscope,' he replied.

'So why didn't you shoot?'

'I don't know really, but I suppose it may have had something to do with the excellent cocktail party you gave us in Mar del Plata.'

I have a lasting impression of all those who took part in Operation Paraquat, the recapture of South Georgia. Top of my list were the exceptional feats of aviation. Indeed one of the SAS echoed my feelings when he said, 'All the airmen involved in Paraquat did a fantastic job. They just never knew when to give up.'

John Coward wrote in his official report: 'Both aircraft and aircrew are more or less dead beat after a week's flat-out flying. They have done absolute wonders and without them the invasion of South Georgia could not have happened. I greatly hope that this will not be overlooked in the accolades which follow this operation.' Happily our gallant aviators did get the recognition they deserved.

The submarine, still berthed alongside the one and only jetty at King Edward Point, was not only taking up valuable space but remained a danger because of its torpedoes and charges. We felt it was best to try to shift it to the whaling station. Captain John

Coward of the *Brilliant*, as a long-serving submariner, drew the short straw on this one. The engines were started up and they managed to get her clear of the jetty. Then she started lurching precariously. Down in the control room Chief Petty Officer Felix Artuso made a dash to blow some of the tanks to maintain buoyancy. The marines who were down there with him thought that he was trying to scuttle the submarine with them on board. In the moments that followed there was both shouting and shooting. John Coward had no idea what was going on but he heard the crack of the guns. Artuso had been shot dead. I was given the unpleasant task of conducting the enquiry. There was plenty of doubt about what exactly had happened amidst the confusion, but the Lance Corporal accused of firing the fatal bullet was cleared. We buried Artuso in the whaler's cemetery at Grytviken, not far from Ernest Shackleton.

Captain Redmond of the *Tidespring* helped us out of an equally tricky situation. He accepted the inevitability of becoming the prison ship and allowed us to transfer some of our prisoners to him. Unfortunately we had to keep Astiz.

We were also able to retrieve the British Antarctic Survey team who had been marooned up on the Lyell Glacier. We were relieved to find them in pretty good shape. After a delivery of food and beer they came down under their own steam.

Then we went round to St Andrew's Bay to collect Cindy and Annie and the BAS men who had been looking after them. It was a great pleasure to find them all in good heart and health.

Next it was a trip to Bird Island and Schlieper Bay. Tony Ellerbeck went in and evacuated the scientists and much of their equipment. There was also a crate containing a pair of South Georgia pintail ducks destined for Peter Scott's Wildfowl Trust at Slimbridge.

And as if to complete the personnel inventory the three missing SAS from Grass Island turned up, a little the worse for wear, but without having suffered serious accident or injury.

Indeed we had been extremely lucky. The *Santa Fe* had virtually surrendered to us by being on the surface. The island had been retaken more by good fortune than design. We had been on a roll. We had inserted forces without proper preparation or observation and had got away with it. Our best information had not come from any military source but from the British Antarctic Survey.

There had also been a reluctance to see *Endurance* in an obvious warlike capacity. This may have been partly a political decision. How would it have looked if *Endurance* had been the command ship for this important operation? At some point this option must have been considered. Could it have been that we were 'unarmed' or had the 'wrong communications' that mattered? Possibly so. But there have been hints at least that Sandy Woodward did not have a completely free hand. All I can say for certain is that in his account of the earlier phases of the Conflict there is very little mention of South Georgia. Much later I asked him about this.

'Were we fighting a different war?'

'No,' he said, 'you had your own group. This was basically the logistic group and the forward operating base. I had the carrier group and General Moore had the land forces.'

'But surely, weren't we all working together?'

'Yes we did, and the whole show was co-ordinated by Northwood. But my story was about my group.'

'But we were never too far away from you and constantly under threat. If I had been an Argentine Admiral with the option of using my two small submarines, and possibly the *Santa Fe*'s sister ship, I'd have sent them to South Georgia knowing that the force there was virtually undefended. The sinking of merchant ships in particular would have been a massive morale boost to Argentina. Look what happened when they sunk the *Conveyor*.'

He noted my comments but really had very little more to say that shed light on the reasons why we were left in such a precarious position.

Now we had our first victory we were free to send home press briefings. There were perhaps half a dozen of these, not one of which was released. None of us had any real doubt why this was.

But Mrs Thatcher was delighted by the news of this first definite advance in the conflict. It was *Antrim* who took the credit. I was not alone among the Captains of the other ships who asked the question, 'Did we not all deserve a share?'

199

Chris Nunn and 'M' Company were given the job of commanding the garrison and producing a full list of British Antarctic Survey equipment. We got the janitor's job of searching the sea bed for any unpleasant surprises and generally tidying up the area.

Brilliant and *Plymouth* left on 28 April to rejoin their group. *Tidespring* and *Antrim* were ordered north towards Ascension and a rendezvous with *Antelope* for the transfer of civilians and Commander Astiz. Once again it seemed very quiet. *Endurance* and 'M' Company were left as the sole custodians of South Georgia.

We believed that the island was likely to become the forward operating base for merchant ships supporting the Task Group. If this was the case somebody either rated our punching power rather more than before or they were taking a terrible gamble. In the background we were aware of discussions at Northwood as to how South Georgia could be defended and whether or not it needed to be.

South Georgia was already yesterday's front page. The focus had shifted elsewhere now. On 2 May an Argentine cruiser, the *General Belgrano*, was torpedoed and sunk by HMS *Conqueror*. Two days later we lost the *Sheffield*.

Our Intelligence gathering, ahead of the *Belgrano* sinking, told us that the Argentine Navy had split into groups not dissimilar to our own. The British Force consisted of the military group containing the assault troops, the carrier group which was led by *Hermes* and Sandy Woodward, and my own group which by now consisted largely of supply ships operating in and out of South Georgia.

At that stage, although we were intercepting signals, we weren't completely sure of the Argentine positions. We had pretty good evidence though that their carrier group (led by the *25th May*) was operating to the north with some modern guided weapon destroyers, whilst the *Belgrano* (with two venerable ex-US destroyers) was employing a pincer movement and operating to the south. It seemed to us that there was more than a possibility that the *Belgrano* group was on the way to South Georgia. The expectation that this was unlikely to be a courtesy visit gave us several days of renewed anxiety. The supply lockers for our fairly meagre weaponry were half-empty, and even had we been well stocked our odds against a cruiser and destroyers were similar to those of a carthorse at Royal Ascot. And here we were charged with the responsibility of defending merchant shipping that floated around us like sitting ducks.

We now know that the delay in further military action, and consequently the run on our loo paper supplies, was mostly to do with the political argument about whether or not the *Conqueror* should attack the *Belgrano* whilst she remained outside the exclusion zone. When we heard of *Conqueror*'s 'hit' there was more than a little jubilation. All that was left to threaten us now was a couple of destroyers. After a submarime at close quarters and a cruiser steaming in our direction, they hardly seemed worth worrying about.

Our joy upon hearing the fate of the *Belgrano* was soon tempered as the reality of what it meant began to sink in. The *Belgrano* had been our host ship in Puerto Belgrano only a few months before; we knew that their standard of training was not particularly high. Combine that with some excitable sailors, little real awareness of damage control procedures, and out-of-date life rafts and it added up to considerable loss of life. It was impossible to feel good about that.

Chapter 11

MOPPING UP

We weren't alone for long as merchant ships began arriving as part of the build up to the invasion of the Falklands. One of the first ships to arrive was the RFA *Blue Rover*. She became our more or less resident tanker. She was followed by the *Yorkshireman* and the *Salvageman*, then the biggest North Sea tugs. We knew they would be a Godsend since merchant ships were very prone to dragging their anchors in heavy wind conditions.

Captain Stockwell of the *Salvageman* entered the bay in darkness. He had been told by the naval communications team on board that the garrison was expecting him and had a bit of a shock when the sea around him was lit by an enormous flare and an unfamiliar voice was heard on the radio saying, 'Stand by to open fire!' Moments later the spent flare drifted down and hit Alan on the head. In fact this alarming incident had happened purely through lack of communication. Chris Nunn had no idea of his likely time of arrival and was taking no chances.

An influx of many vessels followed rapidly. One was *Stena Seaspread*, a diesel electric offshore supply vessel of about 6,000 tonnes which normally operated in the Thistle Oilfield in the North Sea. On board *Seaspread* were specialized damage repair teams with their equipment, under the command of Captain Paul Badcock, who had originated from our own village in Cornwall.

After the departure of *Tidespring*, *Antrim* and *Plymouth* our task in South Georgia changed considerably. I was effectively Group Commander and Harbour Master for all the shipping that arrived to support the main battle group. I was also to provide communications and helicopter support for 'M' Company. All that was fairly straightforward, as was the task of preparing the shore bases and safe anchorages.

Less palatable was the task of clearing up the explosives. In Leith alone this amounted to 1200 kilos of explosives plus detonators. It took us nearly ten days. Our diving teams were led by MCD Officer, Lieutenant David O'Connell. They neutralized TNT and plastic explosive in a dangerous state and dealt with mortars, rockets, and other ammunition. These were either used by our own forces for training purposes or counter-mined. They also uncovered personal effects, kit bags, radio equipment and documents of intelligence value which there had been some attempt to burn.

At this time we also learned of Northwood's assessment that the other Argentine Guppy submarine, *Santiago del Estero*, had sailed a week earlier and could be en route to South Georgia. We believed the threat was more than possible; the Argentines almost certainly knew we had no ASW search capability. Frankly there was little that could be done to protect the 'high value units' (the large merchant ships), but I was determined once again to use the local geography to give us as much protection as possible. We flew, every day at first light, a visual reconnaissance. We also made covert passages across the area from Grytviken to Stromness and covered the entrances to the anchorages as best we could.

One blessing was that the Argentines had stocked their garrison with many months' supply of tinned food and wine. These spoils of war were a considerable morale-booster.

As we were considered to be a mine-sweeping, mine-hunting depot ship, there was always a chance we would be dispatched to the Falklands area to co-ordinate the efforts of the four commandeered trawlers who were steaming south to sweep moored mines. This scheme was abandoned at some stage and we remained at South Georgia. In my view this was the right decision.

This was an extremely busy period for us, and we were all too aware that the more merchant ships and 'heavy units' we had in the area, the more of a target we became. We received a number of signals suggesting that one or more Argentine submarines were going to pay us a visit. The submarine *Salta* was mentioned several times. She was apparently doing very little in the Falkland area and could have easily been tasked with an anti-shipping role in the South Georgia area. Fortunately for us the Argentines did not like operating their small submarines too far away from their own support. And we later learned that, for a large part of the conflict, only one of them was operational.

One cheery event in mid-May was the arrival of a small ship, the *Iris* with 'our' marines on board. These were the same group who had been captured when South Georgia fell and the reunion brought us back to a full ship's company. Some of our sailors who had also been captured were returned to us, as was my First Lieutenant, Mike Green, who had recovered from his appendicitis operation. Being back to full strength was excellent news. And it happened just in time to welcome the large ships – *Canberra*, *Stromness*, *Norland* and the *QE2*, all of which appeared in the bay, complete with their troops and choppers.

QE2 had brought out Five Brigade which consisted of Scots Guards, Welsh Guards and Gurkhas. When you saw that lot mustered together it was almost possible to feel sorry for the Argentine troops on the Falklands. It was to be our task to organize the cross-deck operation – that is to transfer – this large group, with all their weapons and support. This included shifting armoured cars and a first aid post from the *QE2* to *Canberra* and *Norland* who would ship them to the Falkland area.

Unfortunately the BBC World Service announced the exact time of arrival of the *QE2* at South Georgia, and it was pretty obvious from the signal traffic that *Canberra*, *Norland* and *Stromness* were going to be in the bay for the transfer. If the Argentines were going to hit us with submarines this was the optimum time for maximum devastation. I recall thinking that someone should perhaps remind the BBC that their broadcasts were monitored in Argentina.

It was a major operation to transfer this number of troops in such a desolate bay. It was conducted from the bridge of the *QE2*, largely by my own officers, and in particular Lieutenant-

Commander Wills, who had been lent to me as an operations officer. He masterminded the whole of this operation which extraordinarily took only three days. As ships were emptied, or filled, they departed. As each one left we heaved a sigh of relief. The Argentines were constantly overflying the area and only the low cloud base concealed exactly what was going on in Cumberland Bay. If they had seen our Dunkirk-style operation I believe they would have been sufficiently impressed to send a gatecrasher to the party.

It was in many ways almost unreal to see such a mass of shipping in such a place. It was an equally odd experience for our helicopter crews. They had become used to working from the flight decks which looked like table tennis tables alongside the football pitch areas on the big ships.

The consequences of conflict were brought home when the *Stromness* arrived with some 650 survivors from the *Ardent*, *Antelope* and *Coventry*. Among this number was Captain David Hart-Dyke whom I had known for many years. His radar had blown up in his face making his features unrecognizable. One doctor described his injuries as 'superficial burns'. If that was the case I would not wish to see anyone who was badly burned.

On 29 May, the last day of the transfer operation, the weather cleared enough for an Argentine Hercules at some considerable height to target a British tanker passing South Georgia. A whole stick of bombs rained down from the sky. Only one hit the ship. The others created one hell of a fireworks display as they blew up in the sea. Until then I had believed that the only land-based air threat to South Georgia was posed by Canberras carrying just two bombs apiece and operating pretty much at their range limit. The armed Hercules proved that my evaluation was faulty and increased the sense of urgency to get the *QE2* in particular under way. Captain Jackson recognized the threat too and accepted that departing ASAP was a damn good idea. But he was almost as worried about icebergs as Argentines, particularly if he was to get up a fair head of steam. The *QE2* sailed at around 17.00. She took a dogleg course out to the east before making a fast run up to Ascension.

The *Canberra* and *Norland* left soon after. Meanwhile the

Stromness was transferring ammunition from one of the 'STUFT', i.e. one of the ships (in this case the *Lycaon*) taken up from trade.

I was still very concerned about the air threat and thought it was a reasonable assumption that the Argentines may try again. I posted the Wasps high up in the mountains as 'lookouts' and armed up with missiles intended to put as much flak into the path of any incoming Hercules as possible. Ships that were not involved in transfers were sent east to lie up hidden among the icebergs.

We were delighted to intercept a signal from an Argentine recce aircraft saying that there were now no enemy ships at South Georgia. It meant that the ruse of clearing the harbours had worked.

The problem now was transferring stores. Although South Georgia's harbours were reasonably sheltered from a sea state point of view, we were anything but sheltered from wind velocity, so trying to manoeuvre two large merchant ships alongside each other with limited tug resource was not easy. I was relieved when the tugs *Salvageman* and the *Yorkshireman* were despatched back to South Georgia. We had lost them to the main task group so that they could tow the damaged ships, including the *Sheffield*, to South Georgia, but that task failed and there was no longer any point in keeping them with the carrier group.

It was also about that time that the North Sea vessel *Wimpey Seahorse* appeared with a large deck cargo of buoys, mooring chain and shackles. We were able to lay several buoys in the bays for securing merchantmen and helping to avoid anchor dragging problems. I think perhaps we were fortunate not to lose a merchantman or two. The *Saxonia* in particular, had suffered in the storm force winds.

It was now the beginning of the Antarctic winter and the weather was to become an increasing, almost constant source of consternation. Winds of up to 70 knots would spring up rather rapidly, batter us for a few hours and then subside to a gentle breeze. Blizzards were now also arriving with some regularity. But the onset of poorer weather was not altogether a bad thing. We were grateful for the fog and low cloud that shrouded us and for the presence of icebergs to conceal high-value targets.

And we were encouraged by the flow of news from the Falklands. There had been a successful landing at San Carlos and our Paras had won a famous victory at Goose Green. We knew that Royal Marines and Paras would now be yomping their way towards Stanley.

On 2 June *Antrim* was despatched back to South Georgia which was a great relief to us. Now we had a ship with Exocets which, in addition to her anti-aircraft capability, could also be used effectively in an anti-submarine rôle. But the joy we felt at *Antrim*'s return was diluted immediately. On the same day Chris Nunn, the Garrison Commander, was informed that his brother had been killed in the battle for Goose Green. Lieutenant Richard Nunn, also of the Royal Marines, was a helicopter pilot with the Second Battalion Parachute Regiment. Six days earlier he had been flying a shuttle in and out of the area lifting forward ammunition and evacuating casualties. He had been given the task of evacuating Lieutenant Colonel Jones, the dying Battalion Commander, when his Scout helicopter was attacked by a Pucara and shot down.

On the evening before we heard this news Chris Nunn was having dinner with me on board *Endurance*. Out of the blue he had said, 'I think Richard's been killed.' I did my best to convince him to put such nonsense out of his mind but he remained adamant. As the job of informing him that his premonition had been correct fell to me I felt utterly dreadful about the way I had handled things the previous evening.

In all we lost 260 men in the Falklands. The Argentine surrender on 14 June put an end to the killing and we were told quite simply that Operation Corporate had been brought to a successful conclusion. At that moment I can hardly have been the only one who thought that the cost of that success had been far too high.

One effect of the surrender was that most of the merchant ships which had been using South Georgia could now be transferred to Fort William, the deeper harbour outside Port Stanley. They would be able to make a passage direct to the Stanley area rather than the more dangerous passage to San Carlos Water.

Here they would be used to shuttle between South Georgia and Stanley with stores and munitions.

The war was over in the Falklands, the war was over in South Georgia, but for *Endurance* the conflict was to continue a little longer. The Argentines were still in occupation of the Antarctic island of Southern Thule. There was only a small garrison billeted there, but it was still an irritation and had to be removed. Admiral Woodward received his order to evict the Argentines on 15 June. From this Operation Keyhole was born. This would be a race against the Antarctic winter which could lock us in for months.

Sandy Woodward asked me what I needed to do the job. My shopping list opened with a frigate to create a bombardment in case we met opposition. That meant we also needed a tanker, partly for the fuel, but also as accommodation for a modest force and perhaps for prisoners. To make it a belt and braces operation we also required one of the heavy tugs for the 'bollard pull' in case we got caught in the ice.

'What do you think this is Nick? Fucking Gallipolli?' he said after hearing my requests.

'I think it's pretty much a bare bones list,' I said. 'It's not the enemy that worries me. It's the ice.'

Of all the operations that made up the Falklands conflict, this was something I was particularly pleased to be associated with. Southern Thule had been one of the sparks that lit the fire of war. When the Argentines had walked in in 1977 the FO response had been characteristically weak-kneed. Their diplomatic response, such as it was, was to argue that Southern Thule was technically part of the Sandwich Islands which placed it in the Antarctic area. This was therefore a violation of the Antarctic Treaty. But this was hardly the case. Southern Thule is the southernmost island of a long chain of overgrown boulders, like mini-Gibraltars, stretching along a line as far as 59 degrees 30 minutes south. They were first sighted by Captain Cook in 1775 and have since been visited by many of the most famous names in exploration. All of the islands are north of the Antarctic area.

When I had 'spied out the land', under the cover of the Attenborough visit, we had guesstimated there was probably about forty people at the base. What was more important was that the island is within range of Hercules aircraft, either from the Antarctic base at Marambio or from the mainland. The significance of this was that the base could have been reinforced at any time during the Conflict. We therefore had little idea of the strength we would be facing.

At this time of year the pack ice advances north at a rate of approximately six miles a day and this, together with Antarctic winter conditions, made the operation less than straightforward. The rush was on to get there, do the job and get out again in the shortest possible time. We sailed almost immediately and arrived off Southern Thule on 15 June.

My orders, prior to departure, were to issue an ultimatum by radio to try to persuade the occupants to surrender merely by the threat of force. The message was: 'The Falklands and South Georgia are now in British hands. To avoid further bloodshed, you are to give up possession of the base. You will be embarked in British ship *Endurance* to be repatriated to Argentina or we will bomb Thule by overwhelming force.'

The calculated bluff was that they would assume *Endurance* was already in the area. It seemed an age before we received the reply: 'You are navigating in Argentine waters. The base is carrying out scientific work.'

Since this reply did not commit the garrison to anything, we had to proceed with plans for evacuation by force. I was delighted to have my own and 'M' Company marines. This was a golden opportunity for them to enjoy being part of a winning team this time.

Again I was being driven from the back seat at Northwood. Happily this time the 'driver' was to be my old friend Rob Woodard. Because of the rapport between us there would be no doubt that I would be very much my own boss this time. There would be regular liaison of course, but I knew Rob would back my judgement and offer purposeful advice as required.

I asked to be supplied with Blowpipes, hand-held surface to air missiles, and their operators. I had seen only too recently the effect of a Hercules air attack. The Blowpipes were at least some defence against that. We were also given the tug *Salvageman*, the

209

frigate *Yarmouth*, and the tanker RFA *Olmeda*. And, if trials were successful, *Endurance* would embark a Wessex 5 from *Regent* to improve the troop-lift capability and allow a single-lift recce insert. It was planned that I could get the troops in position on the mountain above the base at least 24 hours before the arrival of *Yarmouth* and *Olmeda*. I had been given just about everything I had asked for.

We sailed from South Georgia at about 15.00 on 17 June with our twenty-two marines and a rather large Wessex filling half our hangar. *Salvageman* was in station astern. The weather remained reasonable which helped us to maintain 11.5 knots. Although we encountered various icebergs there were still no signs of the dreaded pack ice.

We arrived in the vicinity of Southern Thule on Saturday, 19 June. The wind was 20–25 knots which hardly counts for a breeze in that part of the world. The main problem was going to be visibility reduced by persistent snow showers.

I had asked for the RAF to fly a Nimrod south from Ascension to check on the advance of the pack ice. We had no idea how tight our schedule had to be. Without aerial photographs we could assume no more than three days. The RAF, however, had obviously decided the war was over. A Nimrod? At the weekend? Out of the question, old chap.

We stopped in the lee of a tabular iceberg five miles south of the island. Shortly after sunrise, we flew a Wasp reconnaissance flight to pick a spot on the ice cap to insert the recce troop. Flying conditions were marginal at best. We put the recce troop in the Wessex with our AS12-armed Wasps riding 'shotgun' at low level. This was the chance for Lieutenant-Commander Blight and his Wessex crew to see if they could live up to the exploits of Tony Ellerbeck. They did extraordinarily well. Unfortunately the Argentines were listening in and rumbled part of our plan. We tried a diversion run and then landed where we had intended.

Endurance and *Salvageman* remained by the iceberg overnight. *Yarmouth* and *Olmeda* closed from the north-west and joined us at about 04.00. But by now the weather had worsened and was too bad for the transfer of orders and maps. We now had to wait for first light for the helicopters to do the job.

I maintained radio contact with the recce troop overnight. In the now atrocious weather conditions they had dug themselves in to the side of the mountain above the base. I asked Sergeant Napier if everything was all right. In his broad Northern Ireland accent he said, 'Ah sure, we're fine, sir, but I went and forgot my hot water bottle, didn't I?'

'What's the temperature?'

'I think it's around minus 52. But don't worry about us sir. We're having a fine time. I've had two invitations to join the Peter Pan Club already.'

The Peter Pan Club was exclusively for those who had fallen down a crevasse. I later learnt he'd fallen about 15 feet the first time but had been lucky. He had chosen a curving crevasse so they were able to haul him out. The second time he'd only dropped about six feet as he led his troop down the side of the mountain. Even the most perfectly smooth snow could conceal a crevasse. Royal Marines do not rope themselves together when they're in action conditions although they do on exercises.

The following morning he reported no activity at the base and no sign of any defensive positions. I called the base on radio to demand a surrender, but was unable to raise any reply. We had to do something now to demand their attention. We set 'H' hour for 13.30 and all the ships moved in to their assault stations. This meant I was going to take *Endurance* as close to the shore as I dared which was a few yards off the ice cliff. From this range our 20 mm guns would encourage a conversation. *Yarmouth* had also moved to her bombardment position with orders to knock hell out of a cluster of rocks at the side of the base.

We were just about ready to open fire and give the order for the recce troop to come down the mountain when someone popped out of the base waving a white flag. The fireworks party was immediately cancelled in favour of sending in the other section of 'M' Company and our own marines. These were to be my insurance policy when I flew ashore to accept the surrender. It was all a bit of an anti-climax but at least we could be content to have reached this stage without anyone being hurt.

The garrison turned out to be military personnel led by a naval crew. Some of them were genuine technicians. This was still outwardly a meteorological station. In the three days since we had informed them of our approach they had systematically destroyed everything of value and had even thrown their arms into the sea. The Garrison Commander calmly admitted that he had destroyed perhaps 2 million dollars worth of equipment. Happily he had been more circumspect about the food and wine which we duly claimed as the plunder of war.

The prisoners were taken off by helicopter and parked in *Olmeda*. We held a ceremonial surrender in *Endurance* at which representatives of all the British units took part. For me this was an especially sweet moment. I had now taken two surrenders in two months.

By 24 June *Endurance* and *Salvageman* had returned to Grytviken. *Yarmouth* and *Olmeda* had returned to the Falkland area two days earlier to transfer the prisoners to one of the merchant ships who were to repatriate them, with some of the Falklands garrison. During our absence the *Antrim* had remained at South Georgia as the air defence unit, together with the *Scottish Eagle*, as the station tanker. RFA *Regent*, whose helicopter we had borrowed, was also there as the station store ship. *Wimpey Seahorse* was still laying moorings and the tug *Yorkshireman* was still helping ships berth. There was also MV *British Enterprise III*, a despatch vessel running between the task groups with mail, signals and official correspondence

M Company had a rough deal. Some of them had been left behind on our jaunt to Southern Thule. I did my best to get them transported back to the UK, or at least to the Falklands where they could join the rest of 42 Commando. Eventually HMS *Ambuscade* arrived with a small detachment of fifty-five Scots Guards to install them in the place of 'M' Company, who were at last to be lifted out. Although they had never been particularly happy with their task there was no evidence of this in their performance.

By now the weather in South Georgia was evil. The winter snow had arrived and the temperature never rose above zero. Tracks that we had been using between the base and the whaling stations became impassable because of the depth of snow, and

Yo por este medio rindo sin condiciones La
Base a Southern Thule South Sandwich Islands
y las cercanias en nombre del Gobierno Argentino
a los representantes de Her Britannic Majesty's
Royal Navy. este 20 dia de junio 1982,

Teniente de Corbeta
Enrique Peralta Martinez
Jefe Est. Cient. "Corbeta Uruguay"

Captain.

Captain Royal Marines

Commander Royal Navy

Captain RFA

P. Stockwell.

THE SURRENDER DOCUMENT

whenever the gale force winds died away they were invariably replaced by blizzards. But despite all this we did enjoy a few gloriously sunny days. Then we had a go at using the snowshoes and skis, but I do not recall anyone who was particularly proficient with the snowshoes.

A day or two after our return to South Georgia we were given a new task – dealing with what remained of the *Santa Fe*. When *Regent* and *Scottish Eagle* sailed on 28 June, and *Antrim* the following day, we began to wonder if we were ever going to get home as we knew we still had to return to the Falklands at some stage.

We were now downgraded to the status of task unit. The salvage operation which I monitored was not only dangerous but carried out in weather conditions that had turned from dreadful to appalling. I really do not know how those involved managed to remain so resolutely cheerful. It was even more extraordinary because the work was carried out without the support of submarine experts until the last day. What expertise we had was supplied by our hydrographer, Lieutenant-Commander David Ives, who had served very briefly in submarines, and by Lieutenant-Commander Arthur Ainsley, our supply officer, who had done a single tour of duty in a Polaris sub. We succeeded, I think, largely because we were blissfully unaware of some of the risks we were taking.

I wrote: 'Everyone was willing that submarine to the surface and as a bunch of amateurs we succeeded where many others would have faltered.'

For an organization which is supposed to be the ultimate in professionalism we really did very badly on advice from our Submarine Command. It would have been very helpful, for instance, to have been instructed on the layout and content of the tanks. The *Santa Fe* had been a fairly typical example of the Guppy 'breed' which as a class had been scattered throughout many of the world's navies.

In the aftermath of the incident when the Argentine submariner, Artuso, had been killed, a diving team from HMS *Brilliant* had disabled her by blowing off the rudder, thus damaging the propulsion system. Subsequently the submarine sank alongside the jetty. We knew that, with her full outfit of torpedoes, mines and charges she was a serious hazard and the sooner we took her out of the area the better. We first used the *Typhoon*, an MOD tug, assisted by *Endurance*'s diving team to pump out as much water as possible. But the pump was not really strong enough and the effort was temporarily abandoned until we could supply better equipment. She was sitting on the sea bottom, with just the fin showing at a 15 degree list to port. The time had now come to raise her.

The salvage began on 28 June. We used portable pumps and pumps from *Salvageman* which was lashed alongside the *Santa Fe*. At first we tried pumping out through the upper conning tower hatch, but were thwarted by the water level being below the lip of the hatch. The lack of any plans meant that we had to rely entirely on folk memory for what we might encounter below. We erected a coffer dam and constructed it round the hatch so we had a watertight area and a place where we could insert a pump. Little by little we managed to take the water out of the conning tower but it was days later before we reached the control room. We could not be sure even then which valves controlled which tank, a necessity if we were to blow air into the tanks or take out fuel and water.

The first man into the control room had a particularly unpleasant welcome. Among other débris there was an oily mass of rotten food and the body parts of a man shot at close range. Next we pierced the main ballast tank from the outside by means of a cox's gun, a handy piece of equipment which makes a hole and then seals it. The idea was to use air from the tug to blow the water out. Here we had at least a limited success. Having more or less dried out the control room, we managed to get into the galley accommodation by removing the sight glass in a door, producing a bore of water into the control room! By trial and error we managed to block that too.

We used crowbars to prise our way into different compartments off the control room. At each stage we managed to create a new flood which in turn had to be sealed. Several of the compartments contained fuel oil sludge and more rotten food floating on the surface of the water.

We also found an extensive collection of armaments which included torpedoes, mines, boxes of small arms, ammunition and charges. Four homing torpedoes were found tossed like scurvy victims on bunks. There were more torpedoes in the after racks, torpedoes on a false deck and torpedoes in the tubes. All appeared to have their detonating devices inserted. The one empty tube probably represented an attempt to sink one of our ships, possibly ourselves! We found a brass plaque on the door of another tube informing us it contained a mine. Was this an accelerated scuttling device or a booby trap for the British?

After days of further pumping we discovered that LP air was still available in the submarine's LP system. By cross-connecting it to the blow panel it was finally possible to blow the main ballast tanks. Now that the bow and safety tanks were filled with air the *Santa Fe* rose three or four feet. Our divers confirmed that she was off the bottom at the bows and only just aground aft of the conning tower. We were getting there. More pumping brought the reward of another rise of two feet. Then we moved aft and started again. There was a great cheer as the submarine rose to the surface. She looked like an injured dolphin with a list of about 25 degrees to port. But she was buoyant! We felt she was probably towable but to avoid the risk of capsize she was lashed to the side of *Salvageman*. Further pumping and plugging improved stability but there was one worrying leak in the motor room which defeated us.

On 15 July an expert team arrived from UK to inspect the *Santa Fe* which was now more or less dry. We all recognized the most worrying problem – a lot of TNT explosives were rapidly drying out and becoming increasingly unstable. Through our efforts the *Santa Fe* had become a floating time bomb. My instinct was to destroy her on the spot but it would be difficult to control the explosion. If all that TNT went up much of the base area would evaporate and the base itself could require an aviation licence.

Our only option was to tow her away and ground her. Warrant Officer Green, one of our team of experts, advised against any further salvage operations. I bowed to his experience but it was all bloody frustrating. It had taken a hell of a lot of effort to get as far as we had. Our divers had logged record times for the number of dives within a month. One of them, Knocker White, had been underwater for 726 minutes, which was in itself a new record. But all this seemed to have achieved was a mounting fear of being blown to Kingdom come.

We decided to beach *Santa Fe* in a position near Hestesletten, approximately four miles away. This was a gently shelving beach so we could take the tug in, still lashed to the submarine, then let the *Santa Fe* go to drift up onto the beach. At least that was the theory of it. I can't say I was particularly confident that it was going to work.

I went with the *Salvageman*. I felt I had to offer something in the way of falsely confident smiles, and anyway if the sub and tug were to blow up it was my duty to be with them. *Endurance* stood by fairly close as we were all towed inshore by *Yorkshireman*. It was not an operation that any of us particularly relished.

The submarine was to be beached with the main hatch and all doors open. As we were moving we tried to empty the motor room and blow the main tanks to give *Santa Fe* a little extra buoyancy for what we sincerely hoped would not become a Viking funeral. Just ahead of the beach we cut all the lines and let her drift. She waddled, but, stubbornly maintaining her 25 degree list, finally planted herself on the rocks. We lost all the pumps but I certainly wasn't going to risk recovering them. After 24 hours the submarine's list had reduced to perhaps 15 degrees and the after end of the casing had settled just below the waterline. We believed that the water would rise to sill level in the accommodation area and this should be enough to ensure stability. More importantly, the TNT would soon become soaked and safe.

Chapter 12

HOMEWARD BOUND

Finally we were sent the signal to proceed to Stanley. The passage to the Falklands was so rough that we had to cancel our stores transfer with *Regent*. We did catch a glimpse of the Carrier Task Force as it passed a few miles to the north. We exchanged signals and congratulations with my old friend Captain (now Admiral Sir) Jeremy Black of the *Invincible*. The tugs were still in company with us but as they had a very low freeboard they behaved more like submarines heading into this heavy sea.

Then, on Monday, 19 July *Endurance* arrived in Stanley. The familiar landscape was crowded with supply ships for the Task Force crammed into all the harbour berths and overflowing into the outer harbour. Overhead there was the constant clatter of helicopters. On shore we could see the streets laden with military vehicles and teeming with men in a wide variety of uniforms. It was a far cry from the peace and quiet we had left behind.

Endurance was given the most heart-warming reception. Sir Rex Hunt, newly styled as Civil Commissioner, gave a party for the officers and senior rates at Government House. I called on Admiral Reffell who by now had relieved Admiral Woodward. He was flying his flag in the *Bristol* and I went there for lunch. I could not resist reminding him of the conversations we had had the previous summer which of course did little to endear me to him. But I saw him as the sort of man who could take it on the chin. I expected something at least conciliatory, perhaps even apologetic. I have to say I was disappointed. He brushed everything aside with some mumblings about 'priorities being priorities'.

I also called on Major General Thorne, known as 'the jumping bean', who had relieved General Moore as the leader of the land force and had become the Military Commissioner.

During the early days of the invasion, the Argentines had captured our rather expensively fitted out survey launch *James Caird*. In South Georgia we had commandeered a vastly inferior Argentine launch which our splendid Scouse engineers tried to repair. They christened her *James Turd*. But we refitted her as best we could with a salvaged engine and some bits and pieces we had 'borrowed' from the Argentines. Finally we gave her a paint job which featured her name in gold lettering in the stern. The *James Turd* was then ceremonially presented by *Endurance* to Rex Hunt. I believe she was used for several years.

We also took Rex on a sea tour of outlying settlements. First it was Fitzroy, which had been the scene of the disastrous attacks on *Sir Tristram* and *Sir Galahad*. But now the bay seemed oddly peaceful. The only signs of the Conflict were some life rafts that had been washed up on the rocks. At Fox Bay, on West Falkland, which the ship had last visited on the way to Cape Horn, the people from both East and West Fox Bay arrived to cheer us and we organized a small celebration for as many of them as we could.

It was all really going too well and I was beginning to feel rather more at peace with the world. It may be this that caused me to drop my guard. On our return to Stanley I was enjoying a constitutional stroll along the 'front' when I was accosted by Jeremy Harris of the BBC. He asked for an interview. At first I was inclined to say 'no' but the more I thought about it the more it seemed like an opportunity to express my pride in the achievements and heroism of an exceptional ship's company. I discussed all this with Rex and his view was broadly similar to my own.

'It's all over now,' he said, 'so I don't see any reason why you shouldn't give him a short interview. You've come through, and that in itself is quite a story. And *Endurance* has achieved more than anybody could possibly expect from a virtually unarmed ship. I can see no harm in putting that in the public domain. Do your interview, Nick.'

I think perhaps if I had been able to make my responses in the same sort of detached and diplomatic way that Rex could have done all would have been well. I was as circumspect as possible. I was asked if I had known if problems were brewing and if I had warned London. I was asked what sort of response I received. I felt that the only way to answer those questions was to tell the truth, although I suspected, even then, that in career terms this was suicide. The interview was transmitted on the BBC's World at One, on 27 July, 1982.

We left Stanley at five o'clock on the evening of 23 July. They put on an unforgettable fireworks display for us and horns blared away from every corner of the bay. I took it for what it was – a delightful way of saying a heartfelt 'thank you'. It did nothing, however, to store up any credit with my boss in the *Bristol*, Admiral Reffell.

Our voyage to Chatham was to take almost a month. This was really too much time to reflect on what had happened and what was to be. I had thought a great deal about the people who were important to me during the darker days of war, but this had never been considered in a conclusive way. Perhaps there had not been enough time for that. Perhaps it all seemed too distant. Certainly there had been times when going home had not seemed to be a probability I could let myself consider. But now there were things I had to think through and properly come to terms with. I had told Elizabeth in February about my feelings for someone I had got to know at the British Embassy. I had been at pains to point out that this was not just 'an affair' but something much more than that.

But at the same time I was immensely proud of the marvellous efforts that Elizabeth had made in maintaining and co-ordinating a network of information and support for the *Endurance* wives and families. This had not always been easy. On two occasions the Argentine Broadcasting Service had reported that *Endurance* was a smouldering wreck. Even though this 'news' was quickly contradicted it had already found its way to several homes and Elizabeth had taken it upon herself to give the necessary reassurances. From what I heard later I know she did this terribly well. And, more remarkably, she accepted these responsibilities in the knowledge that her own marriage was almost certainly over.

My wife was not talking about divorce. Her approach had been to send me a number of emotional letters and tapes, the main thrust of which was asking me to reconsider. There were indeed many questions to which she deserved answers, something which I knew would be difficult to provide partly because I did not fully understand my own feelings, but I knew I wanted to cause her as little pain as possible. Since the Conflict began, and communication became more difficult, I have no doubt that she felt every bit as isolated as me. I knew just how difficult that could be.

My other concern was for the children I adored. How was I to tell them that the marriage was to end? How could I explain that the 'returning hero' no longer wanted to live with their mother?

One decision I made was that for the first month at least there would be a semblance of normality. Elizabeth was at least to take her rightful position as the wife of the Captain of the only ship to return to the Medway. It would be as if nothing had happened. I knew she wanted this and was entitled to it. And the public would see what they expected to see. That was the way it had to be.

I believe Elizabeth still thought there was chance of reconciliation. I could not entirely disillusion her about that at a time when my children, and indeed the families and children of a whole ship's company were so eagerly awaiting our return. Nothing should get in the way of that rejoicing. We were all looking forward to what seemed certain to be perhaps the greatest day of our lives.

The British Embassy had effectively closed immediately after the invasion and the Ambassador had returned to the UK with most of the embassy staff. All that was left behind was a scratch team under a newly arrived First Secretary who had run British interests under the Swiss flag. A small staff had stayed and toughed it out. That cannot have been easy either. After the

Conflict Anthony Williams was given a suitably grand office within the FCO. As an additional reward for his astute diplomatic touch in Argentina he was provided with a similarly suitable support staff which included some former Buenos Aires officials.

Rex Hunt was treated rather differently. His office was more of broom cupboard dimensions and his staff was similarly downsized. I have no doubt that all this had much to do with Sir Michael Palliser who was then Head of the FCO. Anthony Williams had been highly regarded for many years and Argentina was hardly a significant blip on his record. Rex, however, had not only come to the FCO through the Commonwealth Office, but he had, on occasions, voiced opinions that confirmed the opinion that he could not properly be regarded on quite the same basis as Anthony Williams.

I am truly sorry if Rex was tarred with Barker brush but I do not believe that was particularly the case. But clearly both of us had issued warnings that were ignored and the carrot and stick principle was being applied ahead of the enquiry. And I had already done enough damage through the Jeremy Harris interview.

I knew now that *Endurance* was a name that had entered into a wide public consciousness. Her rôle had been heavily reported up to the invasion itself, but then, naturally enough, other matters had taken precedence in media attention. We thought that there may have also been an attempt to steer attention away from *Endurance* because she was carrying all special forces. There was some sense in that. But later a rather different picture was beginning to emerge. There can be no doubt there was deliberate attempt to give the ship as little publicity as possible; this was not unconnected with the fact she had proved to be of greater value that anyone in Whitehall cared to admit.

There was little rejoicing in these same corridors of power when in October the following year the *Endurance* was awarded the Wilkinson Sword of Peace for 1982. This award is given to those who, in the view of the donors, have done most to further international peace and goodwill. Interestingly, this had nothing to do with our military rôle. It was, in fact, a recognition of the worth of the ship over many years in the South Atlantic. The citation made specific reference to the work of the ship on behalf of the British Atlantic Survey and the Scott Polar Research Institute.

Honours and promotions followed, but I felt increasingly incredulous. Rex Hunt and Anthony Williams received knighthoods, at least one of which was hugely deserved. And there were knighthoods and plum jobs for any number of Whitehall 'warriors', including Ure and Fearn.

The odd thing was that only three captains of Corporate ships, including the two aircraft carriers, were promoted to Rear Admiral. Was that jealousy? Or were they just not good enough? I found it staggering that someone with the experience of Mike Clapp, who was Commodore in charge of the Amphibious Warfare Force, was never promoted. It was a dreadful waste of experience and know-how.

On the way home we stopped for a few hours at Ascension Island. The senior civil servant in charge invited us up to his house on what is known as Green Mountain. It is the only patch of grass in the whole of the island and it features a tree. It is an odd thing to realize that for almost six months none of us had encountered such a phenomenon. I made the best of this short encounter with civilization. I played a few holes of golf on the brown course. I also received two letters from Admiral Sir John Fieldhouse. One was extremely congratulatory but the other was a harbinger of what I was to face at home. Part of the first letter read:

> I trust it will be long remembered how you kept the White Ensign flying down south and provided a British presence when all else was in enemy hands and how then you have since done so much to re-establish our presence. You are to be congratulated on a most marvellous performance during the past months. Well done and a happy run home.

But in the second letter, commenting on the Jeremy Harris interview, he said;

Offence in Government circles was taken at your answer to the first question in which you referred to 'green lights' offered by Her Majesty's Government to the Argentines. Taking into account the clear instructions on press interviews you are well aware there is a limit to be observed. Your intimate knowledge of the history of the Conflict, and its sensitivities in political terms, will no doubt be valuable to a parliamentary enquiry currently studying the background of the Argentine invasion of the Falklands. I therefore consider that you displayed a lack of judgement in making these statements to the media. I accept that before recording began you declined to answer political questions and indeed your answers to the later questions were impeccably correct. But even having noted your comments and made allowances you should know that you have incurred my displeasure. This administrative censure will not be recorded in your appointing record, but will be retained in my office for the duration of your present appointment. The fact that you have incurred my displeasure is also to be conveyed to the MOD as part of my report on the incident.

This censure was fair enough. It was something he had to do and of course I already recognized my mistake. And I'm not blaming Rex. I was perhaps naive in not expecting a grilling from an experienced journalist, and equally so in believing this was of less importance now that the war was over. In my defence I was entirely unaware of the sensitivity of the Franks Enquiry. We had our own, and rather more dangerous responsibilities in the immediate aftermath. At that stage we, after all, had been fully heads down either fighting the war or clearing up.

Admiral Fieldhouse made his position completely clear at a private lunch in my cabin after arrival at Chatham.

'Did you get two letters from me?' he said.

'I certainly did, sir.'

'You can take it that one cancels out the other.'

'Thank you, sir.'

Which only confirmed what I had always known. Admiral Fieldhouse was a man who took a fair-minded and balanced view of anything.

Our journey home was uneventful apart from a rendezvous

with HMS *Illustrious* and two escorts who were on their way south to take over as flagship from HMS *Bristol*. Throughout we were bombarded with press summaries. Some of them were pretty fanciful but there were certainly some journalists who were hitting the bulls' eyes. More than one stated that I had already been muzzled. There was also a fair amount of positive comment about *Endurance* and the obvious questions were raised about John Nott's change of opinion.

One Sunday one of the ship's company came to my cabin asking if he could telephone home. I knew his mother was suffering from terminal cancer, so naturally I agreed. We could make calls through our civilian satellite system, but strictly speaking this was 'illegal' because we could have been monitored by the Argentines or by anyone else. But I felt this particular circumstance warranted the risk.

He made the call, and when he returned to thank me he added, 'Sir, you're in the shit again.'

'What have I done now?' I asked.

'My mum says you're all over the front page of *The Observer*.'

'Oh really? What's it all about?'

He described the article his mother had read. It was an incredible mix of truth and distortion, not entirely untypical of quite a lot of the material written that summer. The ship's company enjoyed it all hugely, but I knew the piper would have to be paid.

It was just before we reached the Channel that I received the signal informing me that we would not, after all, be met by Admiral Fieldhouse, the Commander-in-Chief. Instead we were to receive his Chief of Staff, Vice Admiral Ted Anson. At face value this was perfectly acceptable but we had noted that the more senior ships had all been met personally by the C-in-C and many by the Prime Minister.

The question and answer brief I was given was most specific. Events leading up to the Argentine invasion were now the subject of the Franks Enquiry and it would be quite wrong of me to comment or to give my views at this time. It worked like this:

'Has your ship's company been told to have no contact with the press?'

'No. They are in precisely the same position as the company of any other ship returning from the Atlantic.'

'Were you aware that one of your talks to the ship's company was subsequently broadcast on ITV?'

'No, I was unaware that the recording was being made and neither I nor the MOD were consulted about the broadcast.'

And so on.

In the event I played the game to the letter, even if sections of the media may have found me pretty inarticulate. On the plus side I was able to show off a large wad of congratulatory signals and telegrams which did a great deal to boost morale. And Admiral Anson said it as well as anyone: 'It was a privilege to welcome home the longest serving member of Task Force 317 today. You have carried out your duties with distinction and notable success, and your ship's company's evident pride and spirit was a pleasure to see. I wish you a joyful home-coming and a well deserved rest.'

I was perhaps most moved by a letter from the wife of a member of the ship's company. In it were many echoes of the situation in which I had left Elizabeth:

> I have been asked many times what it is like being married to someone serving in HMS *Endurance*. I always admit it is hardly a normal way of life. There is sometimes a feeling of deprivation when being alone for so long. Then there are joyful reunions and adjustments to the family routine to make when he comes home again.
>
> All Naval wives know how the problems grow in magnitude when you face them alone. It is particularly frustrating not to be able to put some of those little things right about the house, and worse still to be unable to find somebody willing to come and make the repair. They are little things but they add up when you are alone.
>
> But we were proud to belong to part of the extended family of the brave little *Plum*, sailing into the romantic vast whiteness of the Antarctic, and perhaps a little envious of the men experiencing the beauty and adventure. The wives have little to compensate them for the long days and nights on their own. They meet on very few occasions at recommissioning ceremonies and the ship's company's dance.

Subsequent events and the knowledge that *Endurance* had played such a major part in the retaking of South Georgia and of Southern Thule did little to allay our fears. But hearing about so many brave deeds filled us with pride, each for her own special hero.

And finally there was the great day when our heroes returned. With flags flying, hearts pounding, and tears of joy it was the most wonderful reunion.'

One contemporary account described the great day like this:

The public had to make their welcomes from the Strand at Gillingham. It is estimated that some 20,000 people watched and cheered as *Endurance* passed 300 yards from the shore. There were other crowded vantage points too, like the power station at Grain and the river front at Hoo. The crowds were simply everywhere to greet the ship the Argentines couldn't sink.

Local pubs offered free beer for the ship's company. There were miniature bottles of rum from Medway Council and free bottles of wine from a local merchant. Inevitably there were civic receptions and special editions of local newspapers.

The welcome began as *Endurance* was led up the Medway by the Queen's Harbourmaster's launch, boats of the Kent County Constabulary and the Ministry of Defence Police. She was followed by an armada of craft large and small. It was a turnout the river is unlikely to see again.

The Bullnose reception was strictly in accordance with tradition. Flag Officer Medway, Rear Admiral William Higgins, took the salute as *Endurance* canalled through the lock into the dockyard. VIPs stood behind the Admiral's saluting base and the Mayor of Rochester and other civic dignitaries were found favourable vantage points nearby.

But formality broke down as she berthed. Relatives and dockyard workers yelled themselves hoarse. Dozens of banners were waved in the sunshine, fireman's hoses threw up multi-coloured sprays. There were balloons, hooters and sirens. It was an expression of spontaneous joy and thanks that nobody who saw it will ever forget.'

It was the greatest day of our lives. The ship's company and I were braced with anticipation. The ship had come in from the cold. HMS *Endurance* was the only HM ship to return from the Falklands to the Medway and the people of south-east England waited to welcome her in their tens of thousands. According to the press this brave little ship, which epitomized the South Atlantic, had refused to die. During the year she had been away from her base port there had been a political furore over her future, adventures in the ice of the Antarctic, a war against Argentina and controversy over her Captain.

The ship had been first in and last out of the Falklands Conflict. She had seen plenty of action and had acquitted herself well. Everyone had played a part in this success story and the rapturous welcome exceeded all expectations. We had been officially welcomed home the day before. We had received wonderful signals and telegrams. And, to our great pleasure, Lord Shackleton had already come out to greet us.

But there were others who now noted that we were the only ship not to be welcomed back personally by the Commander-in-Chief. And why, the question would be asked, were we just one of the few ships not to be welcomed by Mrs Thatcher?

I had already begun to have serious misgivings. The day before a helicopter had been dispatched with special instructions for our arrival at Chatham. Included in the mailbag was a directive from the Deputy Director of Public Relations Navy informing me that two senior MOD Press Officers would be embarked before our arrival. The directive went on to say: 'The point of all this is that your future in the Navy depends more on Friday's Press Conference than anything you have ever done.'

I was furious. And it was not surprising that the headline in the *Daily Mail* read: 'Captain Nick Sails In and the Two Men in Grey have Nothing to do with his Silence.'

Numerous press men, journalists and reporters, five television teams and dozens of VIPs joined the ship for the two-hour river passage. My every word was monitored by the Ministry which was as stupid as it was insensitive. My elation was now tempered with annoyance.

But as we cleared the Bullnose and finally caught sight of our waiting families, it was impossible not to share in the unmitigated joy of the company. 'Balls to the Ministry,' I thought, 'the important thing is to be home at last.'

Chapter 13

POST MORTEM

On 8 July, Mrs Thatcher addressed the House of Commons:

I beg to move that this house approves the decision of Her Majesty's Government to set up a Falkland Islands review as announced in a reply to a question by the Right Honourable Gentleman, the Leader of the Opposition on 6 July, 1982.

As early as 8 April I announced in reply to the Right Honourable Member for Orkney and Shetland (Mr Grimond) that there would be a review of the way in which the Government Departments concerned had discharged their responsibilities in the lead up to the invasion of the Falkland Islands. Since then, although a few have argued that this is not necessary, there is widespread agreement that a review of some sort should be conducted and that there should be prior consultation with the Leader of the Opposition and the leaders of the other opposition parties in the House who are Privy Councillors.

It would be fair to say that the consultations led to broad agreement on the nature, scope and composition of the review. Accordingly, I set out a form of the review and its terms of reference in my reply of Tuesday to the Leader of the Opposition and I welcome the opportunity to explain to the House today the reasons why the Government have decided to appoint a committee of six Privy Councillors to conduct the review, and to give it the terms of reference set out in my answer to the Right Honourable Gentleman.

I wish to deal in turn with the nature of the review, its scope and composition. As to its nature, the overriding considerations are that it should be independent; that it should command confidence; that its members should have access to all relevant papers and persons; and that it should complete its work speedily. Those four considerations taken together lead naturally to a Committee of Privy Councillors. Such a committee has one great advantage over other forms of enquiry as it conducts its deliberations in private and its members are all Privy Councillors. There need be no reservations therefore in providing it with all the relevant evidence including much that is highly sensitive, subject to safeguards upon its use and publication.

A Committee of Privy Councillors can be authorized to see relevant departmental documents, cabinet and cabinet committee memoranda, and minutes and intelligence assessments and reports. Many of these documents could not be made available to a Tribunal of Enquiry, a Select Committee, or a Royal Commission.

We did put in a caveat that the Chairman of the Committee will be consulted if any deletions have to be proposed. The fact that the committee would know that these deletions had been made from its report offers the best assurance to those who might believe that the government would try to make unjustified deletions. Nevertheless, I repeat that it is the Government's aim to present to Parliament the report of the committee in full.

MP Tam Dalyell invited the Prime Minister to outline the membership of the committee. Her response was:

I came to the membership of the committee as announced in my reply to the Right Honourable Gentleman on Tuesday. Lord Franks has agreed to be the chairman. I know that that choice is agreeable, indeed it has been welcomed by all those I have consulted. Lord Franks will bring unrivalled experience to the work of his committee. We are fortunate that he is ready to take on the task.

As I also announced on Tuesday, the other members of the committee will be my noble friend, Lord Barber, Lord Lever of Manchester, Sir Patrick Nairne, the Right Honourable Member for Leeds South, Mr Rees, and my noble friend, Lord Watkinson. The Queen has been graciously pleased to approve that Sir Patrick Nairne be sworn as a member of Her Majesty's Privy Council.

The Right Honourable Gentleman, The Leader of the Opposition proposed the name of the Right Honourable Member for Leeds South and Lord Lever. I hope that the House will share my view that a committee with this membership gives us the best possible assurance that the review will be carried out with independence and integrity.

The Spectator, in its editorial, was less convinced:

There may be those who feel they have read enough of the Falklands War, its origins and its aftermath to be going on with, and that the debate should now be adjourned for a few weeks. Nevertheless, returning to the subject after more than three months I'm tempted to repeat one point. It was the decision by the Secretary of State for Defence, Mr Nott, to scrap HMS *Endurance*, the one armed Royal Naval vessel stationed in the South Atlantic which led directly to the invasion of the Falklands by Argentina. In simple terms once the British Government had determined the time had come to withdraw the White Ensign from that part of the world, General Galtieri concluded, not unreasonably, that we had resolved to give rather lower priority to the defence of the Falkland Islands.

Several distinguished voices were raised in an effort to save the *Endurance*; not only because of its presence, which was seen to constitute a deterrent to invasion, but for its valuable role as support ship to the British Antarctic Survey. It was as much a petty spending cut as the decision to drop some of the BBC's foreign language broadcasts. It smacked of junior Whitehall accounting, without any ministerial thought for the consequences.

Last November, dare I say it, the courageous captain, Nicholas Barker, tried to drum up public support for his ship before she sailed on what was to have been her final voyage. He was told, according to the *Observer* last Sunday, on direct orders from the Prime Minister, to keep his mouth shut. Now Captain Barker is saying that two weeks before the Argentine invasion he warned the MOD that it was about to take place.

His ship monitored flights by Argentine military aircraft and preparations of the Argentine Navy for war. He relayed this information to the MOD throughout the month of March.

232

Apparently it was ignored and not even passed on to Lord Carrington. It looks as if Captain Barker may be one of the most important witnesses at Lord Franks's Committee of Enquiry. The facts, and the allegations, against the MOD are damning indeed. Mrs Thatcher would not let Mr Nott resign when he offered to do so at the beginning of April, but there can be no saving of him now.

This was published among a plethora of similar broadsheet comment about the way in which the Government has mishandled the affair. It was pretty close to the truth although most of the substantive warnings came from Lords Shackleton and Buxton, and concerned Members of Parliament.

From the beginning of the enquiry on 26 July, 1982, until the report was published in January the following year the Franks Committee interviewed forty-two people; most of those were senior politicians or Foreign and Commonwealth Office pillars of the establishment. In my own experience, the questions asked were rarely more penetrating than a shotgun blast at a tank. Certainly they achieved no more than scraping away a few of the outer layers of camouflage paint.

The report, when it appeared, was described by one eminent journalist as 'a marvellous miracle of lucid narrative, detached argument and precise economic prose. But the bloke in the pub is going to find it irrelevant and unsatisfactory. Basically it says it shouldn't have happened and somebody should have stopped it. But then who is to blame? A lot of superannuated politicians and civil servants told the enquiry that nobody could have known, nobody should have stopped it, and therefore nobody is to blame. But given the fact that things went very badly wrong we must conclude that the committee failed to ask the right questions.'

But this is a little unfair to Franks. It is clear the committee turned over a great deal of evidence and came up with at least some of the answers. The report did, for instance, note that the FCO and the JIC should have put more reliance on the possibility of a sudden, early invasion. It was also pointed out that Lord Carrington and his colleagues on the cabinet Defence

233

Committee should not have handed over the initiative to the Argentines after September, 1981, by virtually giving up trying to sell both the British Parliament and the Islanders the 'solution' of ceding sovereignty and lease back. Perhaps the most striking criticisms were that the Defence Committee should have considered the Falkland Islands question during the winter of 1981/2 instead of postponing discussion for six months, and that a nuclear submarine should have been dispatched to the South Atlantic early in March, 1982.

From my point of view I was most pleased that Franks said the announcement that HMS *Endurance* was to be withdrawn was a mistake. It was vindication.

But the report also led up some blind alleys. The Argentine invasion, according to Franks, was unprovoked. That is hardly relevant. What should have been addressed was the breakdown in British diplomatic manoeuvres at the end of 1981 and the equally serious failure to act on our – and other – intelligence reports in early 1982.

We knew that Argentina would have no scruples about using force to seize the Falklands. We knew that Argentine action was always going to be based on an assessment of Britain's commitment. Not only the withdrawal of *Endurance* but plans to run down the surface fleet, and the willingness of the Foreign and Commonwealth Office to consider lease back were pretty unambiguous signals to the Junta.

Lord Carrington could have made an issue of submarine deployment. Perhaps he should have. But he had reason to believe that Mrs Thatcher would not support this. At one point the Prime Minister did raise the matter with Defence Secretary John Nott, but nothing was done. This was the fault of the Defence Secretary rather than the Prime Minister. He should have pressed her on the subject. Five years earlier, in a similar situation, David Owen pestered Prime Minister James Callaghan. The submarine was sent and the Argentine sabre rattling subsided. The fact that this strategy was not repeated was a further signal of appeasement from Britain.

Perhaps what is unique about the developing situation is that there should be massive activity on one side and near indifference on the other. This almost became comedy hour when on 28 March the Argentines put a large fleet, complete with a carrier group, to sea. The reaction from London? Nothing.

On 30 March, US Intelligence and *Endurance* had independently intercepted and passed on alarming Argentine signals to Cheltenham. The reaction? Nothing. And, appropriately enough, on 1 April when an armada was approaching the Falklands Cabinet Office Staff told a frantic FCO official to 'get your minister off our backs about the Falklands!'

John Nott should shoulder most of the blame. He spectacularly failed in his duty to protect a sovereign British territory. Lord Carrington was more perceptive but should have made more of Fortress Falklands in September, 1981, and he should also have insisted on the despatch of a submarine in March, 1982. Mrs Thatcher cannot be exonerated either, but she had at least (in her March memorandum) demanded contingency plans. Nothing was done. And she had personally supported the decision to withdraw *Endurance*.

Very little of this comes across in the Franks Report. This casts doubt, not on the integrity of Franks himself, or the members of his committee, but on the integrity of all Government reports of this kind. They are simply not intended to get at the truth. Few people who might conceivably tread a path outside the establishment line are invited to give evidence. I believe I was 'invited' to Franks only because it would have been a greater scandal if I was not. I cannot say I was asked questions that were particularly searching or relevant.

No one has ever explained how the preparations of such a large force could have been hidden, even within a military dictatorship. The Franks Report said that 'the Military Attaché in Buenos Aires had neither the remit nor the capacity to cover Argentine preparations of this kind, although clearly he was deeply concerned'. In my view it was almost impossible *not* to notice the invasion build-up. If this is the case it seriously begs the question about the remit that MI6 was given and we have no one to blame but ourselves. It was recommended in 1968/9 that the primary function of British Military attachés was the sale of British weapons and military equipment. But this did not exonerate either of the Attachés. It is, after all, their duty to keep an eye on the military activities of the countries to which they are attached.

The report also states: 'We learned from an Argentine source that newspapers within that country were carrying articles about a possible retaking of the Falklands by force from as early as January. We also learned of this through British Embassy staff in Buenos Aires who included military attachés and an MI6 man. But from none of these sources came the information that an invasion of the Falklands by the Argentines was imminent.'

There is no doubt that the resignation of Lord Carrington drew the flack away from Foreign and Commonwealth Office officials. It was a couragous and honourable resignation, as was that of Richard Luce. Putting their necks on the block saved the careers of people like Michael Palliser, Antony Acland, John Ure and Robin Fearn, a quartet who have since been showered with honours.

Mrs Thatcher achieved her aim of course and went on to become the longest serving Prime Minister of the 20th century. The 'Falklands factor' helped to sustain her personal popularity even though a long succession of ministers were to fall by the wayside all too often in pretty seedy circumstances.

Four years after the report was published I had dinner with a member of the Franks Committee. I made the point that in my opinion the whole thing had been a whitewash. I didn't expect him to agree.

'I remember your evidence as if it was given yesterday, Nick,' he said.

'Well you didn't publish much of it, nor did you ask many relevant questions.'

'That's entirely right Nick,' he said. 'The purpose of the enquiry was to clear the Government. That was our brief.'

'I always thought that was the case, but it's good to hear it from the horse's mouth.'

It went further than that, of course. The real agenda was to create a platform for Mrs Thatcher and her ministers to win the hearts and minds of the electorate in 1983. Nothing was going to sully the image of the Iron Lady or her Government.

I remained with the ship for a month following the return to Chatham. During this time I was partly on leave in Dorset with my family and partly in *Endurance* for the continuing round of receptions. There were also courtesy and duty calls to be made in London.

I now had no doubt that my marriage was over but of course it is never as easy as that. There were still a great many practical matters to sort out and I was particularly keen to maintain regular contact with my children. I was now living in Winchester or London. But I also recognized this was a time bomb situation and one which I had to clarify as soon as possible.

In September Mrs Thatcher invited the Falklands Commanding Officers to dinner at Number 10. My name was not on the guest list. By coincidence, perhaps on the very same night, I was invited to speak at a Livery dinner at the Tallow Chandlers' Hall.

Speculation about *Endurance* and her captain was still bubbling in the press. The mood of support was strong, particularly from Desmond Wettern of *The Daily Telegraph* who kept asking why Nick Barker continued to be isolated.

To set against this I recall with great gratitude a dinner for Falklands Commanding Officers given by Admiral Eberle, the Commander-in-Chief of the Home Command, in Nelson's cabin on board the *Victory*. It was an excellent occasion and did much to reassure me that there were those in the Naval hierarchy who recognized the importance of the part that *Endurance* had played in the Conflict.

But I was also sent for by Admiral Reffell, my Flag Officer. He had written a very polite and largely positive final report, but he also questioned my judgement. I felt that his judgement was questionable too. And even if he was right about me I could not help thinking that his errors of judgement had caused unnecessary grief and pain to a large number of families.

'I suppose you are referring to those with whom I made friends in Argentina,' I said, 'and you must know that my marriage is about to break up. But can you really question my judgement in terms of our tactics during the Conflict, or even the strategic case I argued to keep *Endurance* in service?'

He refused to discuss the specifics that added up to my 'errors in judgement'. I was even irritated enough to suggest that he was doing this to distance himself from the decision to axe *Endurance* ahead of the Franks Report and that the same view could be applied to both Admiral Staveley and Captain Kerr. I knew I'd touched the truth and would suffer for it. My biggest error of judgement was to make a point of principle.

For a few further months I was given the job of President of the Admiralty Interview Board in Portsmouth. This was for the selection of potential officers. In many ways it was a dream job and one that I hugely enjoyed. It was also an honourable side-step which gave the still circling press vultures little more to chew on and a six-month breathing space in which my ultimate fate could be decided.

It was during this time that the Franks Report was published. Almost simultaneously a message was sent via my senior officer from Secretary of State, Michael Heseltine, instructing me not to make any comment whatsoever. The General Election was now just five months away.

One irony of this is that there is much that I could have said that the Government would heartily have approved. After the shooting started, the action taken by Admiral Lewin (Chief of Defence Staff) and Admiral Sir Henry Leach (Chief of Naval Staff) and the Prime Minister herself was commendable. Internal disagreements between organizations thrown together to do a job are par for the course; loyalty alone would have prevented me talking about these. There can be no war in history that has been fought with total concord among its commanders. In the end it is outcomes that matter and those had been generally satisfactory. And where things had gone wrong it could only be hoped that lessons would be learned.

The campaign to recapture the Falklands had in some ways been a model of what is achievable with limited resources. It had been well organized and for the most part well led. It was a monumental achievement to win a war 8,000 miles away with generally inferior numbers and certainly inferior air power. Our Harrier pilots had been faced with a Battle of Britain situation

238

and their response had been magnificent. All this I could, and certainly would have said in public. In private I shared the concerns of those who questioned the support given to our ground troops. In part this was because Admiral Sandy Woodward was not experienced in amphibious warfare; he was essentially an extremely bright nuclear submariner.

Quite recently Simon Jenkins, later Editor of *The Times*, called the Franks Report a 'very British cover up'. Like many similar reports over the years, it was merely an exercise in exonerating the Government. 'We conclude that we could not be justified in attaching any criticism or blame to the present Government for the Argentine Junta's decision to commit its act of unprovoked aggression in the invasion of the Falkland Islands on 2 April, 1982.'

What, in Simon Jenkins' opinion, has ten years done to that conclusion?

It was written in the heat of victory and the authors saw no virtue in puncturing military glory. It took its evidence on Argentine motives and strategy only from the British Foreign Office. The evidence indicated ludicrously that the invasion was dreamt up by the Junta overnight, on March 30 or 31. Thus Franks was able to present it as a bolt from the blue, unpredictable and unpreventable. Seldom can such a committee have so wilfully decided to fool itself. It would not have happened without a serious breakdown in British diplomatic and military co-ordination in the latter months of 1981, followed by an equally serious failure of reactive intelligence in March, 1982. These deficiencies were aggravated by a Whitehall climate in which ministers felt unable to convey their worries frankly to Downing Street

Britain knew at the time that Argentina had no scruple about using force to seize The Falklands, and that Argentine plans to do so (dating back to the 1970s) were always based on careful assessments of Britain's response. This assessment changed in 1981 with the withdrawal of HMS *Endurance*, the running down of the surface fleet, and the willingness of the Foreign Office to consider leasing the Islands from Argentina. No Argentine assessment considered that Britain would send a fleet to recapture them, nor did any British Navy plan consider such an operation in advance of the Task Force.

A Defence Ministry Paper on the subject, early in 1982, dismissed recapture as near inconceivable. When a seizure was imminent nobody in Downing Street suggested an ultimatum threatening recapture. It was not until the invasion was accomplished and the First Sea Lord volunteered his fleet did war become a serious option. The final analysis must be that Sir Henry Leach emerges as the star of the show.

The left often accused Margaret Thatcher of deliberately drawing Galtieri onto the punch. This is absurd, but Dr Costa Mendes can be forgiven for thinking otherwise.

But that was all in the future and I had the immediate present more on my mind. There were a number of options discussed for my future. In the end, largely because of the inadvertent manoeuvres of Robin Fearn, who had been accepted for the same course at the RCDS, and of Sir John Fieldhouse, I was accepted by Churchill College, Cambridge, for a one year Defence Fellowship. I am immensely grateful to Robin for that. We had had our differences certainly but there was no rancour and I have always had immense respect for his professionalism.

In part I have no doubt that the fellowship sprang from a need to keep Barker where they could see him – in the Navy. Certainly my resignation at that time would have been regarded as a threat. But this is to some extent churlish. Sir John Fieldhouse was certainly sensitive to my difficult position and the need to find something for me to do that would be mutually acceptable. And it was certainly that. I was to write a thesis on the geo-politics of the South Atlantic which could conceivably be of use to the Ministry of Defence and the Foreign Office in the future. I even had a chance to fulfil my ambition as a frustrated undergraduate. Cambridge got the vote largely because of Correlli (Bill) Barnett, a hugely respected but independent-minded and provocative historian who may even have pipped me at the post in the *persona non grata* Stakes at the Ministry of Defence. But I knew I would learn a great deal from him.

There is nothing quite like being a student. I had missed out the first time round and had something to prove to myself. My room, once belonging to Captain Stephen Roskill, the official

Naval historian, was in Churchill College Archive Section which was an Aladdin's cave of distraction. Time and again I had to pull myself away from avenues where fascination was in inverse proportion to anything relevant to my subject. But somehow I found time to complete my thesis. This focused on a path that could lead to the peaceful exploitation of the resources of the South Atlantic. Although it was prepared with the Ministry of Defence in mind I have never deluded myself into believing that anyone was ever likely to read it.

I believed then that there was a future for the Falklands in fish licences and that has proved to be so. The next phases of economic development may be less easy to achieve. Kelp and krill may well be subjects for international discussion, but I still believe the greatest opportunity, which may also lead to independence, will be based on the exploration for, and exploitation of, oil. I have always believed that hydrocarbons will provide the islands with the economic base for independence.

The question of where economic zones – between the Falklands and Argentina – overlap has yet to be resolved. Our Government clearly has no agenda for this. I sincerely hope I am not proved right when I say this will be forced on us by events at a time when we are too militarily impotent to negotiate from a position of strength. If there is a second Falklands Conflict the economic stakes will be higher and the Argentines better prepared.

But the political situation has also changed. Argentina has now sustained a democracy for 15 years. The present régime has improved things in many ways, not least of which has been the dismantling of Argentina's Third World image. The accountability of government to an electorate may make a repeat of the Junta's military adventure unlikely, but this is not cause for complacency. If a week in politics is a long time it would be unwise of our Government to delay meaningful discussion of unresolved matters indefinitely.

POSTSCRIPT

This book is primarily concerned with my time as Captain of *Endurance* but I hope in the not too distant future to find the time to write something more in the nature of a conventional autobiography. Suffice it to say here that I was retired from the Navy in 1988, but the need to supplement my pension made it necessary for me to keep working.

Life was busy but I kept sufficiently in touch with the MOD to hear some disturbing news about *Endurance*. A plan had been devised to bar her from any further work in ice conditions. Constructors and engineers were despatched from the MOD and more or less directed to report that the ship was unfit and, even worse, she would not be replaced.

It was 1991, almost exactly ten years after our first battle. Once again it would be necessary to bring SWAG to 'action readiness'. It would not be possible to disagree with the MOD over the condition of the ship, although the current Captain did his best. But it would be possible to consult shipbrokers and to propose a replacement as soon as possible. Numerous letters were exchanged between senior politicians. Letters were written to *The Times*, questions were bluntly asked in both Houses. The battle was renewed and the MOD did not like it. Some of the same arguments were deployed, but the bottom line was to find a replacement that was cheap and could fulfil 'all the requirements' for the next 20 years.

Various options were considered and I was in almost daily contact with Lord Shackleton and Commander Michael

Ranken. Eventually Captain Tom Woodfield, himself a ship-broker and a long-serving Commanding Officer of British Antarctic Survey ships found an 18-month-old all-purpose polar vessel, the Norwegian-built *Polar Circle*, Lord Buxton took up the case with Michael Heseltine whilst Lord Shackleton approached the Duke of Edinburgh. On 14 October, 1991, it was finally announced in the Commons that the MOD had chartered MV *Polar Circle* for the forthcoming season after which the performance of the ship would be assessed for the longer term. In the event the new ship was a great success and the next stage of our crusade was to persuade relevant Government Departments to buy her outright or take her on a long-term lease.

There were long discussions over the name of the new ship. Should she be renamed *Endurance* on the day the old ship was paid off? On commissioning she was indeed given this famous name and has performed excellently ever since.

There was to be one last twist of the tale. Various museums, ports and other contenders wanted to buy the *Plum* and turn her into an environmental exhibition centre. The museum keepers could wait until she could run no more. But the MOD had been wounded. Come what may, they were going to sell to the highest bidder, preferably keeping her as a runner even if the sum concerned was only £200,000. This derisory figure reflected their earlier decision to classify her as unfit for normal operation.

I wrote to Lord Cranborne (Permanent Under-Secretary of State for Defence) and asked for a stay of execution. However, the Sales Department of the MOD had already entered a contract with a city broker whose stated intention was to use her as a passenger ship in the Middle East. In the event the new owner had no such plan. He had connived with INCOM (the purchasing broker) to sell the ship on to an Indian scrap dealer.

Three days before she was due to transit the Suez Canal I learnt of her true destination. I was horrified to hear that *Endurance* had been the subject of another MOD cock-up and was to end her life on a beach in India. In the remaining three days I tried

243

to raise the money and a crew to buy her back and drive her home. Sir Jack Hayward offered a substantial contribution and we raised the asking price. But we were too late. The *Red Plum* died in pieces early in 1993.

INDEX

250

251